Performance in a time of terror

MANCHESTER
1824

Manchester University Press

theatre
theory · practice
· performance ·

This series will offer a space for those people who practise theatre to have a dialogue with those who think and write about it.

The series has a flexible format that refocuses the analysis and documentation of performance. It provides, presents and represents material which is written by those who make or create performance history, and offers access to theatre documents, different methodologies and approaches to the art of making theatre.

The books in the series are aimed at students, scholars, practitioners and theatre-visiting readers. They encourage reassessments of periods, companies and figures in twentieth-century and twenty-first-century theatre history, and provoke and take up discussions of cultural strategies and legacies that recognise the heterogeneity of performance studies.

The series editors, with the advisory board, aim to publish innovative challenging and exploratory texts from practitioners, theorists and critics.

also available

The Paris Jigsaw: Internationalism and the city's stages
DAVID BRADBY AND MARIA M. DELGADO (EDS)

Theatre in crisis? Performance manifestos for a new century
MARIA M. DELGADO AND CARIDAD SVICH (EDS)

World stages, local audiences: Essays on performance, place, and politics
PETER DICKINSON

Performing presence: Between the live and the simulated
GABRIELLA GIANNACHI AND NICK KAYE

Jean Genet and the politics of theatre: Spaces of revolution
CARL LAVERY

'Love me or kill me': Sarah Kane and the theatre of extremes
GRAHAM SAUNDERS

Trans-global readings: Crossing theatrical boundaries
CARIDAD SVICH

Negotiating cultures: Eugenio Barba and the intercultural debate
IAN WATSON (ED.)

Performance in a time of terror

Critical mimesis and the age of uncertainty

JENNY HUGHES

Manchester University Press
Manchester and New York

distributed in the United States exclusively by Palgrave Macmillan

Published by Manchester University Press
Oxford Road, Manchester M13 9NR, UK
and Room 400, 175 Fifth Avenue, New York, NY 10010, USA
www.manchesteruniversitypress.co.uk

Distributed in the United States exclusively by
Palgrave Macmillan, 175 Fifth Avenue, New York,
NY 10010, USA

Distributed in Canada exclusively by
UBC Press, University of British Columbia, 2029 West Mall,
Vancouver, BC, Canada V6T 1Z2

British Library Cataloguing-in-Publication Data
A catalogue record for this book is available from the British Library

Library of Congress Cataloging-in-Publication Data applied for

ISBN 978 0 7190 8529 1   hardback
ISBN 978 0 7190 8530 7   paperback

First published 2011

The publisher has no responsibility for the persistence or accuracy of URLs for any external or third-party internet websites referred to in this book, and does not guarantee that any content on such websites is, or will remain, accurate or appropriate.

Typeset by Servis Filmsetting Ltd, Stockport, Cheshire
Printed in Great Britain
by the MPG Books Group, Bodmin

This book is dedicated to Theatre for Everybody, Gaza

CONTENTS

List of figures   ix
Acknowledgements   xi

Prologue: a race across the desert   1

1 Searching for a politics of performance in an age of uncertainty   9

2 A beheading in Iraq: Medusa, the mirror and a performance
   of exception   35

3 Counterinsurgency performance in Northern Ireland:
   street-crowd-balcony-scenes and the ob-scene   59

4 A crisis of voice: democratic performance on the London stage   91

5 Camping up and camping out as antiwar protest performance   124

6 Performance, counterterrorism and community: cops,
   neighbours, lovers and double agents   153

Epilogue: critical mimesis, refusal and waste   188

   References   199
   Index   209

FIGURES

1 *Somewhere over the Balcony*, The Drill Hall, London, 1987.
With the permission of the photographer, Sheila Burnett   82
2 *Called to Account*, Tricycle Theatre, London, 2007. Courtesy
of Tricycle Theatre. Photograph by John Haynes   105
3 *Democracy*, National Theatre, London, 2003. With the
permission of the photographer, Conrad Blakemore, and
the National Theatre Archive   116
4 *Shoot/Get Treasure/Repeat*, Royal Court Theatre, London,
2008. With the permission of the photographer, Stephen
Cummiskey   119
5 Stop the war placard, designed by David Gentleman.
Reproduced with permission of the publisher, from Andrew
Murray and Lindsey German (2005) *Stop the War: The Story
of Britain's Biggest Mass Movement*, London: Bookmarks   137
6 Make tea not war placard, designed by Karmarama.
Reproduced with permission of Karmarama   139
7 Cleaning up after capitalism. Courtesy of the vacuum
cleaner. Image available under Creative Commons licensing   141
8 *Not in my Name*, Theatre Veritae, Lancashire, 2008.
Courtesy of Theatre Veritae   169

9   *One Extreme to the Other*, GW Theatre, Oldham, 2008.
    Courtesy of GW Theatre   171
10 *Hearts and Minds*, Khayaal Theatre Company, London,
    2008. Courtesy of Khayaal Theatre Company. Photograph
    by Masoma Al-Khoee   177
11 *Undercover*, In Place of War and Waters Edge Theatre,
    Manchester, 2007. With kind permission of the cast   181

ACKNOWLEDGEMENTS

The process of writing this book was illuminated by the insights and experiences of a number of theatre practitioners who very generously offered me time as well as the opportunity to investigate their work. I am especially grateful to the following: Luqman Ali (Khayaal Theatre), Alice Bartlett and Andrew Raffle (Theatre Veritae), Mike Harris and all at GW Theatre, Hossam Madhoun and Jamal al-Rozzi (Theatre for Everybody), and Janine Waters (Waters Edge Arts). Thanks are also due to a number of academics, students, theatre makers and activists who supported the work in important ways, especially the following people: Zeenat Azmi, Mona Baker, Jonathan Chadwick, John F. Deeney, Maria Delgado, Maryam Duale, Anton Franks, Viv Gardner, Ashley Hanson, Brian Haw, Paul Heritage, Aneesa Khatoon, Sally Mackey, Joanne McKerr, Carol Moore, Gerri Moriarty, Helen Nicholson, Simon Parry, Pavement Maria and the vacuum cleaner.

In Place of War was funded by the Arts and Humanities Research Council from 2004 to 2008, and by the Leverhulme Trust from 2008 to 2011. Thanks are due to both of these funders for providing opportunities for conversations with artists from places of conflict internationally. The echoes from these conversations carry across the arguments and discussions in this book in many different ways.

On a more personal note, *Performance in a Time of Terror* would not have come to be written without the brilliant insights, extraordinary generosity and remarkable patience of Maggie B. Gale. Special thanks and love to Maggie, then – and also to James Thompson, a long-time source of inspiration, confidence and support. Particular thanks are also due to Ruth Daniel and Alison Jeffers, for brilliant contributions to the discussions, events and scholarship generated by the In Place of War project. I also want to especially thank those who made perhaps less direct but similarly vital contributions to the research, variously providing moments of clarification, comfort, calm, silliness and reviving distraction: Su Carroll, Claire Ebrey, the Geri-Hatricks, Alfred Hughes, Millicent Hughes, Miranda Kaunang, Carly McLachlan, Oscar Partridge, Sol Partridge, Ben Wilson, Kaye Wilson and Louis Wilson.

Prologue: a race across the desert

A race across the desert by a merchant and his coolie, pursuing the concession of oil reserves in advance of competitors, who are in close pursuit. Lost in the desert, water supplies running low, the merchant and coolie pitch camp. The coolie, aware of the likelihood of arrest if he is found alive and the merchant half dead, offers the merchant the last of his water supply. The merchant, fearful of the coolie, who he has ruthlessly driven across the desert, mistakes the water bottle for a stone and shoots the coolie dead. In the final scene of Brecht's play, *The Exception and the Rule* (1930), the Judge clears the merchant of guilt and of the need to pay compensation to the coolie's wife and child. The merchant's terror of a mistreated servant in an uninhabited region without presence of police and law is deemed a legitimate justification for murder. The coolie was an illusory enemy, but given the violence of the race across the desert, one that might reasonably be assumed to exist:

> The rule is this: an eye for an eye.
> A fool hopes for the happy exception.
> A drink from his worst enemy
> That's a thing no rational man can expect. (Brecht 2001: 59)

The Exception and the Rule is a 'learning play' or *lehrstück*, a theatrical innovation by which Brecht sought to interrogate the violence and inequity of capitalist society. In highlighting the sites/cites of exception as an important focus for an examination of social justice, the play opens up lines of thought of relevance to a post-Second World War history of crisis as well as to its moment of conception. These 'politics of exception', for example, were especially evident during the so-called war on terror of the first decade of the twenty-first century. Here, any possibility of a happy exception to the circulation of violence was edged out by the inception of extended and, at the time of writing, ongoing military operations and exercise of extra-juridical powers. During the most recent war on terror, declarations of exceptions to the rule supported the spread of war into new territories and the indefinite detention of prisoners of war held without recourse to legal representation.

Brecht's *The Exception and the Rule* shows how dramatisations of threat and frailty during moments of crisis provide the grounds for an extension of power beyond the rule-bound universe and for symbolic and real violence against apparently threatening others. In the style of the Judge and merchant in Brecht's play, the war on terror was supported by the performance of evidence by political leaders and spectacular violence by military and insurgent groups – a dizzying exchange of projected threats and frailties between powerful enemies that supported extra-legal military and political violence. The move to enlist *performance* as a weapon of war was evident from the early stages of the war on terror, with Hollywood catastrophe movie specialists recruited by the US Pentagon following the 9/11 attacks 'with the aim of imagining possible scenarios for future attacks and how to fight them' (Žižek 2002: 16). As part of this move to more effectively visualise possible attacks and rehearse responses to threat, the official 9/11 Commission report called for 'institutionalising imagination' at the highest levels of military and administrative bodies responsible for the security of the nation (Kean *et al.* 2004: 344).

The war on terror thus confronted artists with a series of challenges. As critical theorist Susan Buck-Morss commented shortly after the 9/11 attacks: 'for us as practitioners of culture, business as usual has become difficult if not impossible, because the very tools of our trade – language and image – are being appropriated as weapons on all sides' (Buck-Morss 2003: 63). The sense of doubt captured by Buck-Morss was repeated in the responses of performance practitioners and scholars to the 9/11 attacks, and whilst it arguably carves out an imperative for *more* rather than less performance, it also demands a re-examination of the politics of performance as a critical and urgent project. Brecht articulated the 'political' as a clearly theorised and practised project for performance. The revelation of violence and inequity in *The Exception and the Rule*, for example, calls for critical, self-conscious reflection and action to bring about a better world. For contemporary performance scholars and practitioners, the political has become more difficult to ascertain. Widespread disengagement from formal politics is especially evident in stable democracies and here, a lack of meaningful alternatives to free market capitalism and a blurring of the distinction between the political left and right have narrowed the terms of critical debate. At the same time, as the examples of performance explored in this book evidence, there has been a *diversification* of ways of thinking about and practising a politics of performance, beyond the projects of identity politics, and left and right political orientations. Alongside rejection of the certain engagements of a leftist 'political theatre', there has been a proliferation of performance activism as part of protest movements concerned, for example, with issues of global justice, environmental damage and war. In the UK, there has also been ongoing interrogation of political violence in the mainstream and fringe theatre, and the development of critical and affective forms of experimental and community performance. These sites provide a provocative terrain for the re-examination of a politics of performance. They also enact novel kinds of politics *by means of* performance.

Performance in a Time of Terror examines an array of performances that caused a stir during the war on terror of the first decade of the twenty-first century. These include performances that played a role as weapons of war as well as performances that determinedly searched for the happy exception to the rule of a neighbour's violence against a neighbour. Starting from the premise that the *radical* in performance can be most clearly identified in acts of performed violence that have obliterated life, the first part of the book explores the use of performance as a strategy and tactic of terrorism and counterterrorism. The spate of carefully scripted and rehearsed beheadings carried out by Islamic insurgents in Iraq in 2004 confronted spectators with the annihilating effects of performance on bodies, and the use of mimesis by the British army during the 'war on terrorism' in Northern Ireland (1969–98) deliberately drew on the performance skills of covert military operatives to enact violence (see chapters 2 and 3 respectively). The second half of the book focuses on performance in more conventional terms – and, in particular, on performances that have critically interrogated the violence of war. Here, an exploration of the resurgence of political theatre in London during the war on terror focuses on examples of verbatim theatre, a form that draws on the uncertain affectivity of the voice to dramatise the diminishment of democracy during a time of crisis. Following this, examples of antiwar protest performance are investigated for the ways in which they reproduce and critically mirror a politics of exception by dramatising the frailty of bodies and spaces during times of terror. Finally, an extraordinary series of community and educational performances commissioned by counterterrorism agencies following the London bombings of 7 July 2005, targeting hotspots of terrorist activity in the UK, are investigated for the way they dramatise the *difficultness* of encounters with neighbours by drawing on a protective practice of performance that is profoundly conservative.

The term 'exception' in the title of Brecht's play introduces the overarching theoretical framework of this book. A year before he wrote *The Exception and the Rule* in 1930, Brecht met the philosopher Walter Benjamin, and the two became friends. One of the many concerns that preoccupied Benjamin at this time was the nature of political violence, in part prompted by the work of Carl Schmitt, the controversial political philosopher whose ideas influenced Hitler's regime. The discourse between Benjamin and Schmitt may have inspired Brecht's play, and is traced by the Italian philosopher Giorgio Agamben (see Agamben 2005: 52–64). The sovereign, according to Schmitt, is the figure who has the power to declare an exception to the rule. Drawing on Schmitt and Benjamin's ideas, Agamben argues that a 'state of exception' has become the rule in contemporary forms of governance, and that this is the obscured political fact of the democratic tradition, concealing the latter's coalitions with lawlessness and violence. For Agamben, sovereign power populates these indefinite and indeterminate zones of exception in order to bind the force of 'anomic space' to itself (*ibid.*: 39). In maintaining order and rule, at the same time as claiming the force of the anomalous *outside* of order and rule, sovereign power also produces a schism between the life of the citizen (protected by law) and natural or 'bare life'. As such, life is held in a state of suspension, both inside and outside of an orderly, rule-bound universe, underpinned by uncertainty and carrying the capacity to be killed without recompense – radically undecidable and potentially expendable. Agamben describes bare life as a founding condition of language, law and politics, as both constituting and constituted by sovereign power, and held in a relation of 'inclusive exclusion' as part of the complex topology of a politics of exception (Agamben 1998: 21).

According to this analysis, the 'political' resides in a biopolitical terrain that traverses the empirical, rule-bound universe and anomalous sites/cites of exception. Here, life is regulated by practices of categorisation, recognition, incorporation, identification, non-identification, suspension and excision. Performance and exception are intimately linked: a state of exception is produced by means of a performance – a declaration – of power that may or may not be written in law, and thus power is both made and contested in an embodied and performative zone that is not securely definable or fixable. Performance, in its play of guises, appearances and disappearances, performative enunciations, shifting empirical and imagined realities, tangible materiality and fantastic pretence, is perfectly suited to act as a key agent in this terrain. The implication here is that the 'political' extends beyond the performances of politicians and formal political process (although it does not exclude them). The 'political' exists in an ontological realm that incorporates the material life of voice, speech, body, time and space, and extends across the domains of intimate relationship, intersubjective exchange, cultural practices, intense experience, and processes of identification and non-identification. Agamben argues that learning to recognise the guises of exception in the contours and forms of everyday life is an urgent task, and one which might provide the conditions of an emergent, potential and perhaps more hopeful politics: 'it is by starting from this uncertain terrain and from this opaque zone of indistinction that today we must once again find the path of another politics, of another body, of another word' (Agamben 2000: 139).

Performance in a Time of Terror explores the ways in which performances engage with, reproduce, practise and poeticise a politics of exception. The book tracks the repeated motifs of bare life across a range of performances, and explores the kinds of critical agency that are potentially opened up to understanding by these dramatisations. The performances documented in this book identify, occupy, agitate and parody a politics of exception by drawing on the dislocating power of undocumented voices, abject bodies, estranged identifications, wasted spaces and provisional encampments of everyday life. These *poetics* of exception evoke and make use of the conditions of possibility and potential in the negation of life of a state of exception. However, the book also documents performances that beautify, cover up and draw on the threatening power of the exceptional and anomalous to annihilate life. The chief concern here is to pay critical attention to the distinctions between the respective dramatisations of bare life across the multiple realms in which performance plays a part – political-legal performance, military performance, staged dramas and the performances of everyday life.

Brecht's play is useful as a starting point for this exploration. In the play, it is in the camp in the desert that the audience is confronted by the life of the coolie stripped of value. Here, the coolie is impelled to offer the merchant the last drops of his water and, in turn, the merchant is impelled to shoot him dead. In the courtroom, the camp in the desert is

the site of exception evoked by the Judge to justify the murder committed by the merchant, as 'the uninhabited character of the region' without
'police or law courts' was 'bound to inspire him with alarm' (Brecht
2001: 60). Agamben draws on an analysis of the Holocaust to suggest
that the 'camp' is the means by which the state of exception is given
form: *the camp is the space that is opened when the state of exception
begins to become the rule* . . . now given a permanent spatial arrangement, which as such nevertheless remains outside the normal order'
(Agamben 1998: 168–9. Italics in original). In Brecht's play, the camp
provides the conditions for a formal declaration of an exception to the
rule by the Judge, and here the coolie's life is stripped of consequence,
and a murder becomes a righteous act rather than a violent crime. The
camp in the desert thus provides a motif by which the uncertainty of life
is dramatised, and it is also used to contest legal definitions of justice and
assert a claim for social justice based on the equity and value of all life.
The play recycles the dramatisation of threat and frailty reconstructed
in the courtroom as part of a critical and affective encounter that
draws attention to injustice and demands a habitable space – a happy
exception – for life in the here and now of its performance.

It is interesting to note that the context for the original production
of *The Exception and the Rule* mirrors the politics of exception that
the play dramatises. According to documented record, *The Exception
and the Rule* received its premiere eight years after it was written, in
Kibbutz Givath Chajim in 1938, in what was then Palestine (Willett
1977: 39). The play's critique of political violence must have been especially resonant for a Jewish audience fleeing persecution and searching for safety in the Middle East, only to be faced with the insecurity
of colonial rule, hostile neighbours and the inception of a seemingly
endless, terrible conflict. The play's original production also evokes
the failed research project that began the journey of this book. During
a short research trip to the Palestinian territory of Gaza in 2005, I met
a number of theatre makers, and intended to return so as to feature
some of the theatre in Gaza here. The visit was facilitated by Theatre
for Everybody, a theatre company that extends an invitation to participate in theatre to the diverse communities of the Gaza Strip. However,
with the closure of the border following the withdrawal of Israeli set-
tlers in 2006, infighting between military groups, the blockade of the
Strip and outright war, a return trip has not been possible. This period
has seen rising levels of poverty, unemployment and dependency on
humanitarian aid in Gaza, the destruction of the economic and political infrastructure, and the loss of approximately 1400 lives during the
war with Israel (2008–9).

Over the course of a week in 2005, I met theatre makers from a number of organisations, including Theatre Day Productions, Massafat Theatre, Fekra Arts as well as performers connected to Theatre for Everybody. Many expressed a sense of unreality and feeling of despair about the prospects for theatre in the exceptional spaces of Gaza, aptly expressed by Hossam Madhoun from Theatre for Everybody in a comment made each time a new artist was introduced: 'he sank in the mud of theatre with the rest of us'. One theatre director commented, 'we do not manage to accomplish any theatre in Gaza, despite what you see . . . like a friend told me once – "things here look real, but they are not as they appear, they do not really exist" – theatre in Gaza is like that . . . doing theatre here is like digging in rock' (Handan 2005). Many theatre makers were continuing their attempts to dig in rock. At the time of my visit, approximately seventy artists had joined a 'theatre league' supported by the Ministry of Culture and there continues to be a high-quality tradition of young people's theatre and educational performance in the Strip (see Thompson *et al.* 2009).

These extraordinary theatre makers articulated a desire to drama-tise their struggle as 'human beings', that is, to utilise performance to counter their global status as victims, terrorists and martyrs, and to display both the frailty and resilience of life in a state of exception. The statements here exemplify this shared desire:

> I make theatre because I want to communicate a message about being human, about love, life, to express, to create, to share values and to communicate awareness of our humanity.

> I do theatre to express sorrow, to express that we are human, we are more than heroes and martyrs. To show that we feel and we can talk about what we feel.

> I believe that acting brings out a feeling towards things, an extra sensitiv-ity. I live in a village near the border with Israel and we have experienced many invasions by the Israelis coming in tanks. When I saw this I wanted to go naked before the tank, to show that I am only human. (Theatre Day Productions graduates: 2005)

These comments are profoundly moving and critically urgent in their demand for an end to violence and call for the protection of life. A con-nected sense of urgency, as well as some searching questions about the capacities and function of theatre during a time of crisis, were voiced by Israeli playwright and screenwriter Motti Lerner, visited during the same period of research:

Theatre needs to ask the question 'how can we live here?' Can we live here without relying on a massive military presence? The consensus is that things cannot change, and if it will not change what is there left to write about? It is too frightening to address this question. If we cannot live here without being in this terrible situation then what can we do? Can we continue to live here at all? (Lerner 2005)

This aching question – 'how can we live here?' – so precisely and powerfully articulated in the Gaza Strip and Israel in 2005 – has a global resonance, and is repeated across the explorations of performance in a time of terror that follow here. Such emotive evocations of bare life – the life held in suspension that Agamben identifies as the site of the political – also provide the absent-present starting point of this book. In citing these comments from Palestinian and Israeli artists, I draw attention to the failure to secure an adequate response – and posit the stalling impact of diminished, threatened and wasted life – as a hesitant, uncertain and possible site for the practice of a hopeful and critical politics of performance in time of terror.

1

Searching for a politics of performance in an age of uncertainty

The Wars against Terror have begun. (Bobbitt 2008: 3)

The war on terror that shaped the first decade of the twenty-first century witnessed the institutionalisation of performance as a strategy and tactic of violence. This book investigates performance in times of terror, and is driven by the proposition that the coalitions of performance and violence that become evident during periods of crisis create a pressing imperative to re-examine what is meant by the phrase 'the politics of performance'. The war on terror was supported by carefully scripted, albeit questionable, performances of evidence conveying the case for war. It also featured military rehearsals of 'preventative' scenarios of attack and defence, spectacular violence, ritualised humiliation and torture of prisoners of war, and melodramatic media reporting of the aggression of the opponent and consequent vulnerability of the 'west'. Such dramatisations of threats to life, and the postures of aggression and protection that they provoke, narrow the conditions in which critical, creative responses to violence by artists might be formulated. *Performance in a Time of Terror* explores the potential of performance to stage critical interruptions of the mimetic circulation of threat and frailty during wars on terror, in which arguably the most radical acts of performance are those taking place as part of the shock and awe tactics, covert military operations and torture scenarios associated with such wars.

This necessary re-examination of the politics of performance has also been prompted by a desire to explore the role of performance in times of crisis more generally, born of recognition that wars on terror are often symptoms of historical contexts shaped by economic, political and environmental crisis. A useful way of thinking about this context is offered by Zygmunt Bauman, who argues that the 'liquid times' of modernity, produced by unbridled economic globalisation, generate 'conditions of endemic uncertainty' (Bauman 2007: 4). In Bauman's work, an 'age of uncertainty', and its accompanying terror and violence, is concomitant with a global economy that prizes unplanned expansion and the search for ever-increasing levels of economic productivity and profitability over the value of life. The performances documented and explored in this book exhibit a range of responses to an age of uncertainty. There are examples of performances that have participated in the stage management of crisis in ways that protect some lives and obliterate others. There are also examples of performances that have critically interrupted the displays of threat and frailty that have become idiomatic of an age of uncertainty.

In terms of an examination of the politics of such performances, an immediate challenge is that the conditions of endemic uncertainty noted by Bauman also extend to a generalised uncertainty about how the critical project of art-making might be conceptualised. For example, using Bauman's 'age of uncertainty', art scholar Janet Wolff develops a series of propositions about an 'aesthetics of uncertainty', looking to the marginal, indirect and oblique in artistic practice for 'a new discourse of value without a foundation in certainties or universals' (Wolff 2008: 5). Wolff's uncertainty usefully challenges any attempt to articulate a politics of performance grounded in a dogmatic set of principles. However, *Performance in a Time of Terror* is also stimulated by the insistent notion that, amidst such spiralling uncertainties, the effort to more securely define and practise a hopeful politics of performance remains a critical – important and urgent – task for artists concerned about the violence and inequity of late capitalist society. Here, I explore these politics by paying close attention to a diverse series of performances produced as part of, or in response to, wars on terror.

In this introductory chapter, I lay out a framework for considering the politics of performance in an age of uncertainty. Concepts are introduced from a range of sources, including performance studies, cultural theory and political philosophy. Some are explored in depth; however, others are briefly referenced and worked on in more detail in the chapters that follow. I begin by reviewing explorations of performance and terror at distinct historical and geographical moments, and move on

to explore selected, contemporary studies of the politics of performance. Following this, I offer a discussion of *mimesis* in performance, in
particular focusing on approaches that identify mimesis as a means by
which we negotiate our relationships with a threatening, unpredictable
and alterable world. As part of this, a repeated motif of mimesis and
waste is identified and developed as a possible conceptual framework
for understanding the politics of performance. Departing from notions
of the radical in performance, the chapter concludes by arguing for the
reclamation of the conservative *as part of* performance's radical project,
and as providing rich possibilities for understanding and practising a
hopeful and critical politics of performance in times of crisis.

Whilst this chapter focuses on theoretical concerns, it should be
noted that the terrain outlined here has arisen in a very direct way
from the examination of the performances in successive chapters. If the
reader enjoys engagements with theoretical writing, reading on here
might be a good choice to make, although it is just as possible to access
the argument by reading about the performances documented later
in the book. In the sequence of writing, the chapters that follow came
first and this introductory chapter's conceptual overview was written
last. Here I provide a theoretically driven account of the argument as
a whole; subsequent chapters provide segments of the same account,
grounded in examples of performance.

Performance and terror, terror and performance

What do cheap theatrics and magic shows have to do with human annihilation? Too much, unfortunately. (Taylor 1997: x)

Performance and terror are intimately and intricately affiliated, and
their relationship has been the subject of accounts of performance from
the ancients to our contemporaries. In his *Poetics*, Aristotle famously
commented on the pity and terror provoked in an audience by the abject
hero of ancient Greek tragedy, producing a catharsis that clarified the
spectator's view and materialised the world in ideal, readily surveyable,
knowable form, purged of uncertainty. Conversely, in the twentieth
century Antonin Artaud, in a comment often cited by performance
scholars writing in response to the 9/11 attacks, understood a spectator's
encounter with performance as a confrontation with a terrifying world:

'we are not free. And the sky can still fall on our heads. And theatre has been created to teach us that' (Artaud 1977: 60). Despite their differences, what underpins both of these perspectives is a notion of performance as an encounter with existential terror, and as providing a means by which this terror might be negotiated – that is, performance as a precarious front line to our encounters with an uncertain and unpredictable world. To focus on performance and terror is to explore our attempts to attain agency and meaning in a world we do not control. It is also to be confronted with our failures in this endeavour, as the performances we make reproduce the conditions of uncertainty on which they are (un) founded.

Terrorist violence itself makes use of performance – display, spectacle, timing, rehearsal, stage management and symbolism for example – to distort expected sequences of appearance and disappearance in an offensive and threatening reality, with de-realising affects and effects. Terror is an affect that is stimulated by the disturbance and collapse of worlds of meaning and processes of sense-making as well as material worlds. Performances of terror that destroy the world, and the means by which we make sense of the world, have inspired artists to explore the limitations as well as the possibilities of performance as a response to terror and terrorism. Graham Coulter-Smith and Maurice Owen (2005), for example, provide a useful edited collection that describes performance artists' responses to the 9/11 attacks. Their collection focuses on artists' explorations of the de-realising and destructive impact of violence, and repeated evocation of the ineffable and unspeakable in response. The ways in which performance reproduces the uncertain appearances and disappearances of bodies and worlds in times of terror are also explored as part of the studies of three scholars that have provided the guiding principles of my investigation in this book. These are: Diana Taylor's exploration of performance during the Dirty War in Argentina (Taylor 1997); Michael Taussig's studies of mimesis and colonial terror in Colombia (Taussig 1993; 1992; 1987); and Anthony Kubiak's conceptual study of the stages of terror of western theatre history (Kubiak 1991). Each of these works predates the global conflict of the first decade of the twenty-first century and their distinct contributions to understanding performance's intimacies with terror make them important sources of inspiration for understanding later events.

For Kubiak 'a terror that is theatre's moment, a terror that is so basic to human life that it remains largely invisible *except* as theatre' underpins both the theatricality of terrorism and staged drama's representations of terror (Kubiak 1991: 2. Italics in original). He finds a language for exploring theatre's relationship to terror in Lacanian psychoanalysis: "'I" am displaced outside the location of "my" self and seem to vanish into the Other. This is the essential performative circumstance of theatre' (*ibid.*: 13). In seeing ourselves represented in moments of theatre, we are both in contact with and alienated from a sense of self and world. We disappear in the mimesis of life on 'stage', and yet without such representations we cannot come to sense or know ourselves or the world. Here, theatre is an *'ontological confrontation with non-being'* and 'any particular historical tracing of terror's threat in the theatre would perhaps do no better than to observe the places where each play folds itself into this disappearance' (*ibid.*: 23. Italics in original). Kubiak argues that social and staged dramas can be explored for the ways in which they conceal, gesture towards or reveal the terrifying disappearances of self and world that occur in performance. Some dramas transform terror into acts of terrorism, and others gesture towards disappearance in ways that sanctify or neutralise terror. A gesture towards the *ineffability* of terror in theatre utilises the gap between terror as an affect and terror as a confrontation with non-being in mimesis in a way that might become a *socialising* force. Therefore: 'it is perhaps theatre itself that can still serve us best as the means by which violence is remembered and resisted within the interval between terror's thought and its appropriation' (*ibid.*: 162).

The relationship between performance, terror and disappearance is a repeated focus of Diana Taylor's investigation of an interconnected series of performances in a very different context of terror – Argentina's Dirty War (1976–83). Taylor explores how the terror performances of the military junta sought to reinvent Argentina by cleansing the nation of those threatening to destabilise a new economic and political order. For her, the disappearance of thousands of citizens was a deliberately theatrical, stage-managed and devastating terrorisation that sought to suppress an entire population. Tracing the playing out of 'disappearing acts' across staged dramas, torture scenarios, forced disappearances of citizens and political protests, she identifies a repeated 'slate-cleaning' gesture of locating toxic threats and expelling them from the national constitution. As part of this, Taylor argues that staged dramas mimetically reproduced the violent erasures of the Dirty War, primarily through an appropriation and exploitation of the feminine and feminised body, despite the resistant intentions of the artists involved. Taylor's examination of the mimetic circulation of the disappearance and erasure of life over different domains of performance in Argentina can be usefully placed alongside Taussig's studies of mimesis and colonial terror in Colombia. Drawing on Theodor Adorno and Max Horkheimer's notion of an 'organised control of mimesis', which I return to below, Taussig describes how colonial powers of the First World controlled its encounters with unknown others by creating a 'savage mirror on the edge of the known world' (Taussig 1993: 78). Here, 'civilised' elites, in extending their powers to new territories, mirrored the threat of the unknown and their own violent trajectories by 'making up' threatening and barbaric others that, in turn, legitimised 'retaliatory' violence.

Importantly, the notion of mimesis explored by Taussig, and inferred by Taylor's tracing of the repeated disappearing acts of the Dirty War in Argentina, extends far beyond a reductive understanding of mimesis as a practice of imitation or reflection of the world. As Taussig shows, mimesis is a practice that both materialises and dissembles, and makes and unmakes bodies and worlds. Here, mimesis is understood as a practice of copying and contact that claims the power and agency of and over bodies and worlds. Mimesis is a form of 'sensuous knowing' that has the capacity to generate experience and knowledge, and also actually produce the matter and substance of the world: 'mimesis sutures the real to the really made up – and no society exists otherwise' (Taussig 1993: 86). For Taussig, an era of globalisation has produced 'mimetic excess' or 'mimetic vertigo' – the multiplication of encounters with unpredictable and unknown others has meant that 'all the land is borderland . . . a postmodern landscape where Self and Other paw at the ghostly imaginings of each other's powers' (ibid.: 249). In a discussion that is particularly prescient of the war on terror that characterised the first decade of the twenty-first century, Taussig describes the perpetual insecurity that results from such mimetic excesses as comprising 'the nervous system' of late capitalism's 'state of emergency', supported by low-intensity warfare 'whose leading characteristic is to blur accustomed realities and boundaries and keep them blurred' (Taussig 1992: 22). This conceptualisation of mimesis as a material practice that makes and unmakes bodies and worlds, and provides an uncertain means of regulating our encounters with a threatening and alterable world, is crucial to the argument that follows in this book. Here, I explore the mimetic processes of performances inspired by the nervous system of late capitalism and pay particular attention to the ways in which performance has variously supported the appearance, disappearance, survival and destruction of life during times of crisis. The key question driving this book is as follows: what appearances and disappearances of bodies and worlds were played out as part of the ordered disorder of the war on terror, and how were these reproduced and critically resisted as part of the mimetic processes of performances that responded to crisis?

In order to identify what might be claimed as distinctly *critical* kinds of mimesis in performance in this context, it is useful to explore the mimetic processes of wars on terror in more detail. Interestingly, there is a point of congruence between left and right political commentators about the importance of mimesis to understanding wars on terror and their situation within a social and political context of uncertainty. From the right, international security scholar Philip Bobbitt argues that increasing security concerns – exhibited by the more prevalent use of emergency powers and steady militarisation of domestic environments – are an inevitable feature of the 'global market states' of late capitalism. He is explicit that 'terror', rather than 'terrorism', is the elusive non-object of wars on terror, as powerful elites are aware that the threats they face have a mimetic relationship to their own global, decentralised and networked constitution (Bobbitt 2008: 45). Wars on terror are necessarily imprecise responses to the multiple, anonymous and unpredictable threats of a world shaped by unbridled economic expansion. Echoing this, and here from a left political perspective, Jean Baudrillard saw in the attacks of 9/11 an image of *'triumphant globalisation battling against itself'* (Baudrillard 2002: 11. Italics in original). The mimetic processes in play here, and their terrible consequences, are globally dispersed and all-encompassing in their world-distorting and world-destroying effects. They are also to some extent 'stage-managed' by political and military elites, as demonstrated by the work of Naomi Klein. She describes how economists in powerful countries deliberately induce, manufacture and stage-manage economic and political crisis as part of a 'shock doctrine', facilitating the forced introduction of privatisation, deregulation and cuts to social spending in powerful as well as economically weaker countries, with devastating costs to life. As such, the war on terror of the first decade of the twenty-first century was 'an almost completely for-profit venture, a booming new industry that has breathed new life into the faltering US economy' (Klein 2007: 13). Klein notes that emerging markets of outsourced torture and interrogation services, military healthcare, counterterrorism and security services, weapons manufacture, humanitarian relief and reconstruction are all secured by the longevity of wars on terror in an age of uncertainty.

Wars on terror are effectively durational performances, lacking a beginning, middle and end, and characterised by temporal and spatial formlessness. The US government's decision to drop the nomenclature 'global war on terror' in 2008 (reported in Luce and Dombey 2009) means that the war on terror of the first decade of the twenty-first century might be dated from US President George Bush's address to the nation following the attacks on the US on 9/11 on 20 September 2001 to some point in late 2008. However, a comment made by William Cohen, US President Bill Clinton's Secretary of Defense in 1997, 'the war against terrorism will be a protracted conflict', troubles efforts to fix the temporal frames of this war (cited in Furedi 2007: 2). Military conflicts in Afghanistan and Iraq, the fight against international terrorism in increasing numbers of countries and the emergence of community-based counterterrorism initiatives in domestic contexts, all of which are ongoing at the time of writing, also highlight the movable spatial and temporal frames of wars on terror. The instability of the terms 'terrorism' and 'war on terror' reflect this generalising formlessness – these are terms that can be usefully assigned to a shifting series of objects and subjects, as captured by Noam Chomsky in his comment that 'terrorism is the violence that *they* commit against *us* – whoever *we* happen to be' (cited in Scraton 2002: 71. Italics in original). To extend the perspectives of Aristotle and Artaud cited above, the war on terror, read 'as' performance as well as in its use of performance as a weapon of war, produces a world that is no longer knowable or controllable by means of conventional practices of surveillance and representation. Here, mimesis is drawn on for its capacity to produce, regulate, control and adapt to an uncertain, unpredictable world, and in ways that are discriminate and devastating in their making and unmaking of bodies and worlds. As part of the mimetic processes of this war, destruction has fallen from the skies onto the heads of people living across its all-consuming, ever-expanding spatial and temporal zones.

In his study of the relationship between tragedy and terror, Terry Eagleton suggests that western powers were unable to recognise their own culpability and frailty in the 'monsters' they imagined following the 9/11 attacks: 'the symptoms of weakness and despair in the raging fury at its gate . . . the wretched of the earth, the garbage of global capitalism' (Eagleton 2005: 133). Echoing Eagleton's identification of 'garbage' as the blind spot of the mimetic excesses of the war on terror, Bauman explores *wasted life* as a defining, albeit repressed, feature of an age of uncertainty. Wasted life is an outcome of an economic system that sustains itself by exploitation, overproduction and overconsumption. For Bauman, the military and security industries constitute a 'waste disposal' industry – obscuring the economic causes of crisis, and also leading to intensifying levels of insecurity and threat. Increasing numbers of refugees, migrants and outcasts make up the wasted life of a system in crisis, and here Bauman makes direct reference to Agamben's 'bare life' (discussed in the prologue) as 'the principal category of human waste' (Bauman 2004: 32). 'Wasted humans' are the 'unintended and unplanned "collateral casualties" of economic progress' – destroyed, or broken down to be recycled when needed by the system (*ibid.*: 39). Bauman also proposes that an array of political, military, social and cultural strategies, characterised by processes of expulsion, excision, containment, beautification and purification, help societies negotiate anxieties about waste and wasted life.

This notion of 'wasted life' thus provides the sociological impetus for a line of thinking about the significance of waste and wasted life to performance in times of terror. To some extent, Bauman's wasted life provides a material foundation for Agamben's more abstract, philosophically driven notion of 'bare life', and this opens up a space to explore the rich and complex relationship between performance – a material as well as symbolic practice – and a politics of exception. Performance is a means by which we encounter and negotiate the troublingly intense, proximate presence of threatened bodies and worlds in a crisis-ridden context. To study performance in times of crisis is to insist on the materiality of life, and the tangible, visceral costs of a world configured by violence and inequity. As will become clear, many of the performances documented and explored in this book negotiate waste and wasted life by means of processes of erasure, excision and beautification. However, others make use of and revalue waste and wasted life as part of their political and aesthetic interventions. To further explore this line of thinking, it is useful to examine existing frameworks for understanding the politics of performance in a little more depth.

Critical mimesis and waste

From postclassical times to the present, theatre has gone through a series of transformations that assert the right of the disparate, partial, absurd and ugly against the postulates of unity, wholeness, reconciliation and sense. (Lehmann 2006: 44)

The disruptions of sense and sense-making that characterise performances of terror, noted above, have also generated critical and creative frameworks for understanding and practising the radical in performance. The same features of performance that facilitate its coalitions with violence therefore – its capacity to make life disappear, its blurring of appearances, its sensual excesses and destabilising affects – have been critically mimicked by performance scholars and practitioners committed to understanding and practising a politics of performance that might counter violence and inequity, and help bring about a better world. In this part of the chapter, I suggest that performance also exhibits a critical capacity by means of engagements with waste and wasted life, making use of the sensual force of the abject to dramatise and resist war and crisis. Implicit here is a proposal for a shift in thinking about the politics of performance, from understanding the critical capacities of performance to be associated with the radical, excessive and transformative (prominent in the accounts of performance's politics that I explore below), to embracing the critical potential and value of waste. This, in turn, provides the impetus for a consideration of the rich possibilities of the *conservative* for understanding and practising a hopeful and critical politics of performance.

Crisis has inspired and mobilised political performance practice across the contemporary history of western performance, from the explosion of workers' theatres in between the two World Wars (1914–18; 1939–45), to the proliferation of alternative theatres of the counter-cultural movement in the 1960s (see Kershaw 1992; Samuel *et al.* 1985; Itzin 1980). However, the emergence of postmodernism as a critical frame in the latter half of the last century problematised understandings of the critical potential of performance. The topographies of body, space and text exhibited by performance came to be understood as ambivalent because they mirror, and therefore reproduce, and potentially refuse the patterns of body, space and text circulating in the hegemonic cultural realm. As such, a stance of pure opposition is no longer possible, and, as performance scholar Baz Kershaw asks, the key question becomes: 'how can performance, in being always already implicated in the dominant, avoid replicating the values of the dominant?' (Kershaw 1999: 70). In this book, I use the term 'critical mimesis' to explore this simultaneous mirroring and refusal of hegemonic values in performance. Critical mimesis is a term that responds to the urgent demand for an interruption of the atrophic, petrified projections of self and other mobilised by the mimetic excesses of a system in crisis. Following the critical philosophy of Max Horkheimer and Theodor Adorno, whose commentary on mimesis is explored below, here the 'critical' privileges self-conscious reflective activity that commits to bringing about a more equitable world as well as understanding and explaining society.

Kershaw responds to uncertainties about how to conceptualise the politics of performance in a postmodern context by embracing the radical in performance. For Kershaw, the radical arises from the 'excesses of performance' – the surplus meanings generated by performance's dynamic interaction with its context and continuous co-production by performers and spectators in ways that cannot be directed, predicted or measured. As such, radical performance generates new possibilities for thinking about, experiencing and making the world: 'much more happens in performance than the production of signs, and it is precisely this experience of performative excess – which *includes* the signifying process – that ushers in the potential of the radical in performance' (Kershaw 1999: 66). Kershaw draws on Raymond Williams' analysis of the radical as being associated with 'vigorous and fundamental change' without ideological orientation, and he welcomes the radical as a gesture 'beyond all forms of the dogmatic, towards kinds of freedom that cannot be envisaged' (*ibid.*: 18). Importantly, he is also troubled by the radical – as Kershaw notes, the radical freedoms associated with Nazi rallies are inferred by this definition and, thus, radical performance 'invites an ideological investment that it cannot of itself determine. In that sense, it is always a creative opportunity to change the world for better or worse, a performative process in need of direction' (*ibid.*: 20).

Echoing this troubling reflection on the radical powers of performance, performance theorist Jon McKenzie suggests that the mutational effects of performance have become normative forces under the conditions of late capitalism, shaping the improved efficiencies of systems of production. He identifies a series of challenges for more efficacious performance in this context: 'perform – or else: be fired, redeployed, institutionally marginalised . . . socially normalised . . . outmoded, undereducated' (McKenzie 2001: 7–12). Here, the excesses of radical performance noted by Kershaw also mobilise a performance-obsessed system of production, and given the debilitating terrors and the perpetual alterability of the nervous system of late capitalism, McKenzie's list might be extended to include 'perform – or else . . . be annihilated'. These challenges to perform make use of performance's affinity with terror and here, the uncertainties and excesses of radical performance become tools for powerful elites and their stage-managed crises. This is a context in which the dogmatic and ideological, as sociologist Patricia Clough suggests, have been replaced by the control of bodies by means of the production, modulation and circulation of *affect*. A biopolitical realm configured by a politics of exception (discussed in the prologue), has instituted an 'affect economy' that measures life's value according to its capacity for affective labour in ways which, in turn, institute hierarchical and divisive categorisations of life as valuable or expendable (Clough 2007: 25). The sensuous excesses, intimate engagements and intense forms of experience associated with radical performance can thus service a politics of exception, and, we might add, also produce political consensus by means of a destabilising circulation of fear. What is urgently needed, then, is a practice of performance that critically mirrors the uncertainties of the nervous system and articulates a contingent and determined revaluing of threatened and wasted life.

One response to this terrain has been to take up performance's capacity for affect as a possible site for working within and against an affect economy that mobilises terror. Here, the ideas of cultural theorist Jacques Rancière have been influential. Rancière searches for a critical politics and aesthetics of art in 'dissensus' – moments of aesthetic rupture whereby different senses of the world, and ways of making sense of the world, are uncannily juxtaposed, leading to 'a dissensual re-configuration of the common experience of the sensible'. Such moments disrupt 'proper' ways of speaking and doing, remake the 'fabric of sensory experience' and generate new kinds of critical subjectivity (Rancière 2010: 139–40). Rancière's 'redistribution of the sensible' is referenced by James Thompson in his account of the extension of the affective realm mobilised by participatory performance (Thompson 2009), and by Alan Read, in his descriptions of the kinds of radical inclusion offered by performance's engagements with 'other worldly' phenomena (Read 2008). Thompson's account is highly suggestive of how performance might work within and against the affect economy of a system in crisis – he stresses the importance of research and practice in performance that sustains the 'difficultness of affect', and also explores resistant moments of joy, beauty and celebration in performances in places of war (Thompson 2009: 10). Read similarly examines how performance reconfigures the sensible world in his analysis of encounters with children, animals and natural environments in performance. For Read, the estrangements of the 'human' that such dissensual performances evoke are what make theatre 'so potentially full of politics' (Read 2008: 27). Thus, an experience of estrangement in performance extends the sensible fabric of the social world and it is in the sociality of performance – in the generation of opportunities for kinds of intimacy and engagement that lack predetermination or definition – that its politics resides. The unsettling qualities of encounters with the beyond-human or non-human are also explored by Kershaw in his later work, where he investigates performances that open up 'a *sense* of the human' which extends beyond the exclusive and logocentric realm of 'liberal humanist visions of political or ethical global commonalities' (Kershaw 2007: 212. Italics in original).

These works, necessarily only briefly referenced here, formulate a combined suggestion about the critical potential of performance's uncanny, dissensual representation of life beyond the frames of the comfortably recognised, familiar 'human' world. That is, performance's capacity to discomfort, unsettle and estrange by providing encounters with life and worlds that exist outside habitual frames of recognition or appreciation. In terms of the direct concerns of this book, this unsettlement might also be generated by performances that provide encounters with the monsters at the gate, the 'garbage' of global capitalism, or waste and wasted life, constituting the blind spot of the mimetic processes of a war on terror. However, these latter encounters also draw attention to another kind of force evoked by dissensual encounters, relating to the discomforting, tangible presence of the *abject* – that which is cast away, surplus or leftover from the representation of the world as beautiful and affectionate. Disturbances of our sensible worlds, as performances of terror exhibit, extend the domains of the affective, but they also bring us into contact with our lack of meaning as discrete, coherent subjects, that is, with an experience of self and world as abject, decaying and disappearing. Here, performance represents life in negated, alienated or threatening forms and thus releases the critical and affective force of the abject to disorder the beautifying schemes of an orderly, rule-bound universe. Conversely, performance might also work to excise, repress and cover up waste and wasted life. Thus, to understand performance's politics in an age of uncertainty defined by the production of waste and wasted life – it may be useful to supplement concerns for the excess and affect of performance with an investigation of performance as a practice intimately affiliated to waste. Following this suggestion, and given the repeated significance of mimesis for understanding performance in times of terror here, it is useful to consider some possible relationships between mimesis and waste in performance.

Whilst acknowledging the insecurity of his categorisation, classics scholar Stephen Halliwell views the 'family of concepts' associated with mimesis as corresponding to two domains – 'world-reflecting' and 'world-creating'. The former refers to understandings of mimesis as corresponding to a reality outside representation, and the latter to mimesis as creating a '"worldlike" consistency or plausibility' that may or may not relate to the 'real' world (Halliwell 2002: 23). What is most significant for the discussion here are the interconnections between these categories and their concomitant inference of a complex, paradoxical and cyclical relationship in mimesis between the *representation* of the world, the *making* or materialisation of the world, and the *decay* of the world. The performances explored and documented in this book show performance's critical potential as corresponding to this cyclical process of representation, materialisation and decay in mimesis. According to this understanding, mimesis offers a mirror reflection of the world, and this reflection carries a forceful presence that claims the power of the original. The subjects and objects of mimesis are estranged – they collapse and decay – mobilising a transfer of power, meaning and substance that generates the material presence and ephemerality, and appearances and disappearances of performance. Paradoxically then, the operation of decay at the centre of a mimetic process thus precisely corresponds to mimesis' materialisation of a coherent, plausible, vivid world of sensation and significance that makes the world anew. The outcomes of this cyclical process of unmaking and making the world are incipient, endless and unfathomable, but they are also always constrained by the contours and forms of an alienating and alterable world (recalling Marx's maxim that we make history, but not in circumstances of our own choosing). As such, mimesis can be understood as a practice that simultaneously secures and threatens self and world as plausible and habitable entities, and there is a close affiliation in mimesis between the mortification, vivification and decay or disappearance of life. A struggle to control the power of mimesis signifies a contest of life and death, and *critical* mimesis in performance might thus be defined as a practice of performance that materialises protective and habitable worlds in which life might encounter its own decay, whilst also securing itself in the world.

The paradoxical relationship between mortification and vivification in mimesis is a repeated feature of performance scholarship that explores the distinction between mimesis and mimicry. McKenzie, for example, notes a distinction between 'the normative repetition of traditional mimesis, which tends to erase differences and anomalies in order to create the *appearance* of a unified, coherent, and originary presence' and 'the mutational repetition of countermimesis or countermimicry, in which repetition is exaggerated to the point that differences proliferate and disseminate themselves' (McKenzie 2001: 214. Italics in original). The ambivalence of mimesis, and its critical potential as mimicry, also preoccupies theatre scholar Elin Diamond in her search for a specifically feminist mimesis. For Diamond, mimicry is a form of mimesis that insists on its doubled and doubling nature, and lacks any original or originating 'truth'. She works up a notion of mimesis as: 'a trick mirror that doubles (makes feminine) in the act of reflection' and as such '"mimesis imposed" becomes mimicry unleashed' (Diamond 1997: vi, xi). Cultural theorist Homi Bhabha also makes a distinction between mimesis and mimicry, drawing attention to the insurgency of mimicry: 'the excess or slippage produced by the ambivalence of mimicry (almost the same, but not quite) does not merely "rupture" the discourse, but becomes transformed into an uncertainty which fixes the colonial subject as a "partial" presence . . . mimicry is at once resemblance and menace' (Bhabha 1994: 123). This scholarship has tended to align the vivifying and insurgent notions of mimicry with critical cultural practices. However, in times of terror and crisis, the affects and effects of mimesis and mimicry are promiscuous in their allegiances, with, for example, the insurgency of mimicry mobilised as part of violent, reactionary performances and normative, mortifying performances constituting a refusal of chaos and disorder. The search for critical mimesis in performance thus needs to attend to the specificities of the politics and aesthetics of performance in contingent times and spaces.

This might be further illustrated by turning to two classic explorations of mimesis and terror: Theodor Adorno and Max Horkheimer's work on the organised control of mimesis that led to the Holocaust and Jacques Lacan's discussion of mimicry as a form of camouflage that diminishes life. In a study published shortly after the Second World War, Adorno and Horkheimer trace a history of civilisation's affinity with disorder and chaos, noting civilisation's repeated attempts to control the world by propagating myths of man's sovereignty over nature. Such myths reduce the terror, unpredictability and alterability of the world to a rational and knowable order, and cancel out what they call the 'animation of nature'. Here, life is protected and preserved by means of static and arthritic forms of mimesis that reproduce and intensify our alienation from nature, and thus self-preservation 'repeatedly culminates in the choice between survival and destruction' (Adorno and Horkheimer 1997: 29–30). Representations of the world as orderly and controllable take the place of forms of mimesis that are fluid, organic and adaptable, and terror, which remains 'ready to break out at any moment', attaches to those who resist order. Adorno and Horkheimer note that this led to the figure of the Jew becoming a repository of terror, arousing intense forms of hatred and disgust that felt 'natural', and culminating in the horrors of the Holocaust. Life seeks refuge from a violent and inequitable world by mirroring its static, arthritic forms, that is, by 'mimesis unto death':

> The reflexes of stiffening and numbness in humans are archaic schemata of the urge to survive: by adaptation to death, life pays the toll of its continued existence. Civilisation has replaced the organic adaptation to others and mimetic behaviour proper, by organised control of mimesis. (Adorno and Horkheimer 1997: 180)

This organised control of mimesis can be seen in the mimetic processes of the war on terror of the first decade of the twenty-first century, where terror came to be pinned to a shifting series of threatening others who stood in for and provided a means of regulating an uncertain world. In a later work on aesthetics, Adorno provides the counterpoint to this notion of mimesis by presenting what might be called an adaptive practice of mimesis or mimetic identification, specifically located in aesthetic experiences that provide encounters with the suffering of the other, and evoke a capacity to 'shudder' (Adorno 1997: 319). I return to the concept of 'shudder' in chapter 4 – but what is notable here is the notion of mimesis as a means by which an encounter with an unpredictable world might be regulated, and that at once mortifies and alienates, and also uncertainly protects and vivifies life by providing adaptive forms of response. This opens up possibilities for different practices of mimesis in performance – organised, adaptive, mortifying and decaying – and creates an imperative to pay close attention to respective performances for their capacities to protect life and enhance the possibilities for living. For Adorno and Horkheimer, the organised control of mimesis in the early part of the twentieth century that led to the Holocaust was founded on the repression of life's natural processes of diminishment and decay. My suggestion here is that better understanding of the coalitions of mortification and decay in cultural processes might support a critical and hopeful practice of mimesis in performance.

To further develop an understanding of mimesis as an uncertain means of negotiating life's survival and resilience in a threatening and alterable world, a turn to Jacques Lacan's notion of mimicry as camouflage is useful (I also return to this as part of chapter 3's exploration of counterinsurgency performance). Lacan understands mimicry as a form of resemblance to an anonymous and alienating world, which brings about the protection, but also the diminishment, of self:

> Mimicry reveals something in so far as it is distinct from what might be called an *itself* that is behind ... It is not a question of harmonising with the background but, against a mottled background, of becoming mottled ... Whenever we are dealing with imitation, we should be very careful not to think too quickly of the other who is being imitated. To imitate is no doubt to reproduce an image. But at bottom, it is, for the subject, to be inserted into a function whose exercise grasps it. (Lacan 1977: 99–100)

Thus, in seeking agency in the world by means of mimetic processes, we lose a sense of ourselves as discrete, secure and sensible objects. What is produced by mimesis is an estranged and estranging, mottled figure of self and world, and this evokes the gap between the sense of self as a meaningful subject and abject figure inferred by the discussions of political performance noted above. Here, self and world appear in broken, blurred and abject form, but importantly, such diminished forms also protect and, perhaps, prefigure kinds of relationship to the world based on assimilation and reciprocity rather than mastery and control. In engaging with rather than seeking sovereignty over life's decay in performance, perhaps an uncertain but also more equitable dwelling place in the world might be sensed, materialised and represented. Mimesis and mimicry represent life in diminished and decayed form and release the sensual forces of the abject, which in turn effect life's vivification, mortification and protection. It is in this complex and paradoxical domain that a notion of critical mimesis in performance might be formulated and developed. What is also suggested here is the interdependency of, rather than the opposition between, the normative and mutational, insurgent and mortifying, exposing and protective functions of mimesis.

Jon McKenzie provides a suggestive contribution to this discussion by evoking the energies released by the degradation of material life – captured by our sense of smell – in his exploration of performance's powers of transformation. McKenzie's 'perfumative' denotes 'atmospheres of flows and nonstratified substances' that are 'the citational mist of any and all performances . . . the becoming-mutational of normative forces, the becoming-normative of mutant forces . . . with odours emitted by certain incorporated remains' (McKenzie 2001: 202–3). This suggestion of the critical potential of performance's decaying materiality might be placed alongside Erika Fischer-Lichte's notion of performance as a self-generating organism that re-enchants the ordinary world by providing encounters with the intense, material presence of beings and things (Fischer-Lichte 2008: 206–7). These precise and focused discussions of the materiality of performance are extremely useful. However, according to the argument developing here, performance's powers of decay and enchantment are also troublingly aligned to the vivifying and mortifying potential of mimesis in performance and thus it is important to resist any reification of the critical potential of performance's material presence. *Performance in a Time of Terror* has been provoked by the coexistence of a theatre that enchants and vivifies with a theatre of atrocity, and the example of performance in chapter 2 explores some of the implications of this coexistence. This terrain needs to be negotiated and untangled, not just because it is here that the critical potential of performance resides, but also because, as Adorno and Horkheimer's analysis suggests, the force of the abject in mimesis mobilises a contest of life and death that is potentially annihilating as well as protective. Before any general claims about the critical potential of performance's vivifying and decaying materiality can be made, the circulations of the abject as part of performance's affects and effects must be explored by making careful reference to specific examples of performance. That is the project of this book.

Within contemporary performance, the abject is an important figure in the distinction drawn out by Hans-Thies Lehmann between 'dramatic theatre' and 'postdramatic theatre'. For Lehmann, 'dramatic theatre' is defined by Aristotelian mimesis – dramatic theatre offers up an abject hero who provokes a cathartic expression of pity and terror, and in turn an uncertain world is restored to a surveyable, knowable and ideal form. Contemporary performance practices that have emerged since the 1960s work differently: these 'postdramatic' performances offer provisional and open-ended encounters often operating across multiple temporal and spatial domains, an experience of community rather than fixed relationship, and a lack of action rather than defining event. Postdramatic theatre offers an all-encompassing 'world' of experience complete with fragmented narratives, breaks in meaning, moments of intensity and failed appearances. In terms of the argument developing here, postdramatic theatre might provoke critical interrogation of, compensate for, provide temporary refuge from, offer the promise of surviving or obscure the unpredictability of an age of uncertainty. It is worth briefly noting here that the notion of mimesis I am proposing subsumes any supposed opposition between mimetic and nonmimetic aspects of performance (Lehmann himself describes postdramatic theatre as 'nonmimetic'). Those aspects of performance generally associated with the nonmimetic – performance's excess, affect, potentiated signification, blurred appearances, fragmented and durational forms – are very much part of the notion of mimesis promoted here. Such supposedly nonmimetic features of performance are also profoundly mimetic of the upheavals and uncertainties of a time of terror.

More important for this discussion is postdramatic theatre's engagements with the abject – its frequent featuring of disfigured bodies, rubbish, broken objects and other signifiers of what Lehmann calls 'grotesque decay and absurdity'. This is concomitant with postdramatic theatre's offer of moments of intensity in performance 'but this time the heightening works downward: where the toilets are, the scum' (Lehmann 2006: 117). It is not possible to offer a history of contemporary theatre's relationship to waste and wasted life here; however, it is important to emphasise, as Lehmann himself implies, that contemporary performance's preoccupation with wasted life and broken form is not new, but signals the re-emergence of what has been a historical feature of theatre. Thus, Joe Kelleher's exploration of theatre and politics is highly suggestive of the relevance of waste to contemporary forms of dramatic as well as postdramatic theatre, in its repeated referral to the motif, 'cycle of shit'. The phrase is taken from a speech in debbie tucker green's play, *random* (2008), which responded to increasing rates of knife crime taking the lives of young people in Britain at the time of its original production. In the middle of a speech about her brother, made from his bedroom after he has been stabbed and killed, Sister exclaims 'Fuck this cycle of shit.' Kelleher uses this moment to investigate how the politics of the play are embedded in its evocation of an exposing and unsettling affectivity:

> something is left behind of what happened before, caught in the teeth or the nostrils or still there in the corner of the eye . . . It is as though, somehow, a few unlucky threads of human being got stuck in the teeth . . . as they were trying to retreat from the 'cycle of shit' that invades the world of the play . . . something has been shown, something has been said, has been brought into appearance, which might not otherwise be shown or spoken of. (Kelleher 2009: 26–7)

The power of this play is described in terms of the estranging, abject force of the live performance, and the terrible waste of life that it directly dramatised. It left behind an invasive, tangible presence of waste and wasted life that was critically resilient – that stayed once the performance was over. Lacan provides a useful concept that draws attention to the exposing and unsettling effects of an encounter with waste in performance that may be connected to what Kelleher is describing here. Lacan's *objet petit a* is an algebraic figure that refers to the surplus remains and leftovers of experience that have a material presence but cannot be securely captured in representational form. These leftover bits are sensual but senseless fragments of experience, evoking the mottled appearances of life seeking habitation in an alienating world denoted by Lacan's notion of mimicry, that become attached to parts of bodies – skin, shit, eyes, voice. Their meaning stays out of reach of comprehensive apprehension and permanently circulates. Sister's exclamation of suffering that got caught under Kelleher's skin, and worked its repetitions across his useful account of theatre and politics, is a perfect example of the critical potential of performance as a practice of waste. Examples of similar abject presences feature across the performances documented and explored in this book, emanating from the lifeless eyes of a bodiless head in Iraq disseminated across the worldwide web, the frail and uncertain voices on London theatre stages, the unhomed bodies of antiwar protest camps, and undecidable hearts and minds of young British Muslims of community-based counterterrorism plays. Lacan's description of the *objet petit a* as 'the object that cannot be swallowed, as it were, which remains stuck in the gullet of the signifier' captures the critically resilient nature of the diminished, intense presence of decay in performance (Lacan 1977: 270). These sensual and senseless parts are recycled as part of the mimesis of performance and mobilise performance's unpinnable affects and effects.

Adorno and Horkheimer's account of the organised control of mimesis warns that the critical and affective force of the abject also culminated in the unbearable presence of the Jew and the horrors of the Holocaust. Similarly, Slavoj Žižek identifies the *objet petit a* as 'a tiny feature' in an encounter 'whose presence magically transubstantiates its bearer into an alien' (Žižek 2006: 67). These small embodied distinctions evoke suffering, mobilise desire and also stimulate neighbourly violence, and are precisely what constitutes the political potential, as well as threat, of mimesis. Such cycles of shit raise questions as to how performance might nurture a capacity to register the inhumanity, anonymity, vulnerability and undecidability of waste and wasted life – critically and affectively. To phrase this in macroscopic terms: the circulations of waste and wasted life in performance evoke uncertainties relating to how we might live together in the unpredictable and exposed zones of crisis and exception without interpersonal violence. Circulations of waste signal the abjectification of bodies and space – but the egalitarian and vivifying nature of life's decay perhaps also provides an opportunity to devise responses to the unpredictability and alterability of the world in ways that protect rather than annihilate. *Performance in a Time of Terror* explores how abject, wasted life in performance supports hopeful and troubling conceptualisations of the conservative potential of performance implied here.

Peggy Phelan's writing on performance, with its concerns for holes in bodies, smashed skulls and archaeological remains, anticipates this terrain. For example, she reads the controversy relating to the preservation of the newly discovered remains of the Renaissance's Rose Theatre in London in 1989 through the metaphor of the rectum. Her resistant reading of the controversy evokes the critical and creative potential of waste and wasted life that I am inspired by here: 'empty cavities, hollow caves, and open holes are consolidated as so much "rubbish" in need of psychic repression [. . .] these remains represent the "excess" that will not stay repressed no matter how carefully mainstream society works to solidify the normative' (Phelan 1997: 77–8). Interestingly, her identification of the disruptive capacities of wasted remains comes from a controversy that was stimulated by a *conservative* impulse to preserve the theatre. The Rose Theatre controversy arose from the determined attempt of a group of people to secure the value of a theatre's ruined remains in the context of an ever-changing present. Wasted remains draw attention to troubling questions about the value of life in the face of the world's alterability – and their mobilisation as part of the critical schemas of performance inspires a desire to preserve, restore and conserve life. As such, critical mimesis in an age of uncertainty can be understood to be world-conserving as much as world-creating or world-transforming.

The radical-conservative in performance

renewal movements begin from the premise that there is no escape from the substantial messes we have created and that there has been enough erasure – of history, of culture, of memory. These are movements that do not seek to start from scratch but rather from scrap, from the rubble that is all around. (Klein 2007: 466)

A consideration of the conservative as a way of thinking about and practising a hopeful and critical politics of performance is thus, in part, prefigured by Peggy Phelan's essay on the excavation and preservation of the remains of the Rose Theatre. It is also evoked by the broader consideration of mimesis and waste here, especially by the paradoxical interconnections between the vivification, decay and mortification of life in mimesis repeatedly noted above. Here, the radical and conservative effects of performance are revealed as aligned rather than in opposition: a conservative impulse might be manifested as part of a radical, critical act, and radical intentions might materialise themselves as conservative responses to an altering and alterable world. In this section of the chapter, I begin to map out the critical potential of a radical-conservative politics and aesthetics of performance, providing some preliminary notes that are challenged and developed as part of the analysis of performances in successive chapters, and summarised in the concluding chapter of this book.

In her introduction to Lehmann's account of postdramatic theatre, Karen Jürs-Munby draws comparisons between a postdramatic aesthetic and the contemporary performance practices of Goat Island and Forced Entertainment, theatre companies that create performance texts 'in need of repair'. Here, performance 'does not add up to an Aristotelian dramatic fictional whole but is instead full of holes. The onus is on the spectator/witness to help 'repair' – perhaps by piecing together information . . . or to help bear the trauma of living in a damaged world' (Lehmann 2006: 12). Steve Bottoms and Matthew Goulish's account of Goat Island performances entitled *Small Acts of Repair*, is also very suggestive of a conservative aesthetic and politics of performance. *When will the September roses bloom? Last night was only a comedy*, the performance made by the company after the 9/11 attacks, was stimulated by the question 'how do you make a repair?', provoked in part by the accidental discovery of a household maintenance manual by a member of the company. The evocative notion of repair, which implicitly critiqued and mourned the damaging effects of the escalation of global violence during this period, is read by Bottoms as an 'attempt to seed a more redemptive environ/mental system' than terrorists' use of knives, planes and buildings (Bottoms and Goulish 2007: 25). The turn to repair also resists the wasteful excesses of an overproducing, over-consuming society, and the company's recycling of redundant, thrown-away objects in their performances carries the same gentle and powerful critique. Importantly, this is a process that revalues the diminished, worn-out and fragile within an aesthetics that repairs without beauti-fying, and thus 'leaves your awareness of the fault in place' (*ibid.*: 95). As such, this project of conservation does not compensate for damage and crisis – there is no uncritical embrace of the possibilities of repair-ing and reviving community here. Rather, marks of decay, damage and diminishment are valued for what they signify and memorialise, and also perhaps, for their promise of a resilient relationship to the world in its alterability. These ruined and decaying marks signal possibility and potential – rather than consensus or commonality – they evoke the rupture of damage, and the possibility of its survival.

The conservative has had a long partnership with, rather than oppo-sition to, left-oriented radical politics, as historian Raphael Samuel has comprehensively argued. He insists on the radical, activist and popular roots of conservation movements. For Samuel, these movements stage rescue operations that stem from 'a vertiginous sense of disappearing worlds . . . born out of a sense of emergency' (Samuel 1994: 150). He finds a 'poetics of the ordinary' in the impulse to preserve and restore small objects, natural worlds and ordinary experiences, including domestic spaces and everyday dwellings – arguing that conservation movements are stimulated by the desire of ordinary people to protect something of their worlds of experience during times of rapid change (*ibid.*: 160). Interestingly, this notion of conservation does not resist change, but reinvents what transformation might mean in a context that values the ordinary and everyday. Conservation is an 'aestheticising process' that *begins* rather than ends a cycle of change and, as part of this, conserved objects and environments are 'living organisms' engaged in processes of change where care for their frailty and survival is the primary impera-tive (*ibid.*: 303–4). The conservative is thus a complex domain – there are many kinds of conservation in practice – and their distinctions show that the ways we ascribe meaning and value to objects, organisms and environments are historically and culturally contingent. So, for example, conservation researcher Salvador Muños Viñas contrasts classical practices of conservation which aim to restore an object to its authentic or 'true' condition by cleaning away and covering up damage and even adding alien parts, to postmodern practices which accept damage and ruin as marks of value. These latter practices also seek to engage communities in democratic and creative processes of decision-making regarding conservation, and as such liberate the multiple meanings and values of objects (Muños Viñas 2005: 104 and 158).

In this chapter I have argued that the challenge of articulating and practising a hopeful and critical politics of performance resides in an examination of performance as a practice of waste and wasted life. The notions of mimesis explored above evoke different possible relationships between performance and waste – from a concerned revaluing of waste as part of aesthetic engagements that materialise equitable encounters with strange and estranging others, to the expulsion and repression of waste in the search for certainty. A motif of waste and wasted life has been repeatedly evoked in accounts of performance in times of terror. To cite examples positioned at the start and end of this chapter – Taylor draws attention to the detoxifying, cleansing erasures of life carried out as part of the military junta's disappearing acts in Argentina, whilst Bottoms and Goulish explore the impulse to repair damage in the Goat Island production that followed 9/11. The distinctions between these two examples highlight the troubling and ambivalent critical potential of waste in performance, and this is also a repeated feature of the examinations of the performances in successive chapters. Life is conserved by means of performances of detoxification and expulsion, as much as by performances which revalue waste for its promise of regeneration and survival. Importantly, within the terms of reference of this book, critically mimetic performances are indiscriminate in their valuing of wasted life and are determinedly non-violent, in contrast to those that demonstrate the frailty of life as part of a staging of threat that supports violence.

Notes on methodology

Whilst the conceptual framework drawn on here is inspired by many international scholars and practitioners from different disciplines, the performances that have been selected for close analysis all exhibit a specifically British response to the war on terror. This, in the end, was a deliberate decision, made in part because of the difficulty of completing a close study of performance and terror in other geographical sites (as described in the prologue), and in part stimulated by a desire to explore the local and global interconnections prevalent in one site's response to global conflict. As such, the focus on a British context is responsive to changing dimensions of space and time in a globalised world and offers, I hope, as useful an opportunity to learn something of the challenges and possibilities of critical performance in an age of uncertainty as a more extensive geographical study. The performances documented here show how conflicts in other places impact upon relationships between neighbours closer to home, and also how the local is implicated in wars fought far away. The beheading of a British citizen explored in the following chapter happened in a country thousands of miles away, but was deliberately constructed for audiences in the UK, and had a shocking and distressing impact on communities in the north-west of England, the home of the victim of the attack and also the place where this book was researched and written. Conversely, the performances by and for young British Muslims in chapter 6 all happened close to the home of this book – in and around the north-west of England – but their aesthetics and politics directly responded to a conflict with international terrorism that, at the time of writing, continues to put pressure on relationships between communities in this and other places around the world.

Diana Taylor describes a methodology appropriate for performance studies that crosses geographical, historical and disciplinary borders, and takes account of the local and global interconnections between performances. She extends this methodological imperative to explore critical links between performances to include analysis of the 'nonevents' of small-scale performances as well as spectacular acts of global prominence. This avoids a focus on the paradigmatic in a way that resists the reproduction of unhelpful hierarchies and divisions between performances of different sorts, and instead identifies a diverse array of interconnected performances and 'asks us to think them together' (D. Taylor 2003: 274). I have used Taylor's invitation as a springboard for my own explorations and here this 'thinking together' places performances that were prominent in the public sphere, such as the global day of action against war on 15 February 2003, alongside small-scale performances to audiences of young people, for example. Responding to this methodological imperative also inspired a broad and inclusive approach to the 'texts' drawn on as part of the research. These texts include stage plays and theatre and performance events, but also a range of other texts read as 'scripts' of the mimetic processes of wars on terror: autobiographical accounts of former Special Forces soldiers in Northern Ireland, media reports on antiwar protest demonstrations, digital clips of beheadings, military field manuals, the practical experience of making a performance, insurgency websites, antiwar literature, interviews with artists and government documents relating to national security. These are drawn upon without respect for constructed hierarchies of academic and non-academic sources, and are used according to their potential explanatory power rather than supposed conceptual sophistication.

The performances that are the focus of successive chapters offer a critical drift that exposes the interdependency of self and other, 'us and them', 'here and there' of hybrid postcolonial realities, travelling from Baghdad to Belfast, from London to Manchester, and finding repeated motifs of waste and degradation differently played out in the mimetic processes of each performance. These juxtapositions are not made with the aim of generating universal statements about performance across very different historical and cultural contexts. The examples were deliberately selected to interrogate the global, culturally and historically hybrid, coalitions between performance and wars on terror evident in political crises past and present. As such, these different examples form the basis for the proposition of this book, that is, that a consideration of the politics of performance in an age of uncertainty might supplement considerations of the radical in performance with an appreciation of performance's relationship with waste and wasted life. Briefly, the conceptual steps made by successive chapters are as follows. Chapter 2 explores the beheading of a British citizen in Iraq in 2004 and highlights the ambivalent role of the abject in performance. A competition of abject spectacles between insurgent and counterinsurgent forces supported escalating violence – and here, proximity with the abject had a protective effect that fortified the respective militaries and wider publics implicated in these spectacles. Chapter 3 explores the use of performance by counterterrorism operatives in Northern Ireland in the 1980s, in particular focusing on the abjectification of space as a strategy of performed violence. Here an example of stage drama drew on a poetics of diminished space to forcefully materialise a dream of habitable space in the threatened realms of the here and now. Chapter 4 explores the resurgence of political theatre on the London stage during the war on terror, in particular focusing on verbatim theatre, a form that exploits the uncertain affectivity of the voice to dramatise a crisis of democracy. The critical potential of these plays resides in their dramatisation of the decay of the voice, and of democracy in times of crisis, rather than their supposed revitalisation of a democratic public sphere. Chapter 5 explores how examples of antiwar protest performance reproduce and critically mirror the mimetic circulation of threat and frailty of a time of terror, drawing on an aesthetics and politics of protest camps and queer camp to make use of and revalue waste and wasted life. The 'poetics of the camp' evidenced by these examples are conservative responses to crisis and this conservative impulse is echoed in the following chapter, which focuses on an extraordinary series of community performances commissioned by counterterrorism agencies following the London bombings of 7 July 2005. Here, artists worked critically with and against the counterterrorism agenda to dramatise the difficultness of encounters with undecidable neighbours, drawing on a loving practice of performance that was profoundly protective.

To close, it is useful to refer again to Naomi Klein's suggestion that 'movements that do not seek to start from scratch but rather from scrap, from the rubble that is all around' might be best placed to stage critical interruptions of a world that produces so much wasted life (Klein 2007: 466). In this chapter, I have not so much proposed a new 'politics of performance', then, but instead have attempted to carefully trace a repeated trope of waste in existing cycles of critical terminology, theoretical concepts and performance practice. This is a project of salvage that starts from and ends with rubble and dust, and to make an initial step in the book's exploration of performance in a time of terror, the focus of attention now moves to the rubble and dust of Iraq in 2004.

2

A beheading in Iraq: Medusa, the mirror and a performance of exception

Homo homini lupus [Man is a wolf to man]. Who, after all that he has learnt from life and history, would be so bold as to disrupt this proposition? (Freud 2004 [1930]: 61)

Once more we see people cutting each other's throats in support of childish theories of how to create paradise on earth . . . Look at all the incredible savagery going on in our so-called civilised world: it all comes from human beings and their mental condition! . . . This ghastly power is mostly explained as fear of the neighbouring nation, which is supposed to be possessed by a malevolent fiend. Since nobody is capable of recognising just where and how much he himself is possessed and unconscious, he simply projects his own condition upon his neighbour, and thus it becomes a sacred duty to have the biggest guns and the most poisonous gas. The worst of it is that he is quite right. All one's neighbours are in the grip of some uncontrollable fear, just like oneself. (Jung 2002 [1937]: 92–3)

Seven men, one just out of shot, in black T-shirts, grey tracksuit trousers and trainers, stand in a line against a red brick wall and face the camera. Balaclavas cover their heads and they hold their guns upright, except the man in the middle, reportedly the leader of Al Qaeda in Iraq, Abu Musab al-Zarqawi. He has a knife tucked into his belt. The banner hung behind the men is black with gold lettering spelling out the name of the group – Tawhid al Jihad – 'The Unification of Holy War'. Kenneth

Bigley, the British engineer, kneeling before the line of men, also faces the camera. The logo of the group, superimposed in the top right-hand corner of the screen, rotates as the video plays.

Cut to a close-up shot of Bigley. He is wearing an orange jumpsuit and speaks English with a Liverpool accent:

> Here I am again Mr Blair and your government, very, very close to the end of my life. You don't appear to have done anything at all to help me. I'm not a difficult person. I'm a simple man who just wants to live a simple life with his family. These people, their patience is wearing very, very thin and they're very serious people.

Cut to a shot of the whole group. Bigley continues:

> Please, please give them what they require, the freedom of the women from Abu Ghraib prison, I beg you, if you do this the problem is solved. The British people, more than ever I need your help, more than ever I need your voices to go out into the street and to demand a better life for the females, women who are imprisoned in Abu Ghraib prison.

Zarqawi begins with the *Shahadah*. He speaks in Arabic:

> The heads of the unbelieving Western governments are pretending to be concerned about their people, they pretend that they are concerned for their subjects and are looking after their interests but they are liars and hypocrites. We extended the deadline for killing the British hostage to give them a chance to release the women prisoners in Abu Ghraib but the British government becomes more arrogant as time goes by . . . Britain is not serious about releasing our sisters so this devious Briton can only be handled by means of the sword. And so, our sisters, take heart, because the fighters who seek jihad are constantly discussing your case and how to rescue you. We are going to continue to think of ways to rescue you until we see you free and safe. We are going to fight the non-believers until we see that you are back with your husbands and fathers, brothers and children.

Third shot. The militants call out praise for god. Zarqawi leans over Bigley and takes the knife to the front of his throat. The other men move to hold Bigley down. The final three shots show the beheading of Kenneth Bigley.

At the time of his kidnapping in September 2004, Bigley was working for Gulf Supplies and Commercial Services, a corporation contracted by the US military to support the reconstruction of Iraq. The war was in its most violent phase, with an array of groups engaged in military action and rising rates of suicide bombings, kidnappings, assassinations and beheadings. The torture and violations committed by members of the US military against prisoners in the Abu Ghraib military prison in Iraq had come to prominence in April of the same year. During his three-week-long period of capture, five separate videos were released, three showing Bigley wearing an orange jumpsuit and two showing him caged and shackled. According to one newspaper report, Bigley had worked in the Middle East for more than ten years and was cavalier about his safety, commenting to neighbours who asked him whether he was frightened, 'you only die once'. He was sixty-two years old, and after this last lucrative job to support life in retirement was due to emigrate to Thailand to live with his wife on a mango farm (Naughton 2004). The video of the beheading was posted to militant websites and disseminated across mainstream media and schlock horror sites, and was one of a spate of videoed beheadings in Iraq carried out, recorded and disseminated via the internet in 2004.[1]

The videos demonstrated militant Islam's awareness of the power of performance as a weapon of war. Set, props and costume were carefully stage-managed as part of these scripted performances, with one newspaper report even suggesting that militants rehearsed by decapitating chickens and sheep 'so as to appear professional' (Carroll 2005). The performances conveyed specific messages for different constituents of their diverse audiences. Journalist Jason Burke, for example, argued that this 'theatre of terror' was intended for an audience of 'the Muslim world in the stalls, the West in the cheap seats' (Burke 2004a). For Burke, Zarqawi aimed to demonstrate both his commitment and faith, and that he is the militant towards whom the fighters should gravitate rather than Osama bin Laden, hiding in the mountains. The symbolism – Bigley's orange jumpsuit, with its mimicry of the 'illegal enemy combatants' held by the US military in Camp X-Ray in Guantánamo Bay at the time – tapped into what Burke calls 'the profound sense of humiliation, disenfranchisement and emasculation felt by hundreds of millions of young Muslim men faced with the apparent military, political and increasingly cultural dominance of the West' (Burke 2004b). In this chapter, I explore the mimetic aspects of this act of performed violence, drawing out their significance for understanding the politics of performance in a time of terror. As part of this, the beheading of Kenneth Bigley is positioned as one of a series of acts that participated in the mimetic circulation of threat and frailty during this period of the war, including the acts of torture and humiliation carried out against prisoners of war by US military personnel in Abu Ghraib prison in Iraq and Camp X-Ray in Guantánamo Bay in Cuba. In the analysis that follows, I therefore pay attention to the beheading as part of a systemic pattern of performed violence, in addition to analysing the eruptive violence of the act itself. Tony Perucci provides a powerful example of how this might be done in his examination of the atrocities in Abu Ghraib, in which he identifies a 'performance complex' of neoliberalism across the prison-industrial and military-industrial complex of US society. He calls the repetition of performed violence across these contexts 'the global staging of America's new penal culture, a culture that celebrates a racialised brutal violence and that is produced by both the economic structures and cultural logic of neoliberalism' (Perucci 2009: 364).

The mimesis in play as part of the performance complex of violence in Iraq at the time, and circulated by the spate of beheadings, made use of the means by which the war was mediated as well as reproduced patterns of performed violence pertaining to a colonial past and present. Philip Bobbitt, for example, described the videoed beheadings as a reaction 'against the values while mimicking the techniques of the prevailing constitutional order' (Bobbitt 2008: 44). For Bobbitt, this mimesis is more lethal and difficult to prevent in an era of the global market state, with insurgency groups like those led by Zarqawi taking advantage of decentralisation, outsourcing and digital technology to become '*more theatrical, producing vivid dramas and tableaux for the global network connected to the Internet, the World Wide Web, satellite television, and video technologies*' (*ibid.* 60. Italics in original). However, the relevance of mimesis to the performance complex of the beheading of Kenneth Bigley extends far beyond the mode of dissemination it adopted and symbolic trappings of the beheading as a performed act noted above. In this chapter, newspaper reports, translated communiqués of Islamic groups and the beheading videos themselves are used to develop an analysis of the beheadings as performances of *exception*. As will become clear in the discussion that follows, the beheadings were miniaturised spectacles of exception, in which the 'headlessness' of Iraq in 2004 – a place rapidly descending into the chaos and civil disorder of a long-term military occupation – was both displayed and contested. The power of this performance arises from its mimetic capture of the felt experiences, political chaos and extra-legal realities of a state of exception. Here, the political administrations of countries leading the military coalition declared an exception to the rule of international law and invaded a country on the basis of a questionable remit. The extreme violence of the beheading mirrors and plays back to sovereign power the chaotic violence and illegality of the invasion, together with its abrogation of human rights and military norms.

Writing about the spate of beheadings during this period of the war, Henry Giroux suggests that 'the implications of the political and market success of the videos cannot be overstated' (Giroux 2006: 52). For Giroux, these abject displays signalled a new relationship between spectacle, violence and the media (a point I return to later). The multiple, complex and powerful effects and affects of these performances were also difficult to control. For example, the beheadings arguably generated the conditions for critical responses to the war that put pressure on governments, but their extreme violence also stimulated passive reactions that, conversely to the militants' intentions, reinforced a growing sense of the legitimacy of the war that had been previously lacking in the public sphere of nations leading the military coalition. The undoubted power of the beheadings was conveyed in one report that highlighted the economic impact of these performances – of the $18.4 billion allocated by the US Congress in 2003 for rebuilding Iraq, barely £1 billion had been spent by the end of 2004, half of which had been diverted from reconstruction to improving security (Claude 2004). It is interesting to note that whilst the beheadings gained Zarqawi's group a visibility and status that he could not have otherwise attained, they were also controversial inside militant Islam, stimulating an extraordinary debate about the politics of performed violence. Perhaps the most remarkable evidence of this comes from a letter to Zarqawi intercepted by US intelligence services and attributed to Ayman al-Zawahiri, Osama bin Laden's 'second in command'. Zawahiri asserts that these 'scenes of slaughter' undermined the 'race for the hearts and minds' of the global Muslim community: 'we are in a battle and that more than half of this battle is taking place in the battlefield of the media . . . we don't need this' (Zawahiri 2005). It is quite startling that this mode of murder was condemned by one of those responsible for the 9/11 attacks as somehow too violent, and this also indicates something of the unpredictable and uncontrollable effects and affects of acts of performed violence.

Perucci warns that a cold analysis of violence risks participating in the terrors it tries to deconstruct by symbolically repeating its violations. In this chapter, I attempt to avoid this by critically analysing the cuts and breaks of this violent act and its performance complex, and by positing these disjunctions as central explanatory motifs. The analysis reveals a repetition of cuts and breaks in the wider performance complex here and by critically recycling these excisions I hope to generate an explanatory narrative that acts against the violence it depicts.

Beheading: a performance complex of a state of exception

Beheadings used to provide dramatic endings. They are now where we begin. (Janes 2005: 40)

Beheading is a terror performance historically prevalent during periods of social upheaval; as literature scholar Regina Janes notes, 'the lesson of the heads is that there has been a fundamental change in social hierarchies and the distribution of power' (Janes 1991: 24). Janes' suggestion that beheadings are intimately linked to a crisis of power is a crucial perspective for the discussion that follows. Here, I consider beheadings as performances of power associated with a particular pattern of crisis that reappears across a colonial past and present. Two historical narratives of beheadings prominent in a European cultural imaginary provide useful pointers. Firstly, the shifting performances of punishment, from the display of heads on spikes, to the 'spectacle of the scaffold', and then to the bodiless, disciplinary power that configured France's transition to a modern political state (Janes 2005; 1991; Foucault 1977). Secondly, the 'black, dried, sunken' heads in Joseph Conrad's turn of the century novel *Heart of Darkness*, forming an ornamental border to the garden of missing company agent Mr Kurtz in the Belgian Congo (Conrad 1973 [1902]: 96). It is likely that Conrad was inspired by reports in London newspapers about Captain Rom, station chief of Stanley Falls in the Belgian Congo at the time Conrad wrote his novel, who decorated his flowerbed with twenty-one native skulls cut off during a raid on a rebellious village (Janes 2005: 140).[2]

According to Foucault, disciplinary society substituted the maintenance of power by displays of bodily violence with technologies of surveillance, multiplying and dispersing power by means of an atomisation and categorisation of the bodies and identities of docile citizens. There was an economic imperative here: the need to preserve rather than destroy bodies and minds as productive forces, in response to capitalism's demands for new forms of labour in a burgeoning industrial economy (Foucault 1977: 25–6). The re-emergence of the display of violence indicated by the war on terror, including the beheadings and torture in Abu Ghraib, may have also had an economic imperative. Here, acts of performed violence participated in a stage-managed expansion and contestation of a neoliberal economic regime by means of performances of terror. Why heads? Heads are one of the bodied sites in which we experience terror – as expressed by the soldier who commented about the Battle of the Somme in World War One: 'it makes your head jump to think of it' (cited by Bourke 2005: 195). In addition, the display of headlessness powerfully and tangibly expresses the uncertainty, crisis and devastation that accompanied unbridled economic expansion in Iraq. The prevalence of headless bodies on a global stage mirrors the insecurity of heads of State and non-State powers alike in the face of globalisation, as reflected by the US politician's comment in 1999, 'that's what is scary . . . the world economy today is just like that Internet: everybody is connected but nobody is in charge' (cited in Janes 2005: 176).

The head is also significant because an attack on the head is an attack on the primary signifier of knowledge, culture and identity: 'the body without a head is a body without a name' (Janes 1991: 30). Importantly then, the cutting off of a head signals the removal of the signs of personhood and citizenship from a body, and the identification, apprehension and obliteration of the meaning and being of the enemy in one, complex, act of performed violence. The cutting off of a head also symbolises the uncertain status of the citizen in relation to sovereign power – State beheadings, for example, are reminders of the unquestionable and unsurpassable power of the State, including its capacity to strip bodies of the marks of citizenship. Jacques Derrida describes the 9/11 attacks as an analogous inversion and contestation of such unsurpassable power – a striking down of the 'capital "head" of world capital' by non-State forces (Derrida in Borradori 2003: 96). The covering of the head as part of torture and execution performances are similarly performative acts that erase the identity of a person in order to claim power over their meaning and being. As part of this, the practice of displaying heads – as an ornamental border to a garden in Kurtz's case, a hooded 'terrorist' or via a globally disseminated digital videoed beheading – signals the transfer of power over meaning and being from one body to another. A practice of capturing, framing and displaying heads as part of a contest of power can be identified in the US government's printing of photographs of the 'most wanted' militants onto the backs of playing cards distributed to US soldiers in Afghanistan and Iraq.[3] Such framings might also be inverted, as exhibited by Osama bin Laden's circulation of hundreds of Pakistani rupee notes stamped with his face in a parody of Saudi and US requests for information about him in 2001 (Burke 2003: 175). In addition, the framing of heads can also constitute a powerful, critical statement about war, as shown by British war artist in Iraq, Steve McQueen, in his artwork *Queen and Country* in 2007. He produced a series of British postage stamps that replaced the image of the Queen that usually appeared there with the faces of soldiers killed in Iraq.[4]

To suggest a point of connection between beheadings that have featured as part of our colonial past and those of our 'colonial present', is to argue against an interpretation of Michel Foucault's work on discipline and punishment as signalling a historical *transition* from bodied punishment to more immaterial forms of discipline associated with the technologies of the modern State.[5] This is also suggested by Achille Mbembe's argument that early and late modern manifestations of violence combine the forces of disciplinary, biopolitical and necropolitical power: 'the perception of the existence of the Other as an attempt on my life, as a mortal threat or absolute danger whose biophysical elimination would strengthen my potential to life and security . . . is one of the many imaginaries of sovereignty characteristic of both early and late modernity' (Mbembe 2003: 18). Following an associated line of argument, Jon McKenzie argues that the atrocities in Abu Ghraib exhibited a contemporary 'spectacle of the scaffold' that reanimated the 'political theatricality' which Foucault associated with pre-disciplinary society, now manifested as displays of violence played out across globally networked screens (McKenzie 2009: 340). Accordingly, the performance complex of the beheadings that emerged at this juncture of the war in Iraq represents the visceral eruption of political violence already latent in liberal democracies, rather than indicates a regression to a former historical moment or a historically unprecedented moment. These performances of exception have maintained some kind of presence throughout a colonial past and present and, it might be argued, their repeated appearances and disappearances frame the broader history of wars on terror.

Both of the historical beheadings noted above – from Foucault and Conrad respectively – are performances that arise at the temporal and spatial limits of sovereign rule, in moments of crisis, during which a sovereign power comes into close contact with the violence that underpins its claims over the life of bodies and territory in those places. An association of beheading, or decapitation, with the exceptional power of the sovereign is suggested by Derek Gregory's useful etymology of 'exception': 'exception – ex-capere – is literally that which is "taken outside", and, as this suggests, it is the result of a process of boundary promulgation *and* boundary perturbation' (Gregory 2004: 62. Italics in original). Beheadings signify a contest for bodies and spaces that exist outside the boundaries of rule – and they symbolise and enact the attempted regulation of those bodies and spaces by separating the head from the body – that is, by reproducing a schism between the life of the citizen, existing inside a recognisable and ordered world, and bare life, which can be killed. These complex performances represent, materialise and critically mimic a politics of exception. As such, the spate of beheadings in Iraq in 2004 confronted an invasive power with a mirror of the violence concealed by its false perception as orderly, democratic and rule-bound. The beheading of Kenneth Bigley aggressively inscribed the threatened border of a nation onto the body of a British citizen supporting the construction of military bases in Iraq. It thus symbolised a stalling and expulsion of the overwhelming and duplicitous global power threatening to newly colonise the Middle East, together with a protective affirmation of the integrity of the body of Iraq. Cutting off a head is a violent excision of the body from the source of its personhood and being, and, as such, the beheading materialised the bare life – life without personhood, identity or rights – produced by an exceptional war and illegal occupation. The creation of a headless body – an abject spectacle of bare and wasted life – can also be interpreted as a direct mimesis of the invasion's production of a stateless country populated by countless, innocent victims of war. The videos mimetically reproduced this display of the violence concomitant with, but obscured by, the political fictions of liberal democracy across the networks of the worldwide web.

It may be useful to briefly draw out the theoretical concepts underpinning this analysis. As noted in the prologue, according to Giorgio Agamben, sovereign power is founded on the declaration of an exception to the rule which produces bare life, included in the political order only in the form of its exclusion and underpinned by uncertainty. For Agamben, this exceptional power is the concealed fact of the democratic tradition, and particularly important to the discussion here is his identification of bare life in a state of exception as a 'state of nature'. Bare life and sovereign power exist on a 'threshold of indistinction' between man and animal, recognisable in the figure of the bandit, wolfman, exile and, we might add, the terrorist and his victim (Agamben 1998: 104). The abject force of the beheading is generated by its precise positioning at this threshold of indistinction. Its display of wasted and degraded life materialises the realm of the exception and thus threatens to decompose and disintegrate the political fictions which separate a rule-bound order from the violence that sustains it. What is being mimicked by the beheading is the power to materialise a reality in which some lives are inside, and other lives outside a recognisable, rule-bound and protective order. This mimesis of exception, which displays and decays the fictions of an orderly, rule-bound universe, and makes use of the degrading forces of abjection, therefore also signals nothing less than a contest for the power of mimesis itself, that is, for power over life's appearances and disappearances, and the making and unmaking of bodies and worlds.

The global breadth of the targets of beheadings in Iraq in 2004 indicates that the toxic enemy to be controlled and excised here was associated with all-surpassing, encroaching global capitalism. To state this is to argue against perceptions of the beheadings as acts of violence by Islamic militants against non-Muslims, or as signalling a global contest between east and west. Victims of beheadings were non-Muslim and Muslim people cooperating with coalition forces, symbols of war and globalisation in Iraq, rather than non-Muslim 'infidels'. This is also indicated by the framing of the severed head via the internet, which performs an inversion of the all-surveying, anonymous and bodiless power of the global media. As Burke comments, these digitally dis-seminated performances of violence locate and then redirect invasive gazes: 'modern television is an unprecedented invasion of local, Islamic and private space. What the execution videos have done is take our technology, the spearhead of our invasion, and turned it back on us' (Burke 2004a). The beheadings returned invasive looks with a petrifying display of a disembodied head and lifeless eyes. Such lifeless looks reveal a cognisance of the atrocities committed by the military coalition and direct attention to the waste of life in Iraq – they say 'we see what you are doing' as well as 'look at what you have done'. As such, Bigley's status as a civilian rather than military target, in reflecting the indiscriminate uncertainty of life in a state of exception, was essential to the overall display.

The descriptions of the framing of heads by militants and artists above also infer something of how performance might be used to critically interrupt these contests of life and death in a state of excep-tion. Judith Butler's concept of 'frames of war', developed as part of an exploration of the display and reception of images of atrocity during times of war, is useful here. She locates a figure of the 'non-human' that permanently haunts – 'negatively determines and potentially unsettles' – the frames of war, that is, the communicative practices by which some lives are recognised as grievable and others expendable (Butler 2009: 64; also see Butler 2004). The term 'precarity' is offered to describe the suf-fering of those spectral lives not recognised as grievable and to argue for the extension of representational and interpretive schemes that respond more equitably to the suffering of others. As Butler notes, 'it is most dif-ficult when in a state of pain to stay responsive to the equal claim of the other to shelter, for conditions of livability and grievability. And yet, this vexed domain is the site of a necessary struggle' (Butler 2009: 184). This positing of difficulty is important here as this vexed domain, of course, is a site for a display of frailty, non-being and the annihilation of the enemy and subsequent fortification of self, as well as a potential site for figuring more equitable relationships. The production of a headless body and bodiless head is a framing of precarity that claims power over life's decay and disappearance: it is a display of the transfer of the founding condition of power – the power to make life matter in all of its empirical and spectral forms. In the following discussion, I explore precarity's role in mobilising performances of violence as well as pay critical attention to its potential to interrupt the mimetic processes of wars on terror. As will become clear, and echoing the discussion in the previous chapter, it is the encounter with the abject – rather than the affect – of a precarious body that provides the most provocative terrain for this investigation.

Arjun Appadurai argues that acts of violence create certainty in the face of the imperilment evoked by encroaching globalisation: 'part of the effort to slow down the whirl of the global and its seeming largeness of reach is by holding it still, and making it small . . . Such violence, in this perspective, is not about old hatreds and primordial fears. It is an effort to exorcise the new, the emergent, and the uncertain' (Appadurai 2006: 47–8). As such, the beheadings in Iraq can be understood as an aggressively embodied stalling of an abstract, all-seeing, encroaching power. Equally, beheadings are attempts to control or stall uncertainty not just by exorcism but by *mimesis* of the threatening properties of the world. Here, it is useful to remember the discussion in chapter 1, which referred to mimesis as a practice of mortification and decay – a mirroring and materialisation of the alienated, diminished forms in which body and world appear in times of crisis. In the following section, I borrow these notions of mortification and decay to develop a more detailed reading of beheadings as performance, and explore their protective and destructive effects. The beheading of Bigley mimicked a politics of exception via the removal of the head, consciousness from the eyes and abjection of the body. Importantly, this transfer of power also signified a return of law, in this case the law of an all-seeing deity which regulates the universe and its powers over life and death.

Medusa's look: petrifaction and degradation

In Holbien's picture I showed you at once . . . the singular object floating in the foreground, which is there to be looked at, in order to catch, I would almost say, *to catch in its trap*, the observer, that is, us . . . we are literally called into the picture, and represented here as caught . . . It reflects our own nothingness, in the figure of the death's head. (Lacan 1977: 92. Italics in original)

According to ancient Greek myth, Medusa was a beautiful woman, very proud of her hair. Because of her beauty and sexual endeavours, she was punished by the god Athena, who turned her hair into snakes. From this point on, anyone who looked at the snake-covered head of Medusa turned into stone. Perseus, armed with a mirror-shield, was given the task of beheading Medusa. He protected himself by taking aim at her neck through the mirror and, following his defeat of this monstrous figure, used Medusa's head to petrify – literally, turn into stone – his enemies.

The penultimate shot of the video of the beheading, depicting Bigley's bloodied head held in the air and surrounded by guns wielded by the militants, strongly evokes Perseus' petrifying display of the snake head of the mythical Medusa. A similar framing of a bodiless head, this time surrounded by the cameras of the world's media rather than the militants' guns, was produced by the US military following the killing of Zarqawi, the alleged murderer of Bigley. Following multiple bogus claims that Zarqawi was dead, the US military finally succeeded in killing him in an air-raid attack in June 2006. A large, framed photograph of the head of his corpse was displayed at a press conference announcing Zarqawi's death (Kennicott 2006). From Perseus' framing of the monstrous woman through his mirror, to the border of skulls in Kurtz's garden in the Belgian Congo, to the competitive framings of bloodied heads during the war in Iraq, heads have been apprehended and displayed to claim exceptional power. Beheadings are bloodily precise and incisive framings of the head that petrify the life of the other and transfer power over life and death to the performer of the incision.

It is useful to turn here to Lacan, for whom the visual realm is a 'trap' for the human subject. He draws on a famous painting, Holbein's *Ambassadors* (1533), which depicts two dignitaries surrounded by the instruments of knowledge and science, to illustrate his notion of the human subject perpetually suspended in an uncertain state of meaning and being in the world. There is an indecipherable grey figure in the foreground of the painting that does not fit with the scene depicted, and when looked at awry it comes into focus as a skull: 'we are literally called into the picture, and represented here as caught . . . It reflects our own nothingness, in the figure of the death's head' (Lacan 1977: 92). For Lacan, our entry into the symbolic world – the realm of identity, knowledge and language – can be understood as a mortifying wound or cut. The price of meaning and identity here is a loss of contact with an experience of being. As such, the means by which life is experienced as sensible, plausible and knowable 'petrify the subject in the same movement in which it calls the subject to function, to speak, as subject' (*ibid.*:

207). Beheadings are acts of petrifaction that assert control over the terrors of this uncertain border between meaning and being. The control over the powers of mimesis exhibited as part of these performances also transforms performance into a killing machine, with the original act and each repeated showing of the bodiless head materialising the original petrifaction, and its claiming of power over life and death. Displaying the lifeless head aggressively asserts the lack of meaning and being of the enemy and transfers the powers of mimesis – over the making and unmaking of worlds – to the performer. Its powerful effects are unpredictable, however, as reflected in Zawahiri's admonition of Zarqawi that these 'scenes of slaughter' are failed political performances because they alienate potential allies. To claim power over the prevarications of meaning and being is to be associated with a quality of degradation and decay that inflects the performer with a peculiar frailty as well as magical power. In the analysis that follows, I trace this complex operation of petrifaction and degradation in relation to the beheading of Kenneth Bigley.

The Medusa myth provides a useful frame for this exploration. Here, power over life and death is regulated by the mirroring moment that helped Perseus behead Medusa by capturing and redirecting her petrifying look. As Marjorie Garber and Nancy Vickers note in their extremely useful survey of representations of the Medusa myth, this 'mirroring moment' can be read in multiple and competing ways (Garber and Vickers 2003: 6). For Lacan, the mirror relation is the 'imaginary' stage in the development of self-consciousness, where we attain an uncertain sense of self by measuring ourselves in the shifting and unpredictable responses of the other. The imaginary denotes the illusory, terrifying, spectral, fragmented, overwhelming and deceptive qualities of the mimetic relation between self and other. To apply this to the beheading of Kenneth Bigley, the militants' turn to performance, like Perseus' use of the mirror, symbolically mediated a threatening world through a mirroring of its monstrous, mortifying and degrading effects. The symbolism of the act – the violence that was mimetically reproduced by dressing Bigley's body in an orange jumpsuit and shackles and placing him in a cage for example – produced a figure that made the killing permissible, possible and imperative. Bigley's killing also mobilised a loss of meaning and being of both killer and killed, and here, there is an end to the 'performance', as well as the relevance of performance to analysing this act. Close attention to the digital performance of the beheading, for example, shows that the performance ended before the moment of killing itself. The beheading is shown in three shots, and the cuts reveal that what is exhibited is in fact the *attempt* to behead rather than the actual beheading. The physical struggle to sever head from the body is edited out of the screen performance as the difficulty of the act undermined the display of mastery over the other and control over mimesis. In the actual *act* of killing, in the final disappearance of life – there was no performance.

However, it might be more accurate to state that the permeability of the border between performance, life and death here is central to the power of this particular performance, and signals the contest for power over mimesis as well as the complex relationship between petrifaction and degradation in mimesis. Allen Feldman's description of how performed violence makes use of and disrupts the symbolic realm, the subsequent collapse of which constitutes political violence, is useful here: 'through violence, matter is semiotised in order for it to feed back narratives of historical transformation and political dominance . . . Violence enables and enacts a one-to-one correspondence or iso-morphism between discourse and the material world' (Feldman 1991: 80). Violent acts thus destroy the distinction between the symbolic capture of the enemy and the material flesh of his body. The process of performed violence can be described therefore as a degradation of the symbolic into *matter*, recomposed as *performance*. The performance complex of beheading exhibits a dual process of petrifaction and deg-radation, in that the cut that targets a head inscribes the identity of the other prior to a transfer of power – and this transfer of power degrades the body, and a sense of the body as mattering. As noted, as a result of its dramatisation of a point of collapse of meaning and being, the performance of beheading claims an exceptional and terrifying power – the power to make and unmake worlds. It thus mimics the contours and forms of exception, and it is only performance, in its combination of symbolic competency and decaying materiality, that can effectively reproduce but also critically contest such exceptional power.

In its claiming of the power of mimesis in this way, a beheading also signals the paradoxical coexistence of protective and destructive forces in acts of performed violence. As the Medusa myth suggests, control over mimesis can provide a resilient resource for the protection of self. The discussion here also draws attention to the importance of a display of abjection – as a means of encountering and regulating life's decay – to securing these powers of protection. A turn to Julia Kristeva's notion of the abject is useful here – the difficult to bear, frightening, tangible presence that cannot be securely represented and threatens to infect and defile. For Kristeva, the abject is an uncertain and estranging presence of otherness that proliferates in a world in which the transgression of borders has become habitual. Control over an estranging, invasive and threatening world, and its concomitant proliferation of abject presences, is maintained by asserting a border between the inside and the outside of the body. The abject haunts order and order defines itself by expelling the abject. In the jettison of the abject, life is secured:

> as in true theatre, without makeup or masks, refuse and corpses *show me* what I permanently thrust aside in order to live . . . There, I am at the border of my condition as a living being. My body extricates itself, as being alive, from that border. Such wastes drop so that I might live . . . If dung signifies the other side of the border, the place where I am not and which permits me to be, the corpse, the most sickening of wastes, is a border that has encroached upon everything. It is no longer I who expel, 'I' is expelled. (Kristeva 1982: 3–4. Italics in original)

The dramatisation of such processes of abjection is a feature of the performance complex of the beheading. The mimetic exchange of bodiless heads and spoiled bodies of the beheadings and torture in Abu Ghraib prison in Iraq, for example, can be regarded as a competition of abject spectacles that attempt to control the threat to borders in times of crisis. As part of these competitive performances, the abject was expelled and contained in the body of the enemy and by displaying his control over this body the militant demonstrates his security in the world. Here, power over mimesis is sustained by controlling the most sensuous of life's excesses – its powers of waste and decay.

To map this more precisely onto the performance complex of the spate of beheadings in Iraq in 2004 – many of the beheading videos showed the Qur'an placed in the space of the severed head, and the head placed on the small of the back. Here, the symbol of war and occupation is placed in a bodily site and the religious text placed in the site of knowledge and identity, denoting an absolute, all-seeing and all-knowing power. As such, worldly sovereign power is replaced by a universal, rule-bound order. The head of the foreigner placed in proximity to the orifice most associated with waste is an act of spoiling and degradation. The Qur'an provides a guide for knowledge and meaning that transcends the human-made messes of worldly life represented by foreign, sightless heads and their abject bodies, and signifies ultimate mastery over life and death. This aspect of the performance, in turn, critically mirrors the degrading performances carried out by US military personnel in Abu Ghraib prison. The militants placed the head of the foreigner on his posterior and substituted the head with a Qur'an; US soldiers penetrated the orifices of Iraqi prisoners with a succession of objects and smeared the Qur'an with faeces and urine. As such, the beheadings asserted religious authority, and, in targeting a head rather than a hole, drew attention to the insurgency's moral superiority to the military occupation, with US soldiers' depraved obsessions with the holes of prisoners' bodies and, in turn, the occupying power's digging of holes in the search for oil in Iraq.

McKenzie analyses the atrocities in Abu Ghraib as a 'tableaux of power and degradation' mobilised by 'plot, dramatic unfolding, and even character development – or rather, the decomposition of character and identity' (McKenzie 2009: 342–3). This was horrifically highlighted by the 'shitboy' theme of the improvised torture of one prisoner in Abu Ghraib, which involved smearing his body with excrement: 'M's identity becomes decomposed into the image of "Shitboy" . . . such decomposition or breakdown of subjectivity is precisely the goal of psychological torture' (*ibid.*: 350). In the scenario McKenzie describes, the victim was assigned a 'character' – or rather, a non-character – he became an abject, pitiful and repellent figure. The beheadings were in one sense an attempt to freeze – to petrify – the wasting of the human and the degradation of identity and culture that the occupation enacted in Iraq and assert divine rule in place of holes and exceptions. Beheadings also degrade in their murderous semiotisation of bodies: the excision of Bigley's head is a degradation of the flesh that produces an abject, headless torso. Both atrocities – the torture of 'shitboy' and the beheading of Bigley – expel the abject by projecting it onto the body of the enemy, and, importantly, in this reading of the performance complex, any claim for moral superiority by either set of perpetrators becomes infected by the loss of meaning and being that such encounters with the abject confer.

However, such encounters with loss are also fortifying. In his analysis of decapitation, for example, Freud argues that such displays are 'apotropaic' acts; that is, beheadings produce a fearful sight of something in order to ward off the presence of something more frightening: 'to decapitate = to castrate. The terror of Medusa is thus a terror of castration that is linked to the sight of something' (Freud 1955: 273–4). Leaving aside a discussion of the sexual politics of Freud's association of fear with the castration of the male body, his analysis of the display of Medusa's head as an assertion of virility that displaces impotence onto the enemy and, as a result, protects the performer, is useful. The circulating petrifaction and degradation in play as part of the mimetic process of the beheadings, then, draws attention to the waste of life in a state of exception, but here, such encounters with waste strengthen the performers. Importantly, these radical, violent acts of performance are conservative and protective at the same time as terribly destructive. What is needed here is more performance, not less, and an understanding and practice of performance that attaches value to all bodies rather than those that perform excisions which mark out some bodies as mattering more than others.

Might other kinds of performance provide a negotiation of the abject that signals the potential and power of the uncertain border between self and other, and meaning and being, more equitably and critically? For Kristeva, the abject can be differently negotiated as part of non-violent communicative exchanges, but to do this successfully, the aesthetic qualities of communicative practices should also be inflected with abjection: 'it is the "poetic" unsettlement of analytic utterance that testifies to its closeness to, cohabitation with and "knowledge" of abjection . . . the affects that can be heard in the breaks in discourse . . . breaking away from identification by means of interpretation, analytic speech is one that becomes "incarnate" in the full sense of the term' (Kristeva 1982: 30–1). In the chapters that follow, I explore how this incarnation of the abject plays out in a range of performances made during the war on terror. However, this chapter concludes with an interrogation of the extended performance complex of the beheading itself, carried out by an investigation of the ways it was scripted by national and international media reporting. What becomes clear here is that the beheading was represented in ways that limited conditions for responding in a critical and compassionate manner. A potential poetics of the abject was thus not successfully achieved, and representational practices and atrophied responses from wider publics uncritically mirrored the original petrifaction and its discriminate, protective and destructive effects.

The mirror: cuts, breaks and holes in the beheading performance complex

Perhaps we should compare this literature with the 'disturbances around the scaffold' in which, through the tortured body of the criminal, the power that condemned confronted the people that was the witness, the participant, the possible and indirect victim of this execution. (Foucault 1977: 68)

Foucault makes reference to the possibility of a critical and compassionate response to the display of abjection that constitutes a beheading; in particular, noting the possibility of resistant responses amongst those audiences that beheadings indirectly target as its victims. Whilst such performances were displayed with an expectation of the audience's fearful collusion, they might also therefore lead to resistant acts that gesture towards more hopeful trajectories. Can we engage with these spectacles of abjection without reproducing their toxic affects and effects? Here, I explore how the frames through which the British public viewed the beheading of Kenneth Bigley did *not* provide the conditions for critical responses. The frames through which this contemporary Medusa was viewed by audiences in the UK was the plethora of image, text and discourse provided by national and international media reports. The predominant narrative framing of the beheading of Kenneth Bigley in newspaper reports configured the act of violence as a demonstration of the barbarism of the enemy, a framing of the event that opposes 'us' and 'them', the 'savage' east and 'civilised' west, that I have argued against here. In these reports, the critical potential of the abject disappeared in the cuts, breaks and holes in the wider performance complex of the beheading, and the reception of the beheading thus repeated the petrifications and degradations of the beheading itself.

Taking up Butler's notion of the figure of the 'non-human' permanently haunting the frames of war, noted above, is useful here. In an essay exploring the circulation of the images of torture and humiliation of Iraqi prisoners in Abu Ghraib prison, she argues that whilst only a proportion of the images were made public and that the affectivity of a photograph of suffering cannot restore the human, the images provide the conditions for public outrage and a critical interrogation of the frames of war. The photographs leave a 'mark of humanity' caused by 'fragments that follow in the wake of an abrogation of the normatively human . . . their occlusion and erasure become the continuing sign of their suffering and of their humanity' (Butler 2009: 94). As part of the following discussion, I explore Butler's schema and suggest, once again, that it is in an encounter with abjection evoked by such abrogations of the human that our ability to respond compassionately and equitably is most challenged. This challenge needs to be urgently explored in order to understand the complexity of acts of violence and begin to shape effective, critical responses.

The beheadings provoked audiences to look at and away from the abject spectacle of a bodiless head, and the challenges this presented work with and against Butler's propositions in provocative ways. The first challenge is that the display of the degraded body, and the decision of whether or not to look, were both acts which had protective as well as destructive effects. These are not separate effects of distinct moments of performance or spectatorship, but interdependent aspects of a complete event of performance and reception. In displaying the degraded body, the militant gained power over threat and, at the same time, sought the protection of women prisoners in Abu Ghraib and the territory of Iraq. In choosing not to look, we protect our sense of integrity and maintain a sense of the legitimacy of a war carried out in our names. Conversely, in choosing to look we may attain a sense of power of and power over the abject image in the same moment as being petrified by it. Thus, the conditions of outrage created by these particular images of atrocity work to affirm a sense of the legitimacy of war as much as provoke critique. This leads to a second challenge presented by the competition of abject spectacles circulating here. The imperative to consider those lives which altogether fail to enter the frames of war becomes a critical project of primary importance, as it is perhaps from attending to these cuts and breaks – from the expulsions and excisions of the abject – in the performance complex that we might locate modes of response that offer the most critical potential. The fragments of some abject lives are displayed as part of the apotropaic effects of power's performance; however, there are those that do not enter the frame – fragments of life that are forever deferred and fail to leave a trace. In this final section of the chapter I pay attention to how these two challenges were played out in the reception of the beheading of Kenneth Bigley.

The wider audiences of the beheading included members of the public in the UK who identified the accent, language and look of Kenneth Bigley as familiar. As he pleaded for his life, these audiences were captured by the image and its circulation of terror. The image of the severed head is deliberately prohibitive, intended to frighten away the encroaching, invasive, all-surveying other through returning their invasive gaze with a petrifying look – ultimately conveyed through the lack of consciousness in the eyes of Bigley's severed head. The provocation to look at this fearful spectacle and the escalating violence in Iraq, enacted via the dissemination of the act across the networks of the worldwide web, represented an extension of the act of violence. This attack was defended against by means of an extensive discussion in newspapers, television and other media outlets relating to whether and how the beheading videos should be shown. Some commentators accused the media of allocating excessive amounts of space to the atrocity, providing publicity for 'terrorists' (for example, see Ashley 2004; Gove 2004). Mainstream television in the UK broadcasted Bigley's pleas but refused to show the execution itself. These debates ultimately affirmed the moral superiority of the British viewer at the same time as closed any possibility of supporting self-critical, reflective and more uncertain responses to violence. However, the videoed beheading was viewed by many people over the internet – testifying to the powerful draw of such abject spectacles during times of crisis as well as the allure of the censored image.

As part of a discussion that counters Butler's hopeful analysis of the critical potential of the reception and circulation of images of atrocity, Henry Giroux argues that an encounter with the abject produces an alienated response that legitimises violence against the other. He reworks Debord's famous assignation of consumerist society as a 'society of the spectacle' wherein 'everything that was directly lived has receded into a representation' (Debord 2006: 7). For Giroux, beheading videos, and the state of permanent war that they are part of, have 'trumped' Debord by producing 'a viscerally moving presence of elemental fear, suffering, abjection, degradation, and death' into the simulacra of the social world (Giroux 2006: 50). Spectacles of terrorism bring the abject into sensate proximity, producing alienated forms of perception and relationship as well as a public consensus centred on fear rather than critical engagement with the world. In a related argument, Feldman offers the concept of an 'actuarial gaze' that protects the viewing subject by manipulating and shrouding the 'depth structures and contingencies of historical emergency and crisis' (Feldman 2005: 213). Within this schema, the affect of circulating images of atrocities in Abu Ghraib, rather than provoking critical engagement, provided 'a continuation of American spectrum dominance over the recalcitrant body of the "terrorist" Other' (*ibid.*: 218). Similar to a beheading's effect of warding off the enemy, the shocking images emanating from Abu Ghraib strengthened and fortified the viewing public. For Feldman, this explains the atrocities themselves as well as what he sees as the passivity of the US public's response to the photos:

> The Americanisation of Iraq had first to be mimetically experienced as visual substance if it was to be credible and tangible to those charged with carrying it out [. . .] these images circulated as protective charms, a sympathetic magic, in which optical appropriation and virtual possession of the subjugated, abstracted body of the Iraqi terrorist mimetically empowered the military spectator. (*ibid.*: 219–20)

The circulation of photos of tortured Iraqi bodies promised their makers and viewers that the US would win the war. Following this reading, the beheading videos can be seen as participating in a horrible 'tit for tat' game of making mementos of the ruined body as a means of strengthening and protecting the self. As such, images of atrocity certainly generate an affectivity that expresses the shared precarity of life. Their production and reception provide encounters with the abject that generate the protective resiliencies which come from locating, confronting and casting out such leakages of being and holes in meaning that proliferate during times of uncertainty.

The shrouding impact of the actuarial gaze and its protective effect was particularly evident in the almost entire lack of reference to the torture and abuse of women prisoners in Abu Ghraib in media reports of the beheading of Kenneth Bigley and in wider reports of the atrocities of Abu Ghraib. Throughout the course of the three-week drama of Bigley's capture, the militants repeated their demands for the release of women in Abu Ghraib. This demand was met with confusion by the US and UK governments, with the US government declaring that they had only two women in their custody, both of whom were scientists connected to Saddam Hussein's regime. According to one report on Bigley's beheading in a British newspaper there had formerly been a small number of women in Abu Ghraib but they had all been released (Harding 2004c). However, previous reports by the same journalist confirmed that the sexualised humiliation and rape of women prisoners by US soldiers were well known to the Iraqi public and international journalists (Harding 2004a; Harding 2004b). One of these earlier reports describes how the authorities' attention was first drawn to atrocities in Abu Ghraib by a letter smuggled out of the prison that claimed US military personnel had raped women detainees, some of whom were now pregnant, and that women had been forced to strip naked and parade in front of men: 'the letter urged the Iraqi resistance to bomb the jail to spare the women from further shame'. In addition, the report stated that Iraqi lawyers claimed the charges against these women were often baseless and that the US military had acknowledged that they arrested female relatives because of their connections to the former regime rather than any offence (Harding 2004a). The official inquiry into the abuse at Abu Ghraib commissioned by the Pentagon in 2004, following the public dissemination of the photos, confirmed some of these reports, including the rape of one woman and sexual violations of others (Taguba 2004). Photographs of the sexual abuse of women prisoners were found amongst the 1800 digital photographs taken by the military of torture and abuse inside Abu Ghraib but these photographs were not released by the US government in order to protect US soldiers in Iraq from attacks. Notably, these photographs were seen as more threatening than those of male prisoners being tortured and sexually abused. More than five years after the first publication of photographs of the atrocities, US President Barack Obama intervened to continue to prevent their release because, in his words, they would 'put our troops lives in danger' (McGreal 2009; Gardham 2009). Images of ruined male bodies, especially when humiliated and degraded by female military personnel, as the ubiquitous circulation of images of the violations and abuse inflicted by US soldier Lynndie England suggests, can be circulated as they have protective effects. Images of the rape and sexual violation of female prisoners by male soldiers carry more threat. It is not that images of women being raped are not powerful, it is that they have an emasculating rather than fortifying impact for the military and publics of coalition countries and therefore must be prevented from joining the affect economy of this particular performance of war. The abject is in play in both sets of photographs. With the abuse of male prisoners the decaying affect of the abject is viscerally attached to the body of the enemy, and with the abuse of female prisoners, the decay attaches to the attackers.

The wider circulations of the performance of the beheading in the media can thus be seen as continuing the process of casting out threat whilst bringing the protective, strengthening effects of the abject inside the circulations of discourse. Bigley is brought inside (he is a simple, ordinary man, one of us), the militants are cast out (they are terrorist monsters) and the women in Abu Ghraib are screened out entirely (their part in the drama undermines the protective effects of the wider performance complex). It may be that the US and UK governments' declarations that there were only two women in custody when Kenneth Bigley was beheaded were accurate. However, might it also be that female relatives of prisoners who, according to Harding's original report, were held inside the prison, were not classed as 'prisoners', and that government statements expressing confusion at the militants' demands were deliberately obfuscating? What is clear is that the contemporaneous and, at the time of writing, ongoing insistence on screening out images of the rape and sexual violation of women in the military prisons of Iraq in the mainstream press is significant. If there is any hopeful possibility for negotiating the uncertain impacts of performances of violence in a more critical and affective manner, it must begin by addressing the complexities pertaining to the mimetic circulations of waste and wasted life in such performance complexes. In particular, it must reflexively address how the protective charms of these performances coincided with the annihilation of the other that they were complicit in. In the chapters that follow I search for performances that demonstrate a different practice of ruin and decay – centring on its uses for adaptability, survival, critical action and compassion. Butler's privileging of affectivity provides an important provocation for this project. What I have highlighted here is the importance of attending to the *abject* in performance, that is, the decay, cuts and holes as well as the remnants and fragments of wasted life generated by the framing excisions of a performance complex of exception and its circulating mimetic effects.

This chapter has made an initial, troubling step towards articulating the possibilities for critical mimesis in an age of uncertainty. I have argued that performed violence is constituted by processes of petrifaction and degradation, and that these processes have both protective and destructive effects in the same moment of enactment. Every production of meaning signals its accompanying decay, producing holes and gaps, fragments and leftovers, that might be brought into touch and negotiated as part of a critical and affective project of performance. In the case of the beheadings in Iraq, what has been emphasised is the deliberate screening in and out of the abject to support a public consensus based on fear and the necessity of violence. In the next chapter I engage with the performed violence of the 'war on terrorism' in Northern Ireland, a conflict that has uncanny resonances with the war in Iraq, and evidences an extension of a performance complex of exception that continues to cause pain and suffering for those communities most directly affected.

Notes

1   According to the BBC Security Correspondent Gordon Corera, 238 foreign nationals were kidnapped in Iraq between May 2003 and November 2005, and 5000 Iraqis were kidnapped over a shorter seventeen-month period (Corera 2005). Between May and October 2004 the videoed beheadings of six foreign nationals in Iraq attracted the attention of the global media. All were reportedly carried out by Zarqawi: Nick Berg (US), Kim Sun-il (South Korea), Eugene Armstrong (US), Jack Hensley (US), Kenneth Bigley (UK) and Shoshei Koda (Japan). The victims were working for companies contracted by the US military, except Shoshei Koda, who was visiting Baghdad as a backpacker.

2   I do not include a discussion of the colonial violence of the Ottoman empire here, and, as such, my examination risks conflating very different historical and cultural contexts. An alternative approach might make more of the historical roots of Ottoman colonial violence and interplay of Islamic and non-Islamic motifs mimetically reproduced as part of the beheading. Undoubtedly, beheading is a form of violence that has multiple religious, cultural and historical roots, including political Islam. Here, I offer an argument that views the emergence of beheading in Iraq in 2004 as a complexly constructed, hybrid response to a multifaceted colonial past and present. I hope that this account complements analyses that take a more nuanced perspective with regards to the culturally contingent motifs of these acts of violence.

3   An innovation of the US intelligence services in 2003. For more information go to: www.defenselink.mil/news/newsarticle.aspx?id=29017 [accessed 21 July 2010].

4 Steve McQueen also wrote and directed the award-winning film about the 1981 hunger strikes by political prisoners in Northern Ireland's prisons, *Hunger* (2008).

5 I have borrowed the phrase 'colonial present' from geographer Derek Gregory's useful and incisive analysis of the war on terror (Gregory 2004).

3

Counterinsurgency performance in Northern Ireland: street-crowd-balcony-scenes and the ob-scene

My hair had long since been trimmed into a casual and unmilitary style, and I was used to changing my parting or back-brushing it quickly in order to alter my appearance from time to time. I also prided myself on a rather good variable gait. Everybody has a visual signature when they are observed walking from a distance; even without being conscious of it we are adept at spotting individuals in a crowd by their unique motion as they walk. By subtly changing my point of balance when walking I could significantly alter both my silhouette and my gait. This, combined with a reversible casual jacket, a rough change of hairstyle and the addition of a pair of spectacles, was an excellent way to increase the amount of time I could spend within sight of a target. (Captain James Rennie, 14th Intelligence Company, Northern Ireland – Rennie 1997: 163)

The phrase 'war on terror' reveals little about a conflict's contingent history, protagonists and antagonists, causes or consequences. It might be assumed from the generality of this phrase that the 9/11 attacks ushered in an unprecedented era of emergency and that there are no connections between the war on terror of the first decade of the twenty-first century and previous wars. I begin this chapter with a short story that highlights the limits of such ahistorical perspectives and illustrates the contiguities between the war in Iraq (2003–8) and Britain's longest counterinsurgency campaign, the 'Troubles' or the 'war on terrorism' in Northern Ireland (1969–98). The story also introduces the primary focus of this chapter: performance as a strategy and tactic of counter-insurgency, with specific attention to the war in Northern Ireland. In particular, the chapter focuses on the spatial dimensions of counterin-surgency performances – on the ways in which the mimetic capacities of space were deliberately exploited as part of an effort to maintain control over territory in the contested sites of Northern Ireland.

The story begins with two members of the British Special Forces who were arrested by Iraqi police in Basra in Iraq in September 2005. At the time of their arrest, these undercover operators were in full Arab dress, sitting in a battered-looking car laden with explosives and expensive reconnaissance equipment, and parked outside the central police station in Basra. The official narrative of British army operations in southern Iraq at the time was that this was a model occupation that implemented lessons learned from a successful campaign in Northern Ireland. Challenging this, British journalist Robert Fisk reminded the public of the covert killings and 'shoot to kill' practices of Special Forces in Northern Ireland, 'which does raise the question, doesn't it, as to just what our two SAS lads were doing cruising round Basra in Arab dress with itsy-bitsy moustaches and guns?' (Fisk 2005). At the time of the arrests, attacks on British army patrols and sectarian killings were rising in frequency, and there were fears that Basra's security forces had been infiltrated by local insurgents. The arrest of the two British Special Forces operators in Arab costume was followed by their rescue by the SAS and regular army. This provoked a lethal confrontation and also produced one of the iconic images of the war in Iraq in that year – of British soldiers throwing themselves out of an armoured vehicle erupting in flames and into the arms of an angry crowd.

A flurry of newspaper reports speculating about the identity of the soldiers in disguise linked them to the Special Reconnaissance Regiment, a unit active in Iraq at the time, and prior to that in Northern Ireland (see for example Evans 2005; Norton-Taylor 2005). The Special Reconnaissance Regiment in Iraq worked alongside another elite unit, the Joint Support Group, which was credited with providing intelligence leading to the killing of Abu Musab al-Zarqawi and preventing a number of suicide bombings in Iraq (Rayment 2007; Smith 2007). These two military units – the Special Reconnaissance Regiment and Joint Support Group – are contemporary manifestations of the 14th Intelligence Company and Forces Research Unit respectively, secret military units which, together with the British Special Air Services (SAS), MI5 and MI6, led the covert war in Northern Ireland in the latter decades of the twentieth century. The 14th Intelligence Company specialised in covert surveillance and the Forces Research Unit focused on recruiting and handling agents and informers from insurgent groups and the communities that they resided within.[1] Heading up the Special Reconnaissance Regiment in Iraq in September 2005 was Brigadier Gordon Kerr, a man who had also commanded the Forces Research Unit in Northern Ireland from 1987 to 1991 (Davies 2004: 131–2). The deployment of Brigadier Gordon Kerr to oversee Special Forces operations in Iraq was seen by some close to the conflict in Northern Ireland as a move that would protect him from prosecution for his activities whilst in Northern Ireland (Mackay 2003).

The sense of interconnected, fantastical and exceptional realities evident in this short account of a street scene in Basra is a repeated feature of the counterinsurgency performances in the pages that follow. Counterinsurgency performances in Northern Ireland included conventional military practices (weapons handling, military manoeuvres, patrolling, open combat) as well as the use of disguise, role play, choreography, rehearsal, improvisation and stage-management expertise as part of covert military operations. Allen Feldman's notion of political and military cultures in Northern Ireland as an 'ensemble of performed practices', including insurgency operations, hunger strikes, parades, public funerals and interrogations, highlights the function of body and space as material units of power through which the war was played out and communicated (Feldman 1991: 1). Here, I extend this ensemble to include counterinsurgency performances, focusing on patrolling practices, ambush and surveillance operations, and informer recruitment and handling. The story of counterinsurgency performance recounted here has a heritage in British colonial warfare, and an alternative focus for the chapter might have been the history of military deception in the Middle East. The decision to focus on Northern Ireland here was prompted in part by the autobiographies of former counterinsurgents published following the peace process in Northern Ireland, many of which provide extraordinary accounts of performance and are well worthy of attention from the perspective of performance studies. Perhaps most importantly, however, the conflict in Northern Ireland highlights the continuity of counterinsurgency performances from Britain's colonial past to the war in Afghanistan (2001–) – not just illustrating the ongoing evolution of performance as a tactic and strategy of counterinsurgency, or involving the same military personnel, but also pointing to an embedded, long-term coalition between mimetic processes, democratic tradition and a politics of exception that deserves comprehensive study.

In this chapter, I pay particular attention to the way counterinsurgency performances drew on the mimetic capacities of space to protect and destroy life, and diminish everyday space for people in Northern

Ireland. Here, the relationship between *space* and performed violence
provides an opportunity to extend this book's examination of a politics
of performance, which began with a focus on the *body* and performed
violence in chapter 2. In the latter half of the chapter, I compare counterinsurgency uses of space with the spatial poetry of a play, paying
attention to the distinct poetics of space that emerges in this very different domain. *Somewhere over the Balcony* was produced by Charabanc
Theatre Company in 1987, inspired by the lives of women living in Divis
flats in West Belfast, famous for the army observation posts stationed
on their highest floors, and as such it dramatises the lived experience of
counterinsurgency war. Counterinsurgency performances were carefully rehearsed and performed operations played out inside the extraordinary appearances of everyday life in Northern Ireland during the war.
Somewhere over the Balcony parodied the capacity of appearance to
provide residence for ob-scene worlds via dramatisations of the gradual
erosion and sudden annihilations of the everyday spaces inhabited by
its female characters. Charabanc Theatre Company (1983–95) was the
only theatre company made up of female performers during this period
in Northern Ireland, and the company's work explored the intersection
between female, working-class perspectives on everyday life in Northern
Ireland and experiences of conflict and sectarianism. Like Field Day
Productions (1980–), the groundbreaking cultural venture prominent
during the same period, Charabanc's work challenged and traversed
sectarian divides in both its methodology and its content. These female
theatre makers, together with playwrights Anne Devlin and Christina
Reid, whilst often facing more economically precarious conditions
than their male counterparts, are amongst the few female artists of the
'golden decade' of Northern Irish drama to receive critical and scholarly
recognition (Harris 2006: ix).

The 'skênê' of ancient Greek tragedy is a theatrical trope that might
be usefully mapped onto an analysis of the counterinsurgency and theatrical performances explored in this chapter. A screen separating the
domestic interiors of the great houses on which tragedies were based
from the visible area of the stage, the 'skênê' materialised an 'ominous
doorway' through which characters moved from the public dramas of
democratic life to encounter their deaths (Wiles 2000: 122). During
the war in Northern Ireland, the 'skênê' separating the transparent
operations of liberal democracy and the ob-scene and lethal dramas of
exception was both manoeuvrable and permeable. Reality accrued an
uncanny, doubling and doubled quality as the 'skênês' of appearance
were manipulated as part of a tactical play of democratic process, overt
war and covert military operations. This chapter considers what can

be learnt about the politics of performance from a study of the moving 'skênês' of counterinsurgency performance and theatrical performance during the war. Both kinds of performance dramatise the uncertain, uncanny, dissimulating qualities of space that are part of the lived experience of wars on terror. However, these performances had very different ends: counterinsurgency performances diminished and destroyed the appearances of space, whilst the play discussed here determinedly materialised habitable space within an environment of threat. In comparing the militaristic appropriation of space exemplified in the first half of the chapter, to the aesthetic and political strategies of *Somewhere over the Balcony*, there is thus an opportunity to investigate the contrasting forms of critical and creative mimesis that become possible during times of terror and crisis.

The 'Troubles' in Northern Ireland as mimetic process

Perhaps more than any other branch of military endeavour, successful deception is an art rather than a science . . . Many of the best practitioners have backgrounds in both the visual and performing arts. (Latimer 2001: 4)

The territory of Northern Ireland has a long history as a space of exception, and the struggle for control over this space has been a feature of British and Irish politics from the beginnings of colonisation in the twelfth century. In terms of contemporary history, the State of Northern Ireland was an outcome of partition following the Anglo-Irish war (1919–21). Northern Ireland remained part of the United Kingdom with a devolved government, and the Irish Free State, which became the Republic of Ireland, was established in the south in 1922. To control nationalist resistance in the North, the Civil Authorities (Special Powers) Act (Northern Ireland) was also established in 1922, prescribing powers of arrest, detention and trial without jury 'normally reserved for a state of emergency' (Mockaitis 1995: 97). These emergency powers were used indiscriminately against the Catholic population, mirroring discrimination against Catholics in other areas of public life that inspired the Irish civil rights movement in the late 1960s (*ibid.*; Iron 2008). An accompanying increase in public disorder led to the eventual deployment of the British army in 1969, the dissolving of the government of Northern Ireland in 1972 and more than thirty years of conflict between Republican, Nationalist and Loyalist paramilitaries and the British army, officially ending with the Good Friday Agreement in 1998. The period of conflict from 1969 also witnessed the periodic updating of anti-terrorism legislation detailing extraordinary powers of arrest and detention, and resulting in 'an unprecedented legal framework whose oddity makes it hard to place in the British tradition' (Townshend 1986: 69). Over the three decades of the Troubles, more than 3600 people were killed and thousands more injured and displaced.

The conflict in Northern Ireland has been described as charac-terised by 'a tendency towards mutual imitation' or 'mimetic process' (Townshend 1986: 32). For historian Charles Townshend, such mimetic processes are strategic – 'mimesis is clearly as necessary as it is dangerous' – as replicating the successful tactics of the opponent facilitates the assertion of control over territory and populations (*ibid.*). However, for historian John Newsinger, this mimesis was counter-productive in Northern Ireland, as it increased support for insurgency groups and produced as much retaliatory violence as it claimed to prevent (Newsinger 1995: 103). Here, it is useful to reintroduce the notion of organised control of mimesis discussed in chapter 1, where acts of violence mirror a distorted and alienating world and also provide an uncertain kind of refuge and protection from that world. In Northern Ireland, the contest to control mimetic processes of the war mobilised by overt and covert military operations distorted appearances to such an extent that in many cases it remains impossible to untangle who was responsible for the acts of violence and atrocity that made up the trajec-tory of the war. I explore examples of this later in the chapter, but for now it is useful to consider how this mimetic process was evident in the overarching history of the Troubles.

A mimetic process is evident, for example, in the coincidence of British army intervention in 1969 with the resurgence of Republican military struggle and the birth of the Provisional Irish Republican Army (IRA). It is also apparent in the British army's shift from a period of overt warfare towards the end of the 1970s, to adopting a strategy of covert war. This move reflected the IRA's adoption of a policy of a 'long war' of attrition following the failure of political negotiations and their realisa-tion that they could not win a conventional military confrontation. The transformation of the IRA into a professional, secret and mobile cell structure at this time was described by former British army covert oper-ator Nick Curtis as 'a kind of dark mirror of our own structure' (Curtis 1998: 140). For the British government, covert operations of the kind discussed in this chapter were married to a policy of 'police primacy', or 'Ulsterisation', that sought to undermine the political legitimacy of the struggle by criminalising paramilitary activity and removing the special category status of political prisoners. Sinn Féin also came to renewed prominence at this time as an autonomous Republican political party participating in the mainstream political arena. The British policy of covert warfare coupled with police primacy was a performance of liberal democracy which was thus a direct mimesis of the IRA's emergence as a professional, cell-based army and Republican politicians' participation in the democratic public sphere.

The longest period of the conflict (from the late 1970s to the 1990s) was therefore characterised by the maintenance of the appearances of liberal democracy in the public sphere whilst at the same time institutionalising military practices 'difficult to support in open society' (Mockaitis 1995: 121–2). In the words of Nick Curtis: 'without doubt we were wading thigh-deep through the filth of the lowest possible human behaviour' (Curtis 1998: 180). Actors from all sides manipulated the appearances of liberal democracy to enact an ob-scene and, to borrow journalist Martin Dillon's term, 'dirty war' (Dillon 1990). Democratic institutions provided additional 'skênês' that obscured the violence and lawlessness of the war. Unprecedented levels of government interference in mainstream broadcasting and media institutions, for example, kept the dirtier aspects of the war from public view (documented by Taylor 2001; Rolston and Miller 1996; Edgerton 1996; Murdock 1991; Curtis 1984). Government interference was famously justified by the then British Prime Minister Margaret Thatcher in 1985 as follows: 'we must try to find ways to starve the terrorist and the hijacker of the oxygen of publicity on which they depend' (cited in *ibid*. Edgerton 1996: 115). This culminated in the broadcasting ban of 1988, which prohibited the broadcast of the voices, but not the words, of representatives from eleven Republican and Loyalist paramilitary and political organisations (including Sinn Féin who at the time had a democratic mandate) as these people 'offend many who see and hear them' (Home Secretary Douglas Hurd, cited in *ibid.*: 123). Broadcasting outlets showed military and political spokespeople talking to camera with their words spoken by an actor with an Irish accent, providing an unexpected, profitable opportunity for Irish actors – journalist Peter Taylor, for example, reports that the actor impersonating Sinn Féin leader Gerry Adams 'is said to have made a small fortune' (Taylor 2001: 299). Gerry Adams himself ironically reflects that the broadcasting ban was introduced at the same time as the removal of the right to silence for criminal suspects in Northern Ireland: 'I liked the contrariness of this coercion. Republicans could not talk on the media. Republicans were compelled to talk in the interrogation centres' (Adams 2003: 83). Thatcher justified the broadcasting ban in 1988 with the statement, 'either one is on the side of justice in these matters or on the side of the terrorists' (cited in Edgerton 1996: 126) – a comment that starkly exemplifies how the mimetic process of the war mobilised a melodramatic, simplistic reframing of the conflict into good and evil.[2]

In order to provide a framework for exploring how performance was employed as part of the mimetic processes of the conflict in Northern Ireland, it is useful to briefly introduce the ways in which performance has been utilised as strategy and tactic throughout the history of counterinsurgency warfare. The classic counterinsurgency theorists, Frank Kitson and Robert Thompson, discussing colonial campaigns in Malaya, Oman, Kenya and Northern Ireland, both stress the importance of civil–military cooperation in the battle to win the 'hearts and minds' of the public and isolate insurgents from public support. Overt uses of performance here included the commissioning of media and cultural projects as part of civil–military cooperation and army propaganda campaigns in Malaya (Thompson 1966: 90–102; see also Kitson 1971: 49–63). Interestingly, these operations occasionally engaged theatrical performance; for example, during the Malaya campaign, former insurgents were reportedly used as performers in plays that toured to remote areas, projecting positive images of the regime (Lloyd 1997: 157). The war in Northern Ireland involved a more subtle use of performance. Covert operators took part in physically, mentally and emotionally demanding training programmes that included features familiar to ensemble performance training: the development of physical resiliency, improvisation skills, mental capacities such as memory and concentration, and an ability to work in teams. In addition, covert operators were trained to transform their appearances as part of a careful stage management of their engagements in enemy territory, by paying precise attention to details of gesture, clothing and physical movement (as Captain James Rennie of 14th Intelligence Company describes in the epigraph to this chapter). The aim was to develop a soldier's capacity to adapt appearances in response to the demands of different scenarios as they unfolded in unpredictable settings.

The principle of improvisation is written into counterinsurgency practice from the classics to the contemporaries. By means of improvisation, the threats accruing from the uncanny appearances of space, perpetually present in a context of terror warfare, were skilfully directed away from the body of the counterinsurgent. In Northern Ireland, these improvisation skills supported a soldier's ability to blend into the background, disappear and adapt to sudden and unexpected events as part of covert surveillance operations. They also supported the stage management of dramatic and terrifying eruptions into space during ambushes. Echoing this principle of improvisation, the controversial *US Army Counterinsurgency Field Manual* produced during the war in Iraq urged armies to become 'learning organisations': 'victory is gained through a tempo or rhythm of adaptation that is beyond the other side's ability to achieve or sustain' (US Army 2007: 196). Former covert operators describe how training regimes involved undoing the routine scripts of conventional army training – the focus of training was on developing a soldier's ability to continuously adapt within an ever-changing, threatening environment. Nick Curtis, for example, points out that the ability to creatively and spontaneously improvise was life saving in a 'terrorist war' which demanded flexible rules of engagement, as 'you can't play by the rules if the rules are only being obeyed by one side' (Curtis 1998: 92). In spaces where the exception had become the rule, performance skills helped a soldier keep one step ahead of an enemy: 'we ought always to have the advantage of surprise on our side, thanks to the combination of our acting skills and our ability to draw a concealed weapon in the blink of an eye' (Rennie 1997: 159). Training exercises demanded soldiers' participation in scenarios that simulated real-life military operations. Instructors occasionally carried this to the extreme by staging shootings during training scenarios that appeared to be *real* accidents. That is, they would stage fake shootings, using sheep's blood and guts to create the appearance of a real accident that had occurred during a simulated training scenario, testing a soldier's ability to respond to emergency (see for example *ibid.*: 132–4). Additional real-life scenario training including the use of live arms in a 'killing house', a specially constructed space for the rehearsal of hostage rescue (George 1999: 92; Rennie 1997: 135 and 168), simulated interrogations (Lewis 1999: 64–7; Rennie 1997: 141–51), and rehearsing for the recruitment and handling of informers by gathering detailed personal information from soldiers at military sites close to the training base 'without raising any suspicions or adverse response from our chosen targets' (Lewis 1999: 93).

All sides engaged in the war in Northern Ireland played with appearances, drawing on the performance skills of covert operators and a network of collaborators, including politicians and the media, to control the mimetic processes of war. In terms of the role of the British army, the shifting 'skênês' of the war are still being played in the silences in response to calls for Public Inquiries and yet to be released official reports about atrocities. Former covert operator Martin Ingram (a pseudonym), in a startling account of how the Forces Research Unit was involved in managing a network of secret agents that penetrated the highest levels of the IRA, outlines the difficulties of bringing the

'Stakeknife' story, discussed below, into the public realm. Ingram's comment that there was a deliberate lack of veracity in army records relating to the operations of the Forces Research Unit in Northern Ireland means that some incidents may never be verified (Ingram and Harkin 2004: 64). A critique of the specific decisions that led to the destruction of life and everyday space in Northern Ireland, however important those decisions are, is beyond the remit of this book. Here, my focus is on identifying opportunities for *critical* and creative responses to the organised control of mimesis of a war on terror. As noted in chapter 1, by 'critical' I mean practices of performance that interrupt the mimetic circulation of violence and inequity in times of crisis.

Thus far I have described the war on terror in Northern Ireland as a mimetic process, supported by counterinsurgency performances that drew on a creative and adaptive practice of mimesis. In order to extend this, and introduce the terrain in which a theatre maker might make an intervention, a return to Taussig is useful. His discussion of the protective and destructive effects of mimesis is worth quoting at length:

> Thus there would seem to be in this world of seeming a deeply puzzling capacity for copying and hence deception in which the 'original' and the 'copy' fight it out for ontological pre-eminence – for a claim to power over the perceptual fidelity, epistemic certainty, and very life of humans. And this is why there have to be 'seers.' This is why there have to be healers, persons capable of judging appearance, able to distinguish the different forms of doubling. Even so, such discernment is insufficient. For the healer's power depends, in its turn, on doubling also! The healer's capacity to diagnose and cure, to restore souls (read double, read image) depends on out-doubling doubling . . . out doubling the doubleness of the world. Until the next time. (Taussig 1993: 127–8)

Perhaps this notion of out doubling carves out a space for the critical intervention of a theatre maker. An intention to out double the doubleness of the world, for example, can be identified in Brecht's epic theatre, with its alienation effects deliberately manufactured as part of a performance aesthetic in order to increase a spectator's awareness of doubleness of the world as represented, and its subsequent potential for transformation. The same impulse might be identified in Rancière's 'dissensus', which identifies the critical potential of art in moments of aesthetic rupture, signalling the presence of multiple worlds of experience contained in space. Moments of dissensus counter the operations of the 'police', whose slogan is 'move along! There's nothing to see here' (Rancière 2010: 37). Drawing attention to the mimetic capacities of spatial practices, Henri Lefebvre offers a concept of 'social space' as a socially constructed phenomenon that communicates and materialises the power dynamics of an alienating and dissembling realm: 'any space implies, contains and dissimulates social relationships' (Lefebvre 1991: 82–3). For Lefebvre, any encounter with space is necessarily provisional, relational, potential and multidirectional, and reproduces as well as uses the simulations and dissimulations inherent in the social construction of space.

However, the same alienating, dissembling and dissensual effects are a notable feature of the spatial practice of counterinsurgency, used flexibly as part of a violent competition to out double the doubleness of the world and direct threat away from the body of the counterinsurgent and onto the bodies and spaces of the enemy and enemy territory. Here space accrues an uncanny quality, and like the performed violence explored in chapter 2, the circulations of mimesis in this context culminated in a contest of life that resolved itself in the protection of some lives, and destruction or diminishment of others. Troubling any easy attribution of critical potential to a practice of out doubling the doubleness of reality, during the war in Northern Ireland, the multiple, dissensual worlds of experience hidden in space were always already occupied by the counterinsurgent. This might be usefully understood in relation to the practice of camouflage, a mimesis of the dissensual and dissembling capacities of space invented by French avant-garde artists working with the military in the 1920s, where fragmented, broken lines were employed to disrupt the surveillance of space and provide folds in appearance that concealed hidden worlds prior to an attack (see Latimer 2001: 57–8). As noted in chapter 1, Lacan aligned camouflage to mimicry, a form of resemblance to an anonymous and alienating world that blurs the appearances of self and brings about the protection, but also the diminishment, of self: 'It is not a question of harmonising with the background but, against a mottled background, of becoming mottled . . . to imitate is no doubt to reproduce an image. But at bottom, it is, for the subject, to be inserted into a function whose exercise grasps it' (Lacan 1977: 100).

As such, it becomes possible to consider the *critical* force of mimesis as constituted at least in part by its provision of a protective domain for diminished life, and as a form of engagement with spatial uncertainty that has conservative, restorative ends rather than aggressively asserts power and control over space. Of course, this conservative domain is also mobilised as part of the counterinsurgency performances to protect some lives and destroy others. However, it is recycled in Charabanc's play, *Somewhere over the Balcony*, to materialise a habitable space that generates diverse and indiscriminate possibilities for survival and resilience, and turns to the diminished, mottled appearances of self and world as a cite/site of abundant critical and creative potential. The distinction between the examples of counterinsurgency performance and a stage drama, both of which out double the doubleness of the world, is thus located in a use of mimesis to create habitable spaces that protect worlds in times of crisis, rather than in an aesthetics and politics that somehow prefigure new spatial domains or transform the world. The play explores how the uncanny appearances of space might be creatively employed to secure a terrain that ensures liveability and survival, rather than to protect some lives and obliterate others.

Before offering a more detailed exploration of the play, I investigate three categories of counterinsurgency performance that exhibited different uses of the dissimulating capacities of space as part of the war in Northern Ireland: 'street scenes', 'crowd scenes' and 'the double'.

Street scenes: overt choreographies of counterinsurgency performance

We returned one night after another successful high-wire act through the Ardoyne; walking the tightrope in the dark through streets and alleys. (Curtis 1998: 84)

Classic counterinsurgency theory stresses the importance of maintaining a visible military presence in enemy territory. The 'same-element' theory of counterinsurgency, for example, advocates overt army operations in the same spaces as the insurgency to disperse resistance, control movement of populations and isolate insurgents (Thompson 1966: 115). In the spaces of Northern Ireland, staged and improvised contests of space between army units and paramilitary groups became 'contests of nerve' (Urban 1992: 214). The strategy of overt presence led to heavy losses sustained by army patrols in Republican areas as a result of attacks by IRA snipers early in the campaign in Northern Ireland, and forced a change in patrolling practices. 'Multiple patrolling' introduced a fragmented form of non-linear movement that disrupted perceptible and predictable patterns at the same time as producing an effect of dominance over space. A sophisticated spatial practice which required choreography as well as improvisation, multiple patrolling engaged a number of teams of four-man patrols in separate but connected movements through the streets. Frequent reversals in order, changes of direction and crossings over with each other aimed to 'make the movement of the satellite teams so unpredictable that it was almost impossible to determine where all teams were at any time and thus create uncertainty in the mind of the terrorist' (Iron 2008: 176). Conversely, army checkpoints were static spatial practices that sought to control the unpredictable movements of the IRA and similarly generate uncertainty. Army checkpoints were deliberately staged in and around spaces where it was suspected that a paramilitary attack was planned, as it was known that IRA concerns for the safety of their soldiers would lead to aborted operations. These spatial practices had a significant impact on the campaign and saved many lives: 'by 1992 it is estimated that in many areas, five out of six IRA attacks were aborted due to security force activity' (*ibid.*: 177). Interestingly, the *US Counterinsurgency Field Manual* comments that one of the failures of the counterinsurgency in Iraq was its inability to produce this effect of dominance over space, which handed the initiative to insurgent groups (US Army 2007: 48). The manual similarly emphasises the importance of competency in spatial practice, exhorting soldiers to (just as soldiers in Northern Ireland were required to) 'read the map like a book. Study it every night before sleep and redraw it from memory every morning. Do this until its patterns become second nature' (*ibid.*: 288).

Ambush operations were controversial spatial practices, involving a specific unit of the Special Forces, the SAS, who exploited the dissimulations of space to conceal their presence prior to attacks, leading to allegations of a 'shoot to kill' policy in the British army. SAS soldiers staged carefully timed eruptions that annihilated the appearances of space together with the bodies of the enemy. Former soldier turned journalist Mark Urban provides a useful description of the spatial dimensions of ambushes. He notes how the staging of an ambush involves placing a 'killer' group and 'cut off groups' in the targeted area, with the killer group aiming to destroy the insurgents and the latter preventing escape (Urban 1992: 161–2). Unpacking a specific example – the SAS ambush of an IRA attack on Loughgall police station in May 1987 – provides an opportunity to explore these spatial practices further. Here, placing the killer group inside Loughgall police station pre-empted public controversy, as the presence inside the station of soldiers at the time of the attack justified the use of lethal force. Urban's research suggested that the decision to conduct an ambush may have been unnecessary – the bomb to be used, for example, could have been defused and the perpetrators arrested prior to the attack. The ambush led to eight members of the IRA and one civilian being killed, and another civilian injured (see *ibid.*: 230–4).

Northern Ireland was a space of exception, and this is important to understanding the decision to counter the IRA attack with an ambush rather than more legally supportable methods. Loughgall is situated in rural Northern Ireland, and was targeted by the IRA as part of a strategy to weaken sovereign control at the borders of the British army's influence, destroying remote police stations and creating 'liberated' zones (Taylor 2001: 272). An ambush represents a dramatic eruption of sovereign power that both draws on and then obliterates the double and doubling capacities of space, and reduces space to an effect of power. In areas where British army control over space was most uncertain, the excessive and spectacular violence of the SAS was a stage-managed performance of superior military power that purposely directed terror onto the body and space of the enemy. The 'success' of these performances was based on the SAS's ability to traverse and occupy the dissensual worlds concealed in space, producing terrifying eruptions of ob-scene, exceptional power in the sites in which that power was most uncertain.

This play of appearance and disappearance, absence and presence, and order and disorder in the performances of terror, is also evident in the way in which special operations such as the ambush at Loughgall were formulated. Urban reports that approval for the ambush was given by representatives of successive levels of the military and political administration, each of which mirrored the approval of the representative of another layer of the hierarchy. Note here that mirroring the consent of the previous approver allows each officer and politician distance from responsibility should operations attract controversy, much like, 'the idea of loading the rifle of one soldier in a firing squad with a blank bullet. This has sometimes been done to allow all members of the firing squad to believe that they were personally not responsible for the death of the target' (Urban 1992: 170). From the soldiers directly involved at the end points of performed violence, to the political and military directors of performances of terror, the move to commission murder is made in the domains of mimesis rather than by a discrete identity making an explicit decision. By 'performing' approval in this way, the commissioning of atrocity and murder does not disturb fictions of a rule-bound universe and thus maintains a liberal democracy's illusions of legitimacy.

The exploitation of space exhibited by ambush operations is also notable in other forms of counterinsurgency performance, including the recruitment of informers and agents to work covertly for the British army. Here, rehearsed approaches were made to members of the public or paramilitaries that might be amenable to cooperation with the army. Recruitment of informers and agents involved the scripting, rehearsal and performance of 'scenarios' that engaged a potential informer or agent in a seemingly innocuous interaction with a covert operator. Former covert operator Rob Lewis provides detailed descriptions of such scenarios, which took account of the multiple directions of an encounter, involved rehearsals of planned approaches and required research into 'the background picture of the character we would be trying to deal with' (Lewis 1999: 123). The improvised quality of this play with appearance meant that scenarios did not always go according to plan: 'the unit's tradecraft involved contact with human sources and not pre-programmed computers' (*ibid.*: 96). A series of these performances led to the successful recruitment of Frank Hegarty, a high-profile agent working for the British army during the Troubles. At the time of the initial approach, Hegarty's active involvement in the IRA had lapsed (following earlier engagement during the 1970s, when he also reportedly provided information on IRA activities to the British army). The following successful attempt was made to reactivate Hegarty in 1982, and again, what is notable is the exploitation of the dissimulations of space in the management of the performance here:

> While out walking in the open countryside on the outskirts of Derry, Franko would quite often see a lone man off in the distance slowly moving away. Franko, who was a very amiable man, would hurry along to try and catch up with this man, who was always just a few hundred yards away . . . What Franko never realised was that this whole scene was being orchestrated just for him. It was known that because of his friendly nature he would try and chat to strangers. (*ibid.*: 187)

This 'cat and mouse game' was played out over a number of weeks and led to the eventual recruitment of Hegarty, who was encouraged to rejoin the IRA and subsequently worked his way up to the Quartermasters unit, responsible for the storage, allocation and deployment of weaponry. The information passed to the army by Hegarty led to British Prime Minister Margaret Thatcher's intervention in early 1986, when she ordered the release of details he provided relating to an arms dump in the Republic of Ireland to the Dublin government (Ingram and Harkin 2004: 118–22). The release of this information meant that the IRA was able to identify Hegarty as an informer. He was taken into hiding in England and eventually executed by the IRA after returning to Northern Ireland suffering from homesickness. In an example of the extraordinary shifting 'skênês' of appearance of this mimetic war, it has been reported that Hegarty was executed by another British agent who was also a senior member of the IRA, Freddie Scappaticci, to whom I return below (*ibid.*: 81).

Here, it is useful to consider Brecht's famous essay, 'The Street Scene', which explains his notion of epic theatre. As noted above, epic theatre draws attention to the deceptive appearances of the world by creating alienation effects that support the appearance of the world as provisional and changeable. For Brecht, the eyewitness on the street corner, demonstrating the occurrence of a traffic accident to passers-by, is an appropriate model for the epic performer. By 'demonstration' rather than an imitation of reality, the performer represents events as striking acts that call for explanation and intervention (Brecht 1978: 121–9). What do the street scenes of counterinsurgency performance during Northern Ireland's covert war suggest in response to these principles of performance? It is useful to again turn to Taussig here, who notes that surviving the state of emergency in Colombia in the 1980s required awareness of the dissimulating capacities of appearance, 'knowing how to stand in an atmosphere of clarity and opacity, seeing both ways at once . . . a state of doubleness of social being' (Taussig 1992: 17–18). Counterinsurgency performances in Northern Ireland aggressively controlled spaces and the lives that inhabited those spaces, generating the permanent alienation effects of a state of exception. Here, awareness of the doubleness of social being, including an ability to imitate and blend in with rather than demonstrate the alterability of the world, provided a means of surviving an extraordinary reality. Again, *critical* mimesis here might be most effectively supported by a concern to create habitable spaces in threatened worlds, rather than radically transform the world by doubling its mimetic effects.

Crowd scenes: covert choreographies of counterinsurgency performance

You wouldn't pick them out of a crowded room as being anything other than office workers, farm labourers or bus conductors. This easy ability to appear ordinary was our greatest strength. (Rennie 1997: 168)

Covert operators engaging in military operations in hostile territory learn to project an image of self that is congruent with the environments that they traverse, deliberately constructing an appearance of ordinariness via onstage behaviour that conceals an ob-scene reality. The manipulation of appearance was a particular area of expertise for covert operators who were part of the 14th Intelligence Company, a unit specially trained in covert surveillance, called 'The Muppets' by regular soldiers 'because of their various disguises' (Taylor 2001: 1). Former operators emphasise the focus on performance necessary for covert surveillance, not as a means of drawing attention to self, but to maintain a 'normal' appearance – relying on the appearance of the everyday as a form of protection that permitted deep penetration of enemy territory. This included the use of costume, props, body language and ventriloquism skills – the ability to perform contradictory movements of head and hands – to conceal speaking into hidden radios (Rennie 1997: 91). In addition, covert operators learnt how to mimic the distinct dialects of Northern Ireland and codes of appearance and behaviour expected in working- and middle-class, and Loyalist and Republican areas (*ibid.*: 94, 164; Curtis 1998: 142).

In his study of performance in everyday life, sociologist Erving Goffman explores the contradictions of social communication, in which we utilise visible appearances to control impressions on our audiences, and where 'there are few signs that cannot be used to attest to the presence of something that is not really there' (Goffman 1959: 59). During the covert war in Northern Ireland, it was the appearance of the ordinary and everyday that was the crucial deception – and as the discussion throughout this chapter shows, such appearances became threatened and fractured in times of crisis. Covert surveillance in Northern Ireland involved a delicate and dangerous process of maintaining control over the fragile appearances of everyday life whilst immersed in the environment of, and up close with, the enemy. The contest to control appearances of space between the army and the Republican community included the use of 'dickers' (young members of the IRA) watching for covert operators on street corners, army and paramilitary observation posts in high-rise flats and increasingly sophisticated human and technological surveillance strategies used by both sides (see Urban 1992: 113–14). Of course, the performances of everyday life that were part of this contest of space did not always succeed. One of the original covert operators connected to 14th Intelligence Company in Northern Ireland, Robert Nairac, had such confidence in his ability to manipulate his appearance that he operated in some of the most dangerous territory for British soldiers in Northern Ireland. His alleged execution by the IRA may have resulted from over-confidence in his performance skills: journalist Martin Dillon reports that the IRA always knew his true identity and carefully monitored his activities (Dillon 1990: 185).

Like the practice of 'multiple patrolling' described above, covert surveillance in Northern Ireland involved teams of operators engaged in non-linear and broken, but also choreographed and coordinated, movement through space. Here the focus was on producing invisibility – of maintaining the 'skênê' of ordinary appearance as a means of concealing an ob-scene reality – rather than introducing fragmented forms of visibility to create uncertainty. During surveillance operations only one or two members of a team had sight of a target at any one moment, with the movements of others coordinated by hidden radios: 'the team's invisible web was holding the targets in its centre as they moved through the streets' (Rennie 1997: 3). This demanded an ability to imaginatively project different scenarios across multiple spatial and temporal realms, as team members without direct contact sought to cover the possible next steps of the target: 'to do this as a team, within a hostile environment, is an art form' (Lewis 1999: 60). Moving ahead, falling behind, overtaking, allowing yourself to be overtaken, improvisation, blending into the background and disappearing were key technical aspects of this art form, and, just as competent performers who make a complex art appear simple, 'the trick is to be able to do it without making it look too obvious or outrageous' (Rennie 1997: 93). The spatial competence described here was also a characteristic of the paramilitaries, who became intuitively aware of surveillance operations by detecting slight shifts in the 'skênês' of appearance – the sights, atmospheres, sounds and senses of space: 'when an Army helicopter is overhead and there are no uniformed personnel in the neighbourhood you can be sure that the Army has created a sterile area so that undercover patrols can move into the area and work without interference . . . IRA people on the ground know by instinct that it is happening' (IRA member, cited in Dillon 1990: 477–8).

One former covert operator comments that 'we had to blend into the background wherever we happened to be. We were to become "grey men and women"' (George 1999: 95). Unlike other army units involved in the covert war, the 14th Intelligence Company recruited women as they provided improved access to the diverse guises of the ordinary and everyday: 'we blended in well with the genuine shoppers. The men fared less well as they looked awkward and out of place' (*ibid.*). The importance of appearing grey, indistinct and anonymous was also stressed in training for covert operators: recruits were told to adopt new identities and never communicate personal information to other operators, and any distinguishing marks such as scars or tattoos would rule a candidate out of selection (Lewis 1999: 50; Rennie 1997: 20; Urban 1992: 38). Again like competent performers, 'grey people' can look like anyone. The use of bland titles to name the various units involved in covert war in Northern Ireland was a deliberate strategy that also sought the protection of grey spaces and non-identities. The innocuously named 'Forces Research Unit' and '14th Intelligence Company' (also known as the 'Dets', 'The Group' and 'Joint Services Group'), provided a successful 'screen of secrecy' that was maintained for many years (Urban 1992: 39). A lack of competence in utilising such shades of grey is highlighted by one covert operator's humorous commentary on SAS soldiers' failed attempts to participate in joint operations with the 14th Intelligence Company: 'SAS troopers in plain clothes always seemed to look like SAS troopers in plain clothes. To a man they liked to dress in tight blue jeans, trainers, sweatshirts and bomber jackets; and their notion of a civilian hairstyle invariably matched that of the average professional footballer' (Rennie 1997: 223).

What is notable about these descriptions of the 14th Intelligence Company is covert operators' expertise in negotiating the murky terrain – the spaces of exception – that exist beyond the readily and securely visible, identifiable and readable. During surveillance operations, the ordinary appearances of prosaic, everyday realities concealed the grey spaces of exception that constituted the ordered disorder of the streets of Northern Ireland. Here, the counterinsurgent is the shadow, the grey figure, competently controlling the mimetic process and ascribing the forces of anomie – the shifting contours and forms of an exceptional reality – to herself. As such, the surveillance operations of the 14th Intelligence Company were also postmodern and postdramatic forms of performance, played out across multiple spaces, identities, narratives and temporal frames – durational, provisional, incomplete and rarely culminating in a defining event. Bottom-up improvisations of surveillance practices in the spaces of crisis exhibited durational, creative and adaptive relationships with space, and these relationships served an aggressive agenda.

The street and crowd scenes explored here complicate any simplistic alignment of the aesthetics of creative spatial practice with a counter-hegemonic aesthetic. Here, the resistant possibilities of mimesis and space reveal themselves as promiscuous in their allegiances. For example, Michel de Certeau's formulation of the spatial practices of everyday life as providing a means of counter-hegemonic resistance, of operating beyond the gaze of an all-surveying presence of hegemonic power, appears too simplistic when placed alongside these examples of counterinsurgency performance (see de Certeau 1984: 91–110). Similarly, Peggy Phelan's identification of that which is resistant to representation as a site of critical potential – 'the immateriality of the unmarked' which 'shows itself through the negative and through disappearance' – is similarly challenged (Phelan 1993: 19). These examples of counterinsurgency performance highlight the entrapping function of appearance and disappearance, stasis and movement, visibility and invisibility, absence and presence. The invisible, the unmarked, the creative, the sensory, the dissensual, the affective or embodied, the improvised, the provisional, the surreptitious, the unreadable – familiar terms of reference in discussions of critical cultural practice also define counterinsurgency performance in a time of terror – and the spaces they infer are always already populated by a violent, alienating power.

The doubles

> All the world is not, of course, a stage, but the crucial ways in which it isn't are not easy to specify. (Goffman 1959: 72)

And so to the extraordinary story of the control of the war by means of informers, where 'handlers' and their 'agents' became experts in out doubling the doubleness of appearance to intervene in the armed struggle on behalf of the British government, with agents frequently maintaining their deception for many years, often concealed from close family and friends. Handlers and agents depended upon the uncanny, deceptive appearances generated by the mimetic processes of the war for protection, and this had de-realising effects, as noted by one member of the IRA: 'you begin to wonder what is going on and where the reality lies. This aspect of the war is like a room full of mirrors, not just for us but for the Army' (cited in Dillon 1990: 74).

For Freud, the 'uncanny' denotes a particular class of terrifying experiences wherein the unfamiliar emerges in the context of the familiar: an affect and effect that Freud traces to the German word *unheimlich*, literally translated as 'unhomely' or 'unhoming' (Freud 2003: 124–5). An uncanny or unhoming effect is associated with a number of motifs that Freud found repeated in art, literature and dreams, including the fear of damage to one's sight and the 'double' or 'doppelgänger'. The 'double', in turn, refers to a psychological mechanism Freud associated with early childhood, whereby the subject defends himself against terror by inventing a 'double' onto which the self can be safely projected, and that later in the development of the ego becomes a threatening object. To consider this in terms of counterinsurgency performance, it is possible to view agents who were active members of the IRA whilst working closely with the British army as dependent upon the uncanny, doubling capacities of appearance as protective cover for the self. In the account that follows, a 'double' was also materialised in the body of another person, providing temporary protection for an agent during a particular moment of risk, a protection that was afforded ultimately at the cost of the double's life.

Responsibility for handling high-profile agents in Northern Ireland belonged to the Forces Research Unit (FRU).[3] Whilst this is not the place to give a full account of the history of the unit, it is important to note that the FRU, unlike the 14th Intelligence Company or the SAS in Northern Ireland, was not under the command of the police force but operated independently, offering operational flexibility (Ingram and Harkin 2004: 210–11). This independence was secured, following the IRA bombing of the Conservative Party conference in 1984, by British Prime Minister Margaret Thatcher's direct funding and support. Thatcher saw the FRU, rather than the 'too civil, too refined and too sensitive' MI5, as more capable of meeting the challenge posed by the IRA (Davies 2004: 58–9). Her intuitive judgement echoes the principles of mimesis identified as a potent counterinsurgency weapon throughout this chapter. Favouring military intelligence units over the MI5 guaranteed that the war in Northern Ireland was fought on the front line by men of a similar class background to the paramilitaries.

Freddie Scappaticci, codenamed 'Stake Knife', was a valuable asset as an agent during the Troubles and was so respected by Margaret Thatcher that in 1986 she allegedly invited him to her official residence at Chequers. It was here that she insisted on paying him for his services, which up to that point he had offered for free (Davies 2004: 88). Scappaticci was paid £75,000 a year by the British government (Taylor 2001: 295), an extraordinary amount, especially when contrasted to average annual earnings in the UK in 1986, which were £12,615.[4] Scappaticci grew up in a family of Italian descent with staunch Republican affiliations. During his time as an agent he was responsible for IRA internal security, including the interrogation of suspected informers and agents: 'playing the interrogator and torturer at the very heart of the IRA was, of course, also the perfect cover for an undercover agent working for the British' (*ibid.*: 82). During this time it is estimated that thirty-five people were victims of IRA execution, some of whom were 'sacrificed' by the FRU in order to protect Scappaticci's identity (Ingram and Harkin 2004: 83). The autobiographies of former covert operators drawn on throughout this chapter contain startling accounts of atrocities that were committed as a result of informer and agent handling operations. However, they also contain accounts of atrocities that were prevented – many British and Irish lives were saved by Scappaticci and the agent running operations of the FRU (Davies 2004: 114; Lewis 1999: 236).

Francisco Notarantonio was a pensioner and former IRA member (although not active for many years at the time of his death), and, like Scappaticci, was of Italian descent. It is alleged that details of the identity and residence of Notarantonio were passed by the FRU to Loyalist paramilitaries. This was done in order to protect Scappaticci's identity at a time when there was a rumour amongst Republican groups that a mature member of the IRA, probably of Italian descent, was in the pay of the British army. By killing Notarantonio, this rumour might therefore be dispelled and Scappaticci protected (Davies 2004: 114–15).[5] Notarantonio was an astute choice as a double for Scappaticci, similar enough in terms of personal history to provide a credible match. In a moment of crisis for Scappaticci and his handlers, when the 'double' Scappaticci had performed for many years was showing signs of frailty, a 'real' double was identified to stand in his place, and this saved Scappaticci's life but ended Notarantonio's: 'someone remembered poor old Francisco and decided that on this occasion he would fit the bill perfectly' (*ibid.*: 115). Notarantonio was shot by Loyalist paramilitaries whilst lying in bed next to his wife in October 1987.

In chapter 2, I explored the apotropaic – protective and destructive – effects of acts of violence. The murder of Notarantonio demonstrates this apotropaic effect, again highlighting the coalition of protection and destruction evident in the mimesis of performance in times of terror. The figure of the double protected one man's life whilst facilitating the annihilation of another. As with the SAS ambushes and surveillance operations discussed above, this annihilation is played out in a grey, ob-scene zone beyond the secure and proper domains of ordinary appearance, discourse and law. Here, an absent – 'someone' – decided Notarantonio 'fitted the bill', and in addition, my entire account of this act is constructed without making recourse to proper evidence, and instead draws on unsubstantiated autobiographical information and journalistic accounts. The uncanny play of appearances here is part of a culture of dissimulation that, at the time of writing, is still unresolved: Scappaticci is in hiding, there has been no official confirmation of Scappaticci's identity as an agent and nobody has admitted liability for Notarantonio's murder. Here, the survival of one life was guaranteed by the loss of another, and this process was mobilised by a performance that lacks substantial meaning or recognition, that is, a process in which reality is diminished and substituted for an appearance of reality that depends on a deceptive covering up of its lack.

The double is therefore an estranged and estranging form of appearance, both self and not self, and the smallest of differences between the two, and between Notarantonio and Scappaticci, constituted the mimetic slippage that killed one man and protected another. During times of crisis, these slippages become threatening fractures and their doubling and unhoming appearances threaten a total collapse of the performances of everyday life on which the protection of self uncertainly depends. As appearances fracture, life's unhoming and alienating suspension in the world is revealed, and small distinctions become matters of life and death, mobilised, exchanged and recycled in exclusive – protective and destructive – identifications of self and other. It is only in the realm of performance that these slippages acquire meaning, and the part they played in the particular counterinsurgency performance detailed here culminated in a waste of life. The final section of this chapter explores how theatre during the Troubles in Northern Ireland played a role in the mimetic processes of a counterinsurgency war, and its bartering of bits of life for their protective and destructive effects.

'On a day like today you could be anywhere': Charabanc's *Somewhere over the Balcony*

I can't see your eyes, I can't look on your face,
But I feel your presence all over this place.
(*Somewhere over the Balcony*, Charabanc Theatre Company [Harris 2006: 184])

In the same year as the murder of Francisco Notarantonio, the ambush at Loughgall, the beginning of Gordon Kerr's command of the Forces Research Unit and the broadcasting ban, *Somewhere over the Balcony*, a play by Charabanc Theatre Company, premiered in London and Belfast and toured to Dublin and the US (1987–88) (figure 1). Charabanc Theatre Company was formed in Belfast in 1983 by five unemployed female actors (Marie Jones, Maureen Macauley, Eleanor Methven, Carol Scanlan and Brenda Winter). It was set up with the support of Action for Community Employment (ACE), a government initiative that funded small businesses and aimed to counter high levels of unemployment in Northern Ireland. The five actresses had experienced significant levels of unemployment, partly as a result of a professional theatre scene diminished by lack of financial investment, but also because of the lack of good roles for Irish women and the discriminatory practices of theatres at the time (Harris 2006: xvi). *Somewhere over the Balcony* is based on the lives of women living in Divis flats, a high-rise block of flats that had a permanent army observation post positioned on its top floors, providing twenty-four-hour surveillance over a staunchly Republican area of West

Figure 1 Eleanor Methven, Marie Jones and Carol Moore in *Somewhere over the Balcony*, The Drill Hall, London, 1987. Photograph by Sheila Burnett.

Belfast. The play explores the lives of three women on the balcony of the condemned flats, conducting surveillance on the British army above their heads and an increasingly surreal series of events that unfold on the streets below. It combines humour, song, farce, slapstick and moments of serious drama in a parody of the 'ordinary' appearances of the streets of West Belfast at a time when nothing was as it seemed, as noted in the programme of the original production: 'when people have lived all or most of their lives in a "war-zone", everything changes – especially the definitions of what is normal' (Charabanc 1987).

The recurring motif of the counterinsurgency performances described above is the shifting 'skênês' of appearance threatening to materialise an ob-scene war in the spaces of everyday life in Northern Ireland. Within theatrical space, a shifting 'skênê' offers the possibility of creatively negotiating and reinscribing those appearances as well as dramatising their uncertainties. The analysis of *Somewhere over the Balcony* offered here identifies how the production negotiated the unstable appearances of everyday life and enacted a critical interruption of the mimetic processes of the war. This play and other Charabanc productions have been written about from the perspectives of feminist scholarship (Harris 2006; Foley 2003; DiCenzo 1993; Martin 1987), postcolonial theory (Gilbert 2001) and the politics of Northern Irish drama (Maguire 2006; Lojek 1999). Looking at the play from the perspective of a society deeply impacted by counterinsurgency war adds to this body of work, and provides an understanding responsive to the context of the play as well as useful to the attempt to understand a politics of performance in a time of terror pursued here. Tom Maguire argues that the critical potential of performance in Northern Ireland was diluted by a funding system that supported 'manufactured political consensus', avoiding politically sensitive projects and operating within a frame of 'cultural commodification' (Maguire 2006: 169). However, Lionel Pilkington notes that despite their awareness of the consensus-building intention of much available funding, many theatre groups were committed to appropriating theatre as a cultural resource that offered a political critique (Pilkington in Colleran and Spencer 1998: 22–3). In the analysis that follows I argue that the *conservative* impetus of theatre during the Troubles demonstrates critical potential precisely because of its lack of direct engagement with or exposure of the threatening uncertainties of the wider context of war.

The story of Divis flats shows how artists and communities are awkwardly positioned at the intersections of various hegemonic agendas particularly difficult to negotiate during times of war. In a review of the British army campaign in Northern Ireland, a Ministry of Defence report comments that, 'the long-term solution was not to deploy three battalions into the Divis flats but rather to bulldoze them and build decent, respectable homes with proper amenities' (Ministry of Defence 2006: 8–3). In the programme of *Somewhere over the Balcony*, Divis flats were described as 'the worst housing project in Western Europe', with journalist John Pilger, writing in the programme, describing their characteristics of overcrowding, frequent flooding, water cuts and front rooms used as impoverished shops (Charabanc 1987). Pilger argues that the negative impact of cuts to public services arising from Thatcher's embracing of a free market economy disproportionately affected housing and employment schemes in Northern Ireland. However, the deprivation of Divis flats was also a result of economic racketeering by paramilitary groups. Building firms contracted to the Northern Ireland Housing Executive during the Troubles charged 25 per cent on top of tenders to work in areas most directly affected by violence in order to pay extortion money to paramilitaries, who raised 'several million pounds' from the Housing Executive over a ten-year period, reinvesting money in the armed struggle (Dillon 1990: 424). The violence of the war took many forms and impacted upon multiple public and private domains, including the extreme levels of poverty and deprivation in Divis flats. This account highlights how the mimetic processes of the war, which recruited space and bodies as 'performers' in a deadly contest of appearances, extended to the invasion of domestic, habitable space as well as the urban and rural environments of Northern Ireland. In turn, this signals the importance of theatre's relationship to habitable space to understanding the critical potential of performance in a time of terror.

The consigning of the violent realities of the Troubles to the ob-scene or offstage is a frequently critiqued feature of the 'Troubles play'. Thus, 'the visible world of the stage provides the frame for an offstage presence of some force too vast or amorphous to be seen. However, when that offstage world swells into a timeless, unappeasable horde of sectarian Bacchants . . . it makes political violence appear mindless and unmotivated because it is unrepresentable' (Morash 2002: 246). Countering this argument, Joe Cleary draws on Auerbach's work on mimesis to argue that the privileging of domestic space in naturalistic drama also enacts an implicit critique of social and economic inequity (Cleary 1999: 524). Following Cleary's inference, it is possible to view the Troubles play's relegation of violence to the ob-scene as a critical refusal to accept violence as part of habitable spaces of stage and everyday life, and as mobilising a deeper critique of the degradation of everyday life caused by a social and economic system that supports war. Violence is an ever-present possibility that is deliberately refused. Feminist analysis of Irish theatre has taken up a discussion of domestic space; for example, theatre scholar Melissa Sihra notes that familial, feminine and homely spaces on the Irish stage are often depicted as threatened by encroaching violence and 'within this site of instability and violation, women seek agency and subjective accommodation' (Sihra 2007: 3).

Sihra's suggestion of women's agency within precarious sites is important in relation to *Somewhere over the Balcony*, and is a point that counters critical commentary that the play *denies* agency to its three female characters. For example, according to Maguire, 'like a Greek chorus, the women can narrate and pass comment on the actions of others, but they are never actors themselves' (Maguire 2006: 113). The play, in its depiction of water cuts, the noise of British army helicop-ters, lost children and pets, arrests and interrogations, claustrophobic atmosphere and increasing diminishment of intimate space, powerfully communicates an experience of powerlessness and alienation. This is most dramatically portrayed by Kate's anxiety about the fragility of the walls of her flat which are eventually destroyed by a controlled explo-sion, leaving her to start the second act sitting on the toilet covered only by a sheet. However, the three characters in the play, Ceely Cash, Kate Tidy and Rose Marie Noble, whose surnames might be said to denote distinct strategies of female resilience, are constantly engaged in energetic attempts to resist the invasion of their space by a threatening outside. The play depicts the women's agency as well as exposure and diminishment in this regard, primarily by their reversal and parody of the gaze of army surveillance. For example, early in the play the women mimic the hand movements that guide a helicopter in to land on the top of the block of flats opposite their balcony, bringing a new battalion of soldiers to the area, and, shortly after, they pose for photographs for the new arrivals. During Ceely's short monologue in the first half of the play, she lusts after the soldiers, 'just look at him, joggin' round and round . . . I wonder what he's like out of that uniform. Sexy . . . Jesus Ceely Cash, he is a Brit.' She also conducts her own surveillance of the streets, below: 'May Day! May Day! Slimy the dole snooper is in the area. He is disguised as a paratrooper. Anybody doing the "double" down tools immediately' (Harris 2006: 196).

The subtlety of this parody is easy to miss: the choice of an army uniform as a disguise for the dole snooper is a humorous play on the ubiquitous presence of British army soldiers and covert operators in plain clothes that produced the uncanny appearances of street life in West Belfast at the time of the play. In addition, the reference to 'doing the double' surely refers to the presence of informers and agents in those streets as much as those committing dole fraud: an implicit reference to the extraordinarily elusive appearances of the streets of Belfast that may well have had a cathartic value for a local audience. Ceely's illegal radio station facilitates the women's conduct of their own covert operations from the balcony, including passing information gleaned from their surveillance to other residents, acting as an information point by communicating with those trapped in a surreal siege in the cathedral opposite and, perhaps most importantly, facilitating a game of bingo specially adapted for Northern Ireland: 'two rubber bullets, 22; armalite gun, 21; on the run, 31; . . . doin' time, 29; two dead men, number 10 . . . Prods are dirty, number 30; Pope's a mick, 26' (Harris 2006: 206–7). The positioning of the women on the balcony of the flats means that they do far more than simply narrate the actions that occur offstage. They are, in fact, engaged in a relentless, humorous, critical inversion of the appearances of space, and their parody refers directly to the lives of the women in Divis flats who inspired the play.

The setting of the play on the balcony subverts conventional practices of spectatorship in the theatre and counterinsurgency war, where the objects on stage and streets are looked at by spectators or counterinsurgents respectively. The balcony situates the characters on the cusp of inside and outside, public and private, onstage and ob-scene – a powerful yet vulnerable position where they enact their own surveillance and engage in uncertain dreams of somewhere 'over the rainbow', as evoked by the witty title of the play. Thus, the balcony is also a place from which other spaces can be imagined, echoing Gaston Bachelard's comments on the poetic force of literary descriptions of dream houses, which insist that 'a daydream of elsewhere should be left open therefore, at all times' (Bachelard 1994: 62). However, the women are also trapped visually and spatially on the narrow concrete strip. Costume changes and prop manipulations centre on Kate and Rose's army uniforms and use of military paraphernalia during the different 'operations' of the women, contrasted with Ceely's nightdress, which she remains in throughout the play. These different appearances in themselves signify the precariousness of this spatial setting and the women's competing postures of protection and exposure.

It is precisely the ambivalence of this site that constitutes the dramatic power of the play. Gaston Bachelard comments that: 'come what may, the house enables us to say: I will be an inhabitant of the world, in spite of the world' (Bachelard 1994: 46–7). By means of their situation on the balcony, on the cusp of habitable space and a threatening, uncanny and bizarre outside, the women exhibit uncertain kinds of agency and resilience, at the same time as a powerful determination to inhabit the world. The balcony promises a diminished and exposed habitation; a space to hide where one is also at perpetual risk of discovery. However, the spatial poetry of the balcony also opens up the possibility for other kinds of encounter with the world, and in the play this possibility is given the form of intimate, supportive and humorous relationships between the women and their dreams of somewhere else. This site is also significant, then, as it allows the dream of somewhere else to emerge inside the familiar, albeit uncanny, spaces of the everyday, rather than as a utopian dream of a faraway place of escape. The play determinedly insists on the women's resilience and their right to a habitable space that offers a hopeful future in the here and now. It also recognises the exceptional realities in which these dreams persist. The humorous and moving moment when Ceely and Kate look over the balcony before leaving the flats so that a controlled explosion can be carried out is a powerful and ironic expression of this hopeful perspective:

Ceely: That is a beautiful day isn't it?
Kate: That's what I love about this place. On a day like today you could be anywhere. *They pause and take in the sun.* Ceely, are you not going to put some clothes on?
Ceely: Sure, I'm only going to the Falls Road. *As they exit. . . SFX bomb exploding.* (Harris 2006: 204)

The balcony is not the domestic space of the Troubles play with its private onstage and threatening offstage, but a space that allows for the women's observation of the world and imagination of other worlds. By utilising this site, the play dramatises uncertainty whilst also celebrating the humour, imagination and resilience of the women inhabiting that space. As well as surveying the uncertain appearances of the streets below, and returning the gaze of the military above, the play searches for the kinds of agency offered by these exposed sites, and answers with an image of women in stolen army uniforms and nightdresses, playing bingo, and dreaming of the potentiality and impossibility of their everyday worlds. This dramatisation of space culminates in a play that exhibits a deeply hopeful, ironic and poetic resistance to the war's encroachment on and destruction of habitable space.

The play's search for habitable space was also mobilised by Charabanc's creative methodology. As a company, Charabanc was noted for its successful operation across alternative, professional and community theatre contexts regionally, nationally and internationally, and for its collaborative methodologies (see Maguire 2006; Harris 2006; Byrne 2001). The creative collaboration that led to *Somewhere over the Balcony* involved extensive time spent in Divis flats with residents, who reportedly became enthusiastic audience members of Charabanc's future productions (DiCenzo 1993: 183), with journeys to the city centre to see shows involving traversals of cultural, imagined, sectarian and class divides. This determined expansion of liveable space is conveyed by the name of the company, Charabanc, which refers to the benched buses that offered day trips for groups of workers in the nineteenth century. Commenting on the collaborative methodology of *Somewhere over the Balcony*, one review of the play noted that, 'people thought [the actors] were crazy to want to penetrate the area and get to know the women there. The residents were taken aback' (Fowler 1987). Company members report that as women they were able to traverse such divisions more easily as 'women's culture cuts across the narrow sectarian divide' and, in addition, the commitment of the company to represent the 'ordinary view' enabled audiences to imaginatively experience a perspective of Northern Ireland not wholly determined by the conflict (Byrne 2001: 90).

The set design of *Somewhere over the Balcony* was an important aspect of its spatial poetry. Divis flats were represented by parallel wooden frames that had a cage-like effect, mimicking the architectural structure of high-rise flats and conveying something of its poetics of protection and exposure. However, the easily transportable, minimalist staging also reflected the company's commitment to tour to non-theatrical venues and engage with diverse audiences. As one of the actresses, Eleanor Methven, commented, 'in our plays, a Protestant might sit next to a Catholic and watch the enemy on stage . . . you get to like the characters and identify with them . . . that creates a dilemma for the audience' (Byrne 2001: 90). The spatial poetry exhibited by the methodology, dramatic material and staging of the play, thus combined to offer a poetic, critical resistance to the mimetic processes of a war on terror. It gently illuminated and countered the ob-scene realities of the war via its bizarre encounters and surreal escapades, and as such sustained a felt connection with the complexities of its context, as one reviewer commented: 'improbability piles upon unlikelihood. Yet a crazy authenticity is maintained throughout' (Nowlan 1987). The play forged a powerful contract with the potential of imagination, as well as determinedly insisting on a body's right to habitable space. The power of *Somewhere over the Balcony* resides in its dream of kinds of mimesis that celebrate resilience and survival, and the power to restore worlds in a time of threat and uncertainty.

However, the story of the play's tour warns against any reification of theatre's ability to marry dream and reality. Although this is regarded as Charabanc's 'finest play' (Harris 2006: xi), it was not widely shown across Northern Ireland or the Republic of Ireland at the time. There were performances of the play in Belfast, including a performance at the Divis Community Centre in May 1988, but nonetheless, this remains a very limited tour compared to the company's other productions (for the production history of Charabanc plays see Harris 2006: 237–57). A review in *The Irish News* states that the performance in the Divis Community Centre was a 'gesture of thanks' played out to a largely female audience 'plainly delighted to be given the opportunity to see professional drama in their own community'. Interestingly, this review cites complaints from the company that funding cuts meant that they had to cut short performances to community venues 'where our real audiences are' (Coyle 1988). The lack of funding referred to here was connected to Belfast City Council's protests against the Anglo-Irish Agreement in 1985. These protests disrupted the administration and led to cuts in arts funding which left Charabanc 'in the bizarre position of being able to obtain grants to tour internationally but not locally' (Harris 2006: xxiv). Demonstrating an uncanny interconnection between the different domains of performance examined in this chapter, this disruption prompted British Prime Minister Margaret Thatcher's order of the release of information relating to an arms dump in the Republic of Ireland provided by the IRA member and covert agent Frank Hegarty, leading to the IRA identifying Hegarty as an agent and his eventual execution. Thatcher wanted to highlight the benefits of the Agreement and appease Protestant groups in the North opposed to the accord with the Republic of Ireland (Ingram and Harkin 2004: 119).

This chapter has explored the mimetic processes of the war in Northern Ireland, from the manipulation of ordinary appearance by the grey people of the British army, to the choreographed and dramatic eruptions of the SAS and regular army that produced an effect of dominating space, to the diminishments of habitable space resisted and recycled in *Somewhere over the Balcony*. The play provides the grounds for exploring how performance might offer a poetics of exception through forms of spatial poetry, imaginative and collaborative practice and creativity – linked by a concern to protect habitable space and recognition of the abundant possibilities of dreaming. Here, an intensely performative reality mobilised shifting 'skênês' of appearance as a weapon of war, helping to conceal the complicities of a liberal democracy with an ob-scene war. In the following chapter, I explore the performance of plays that were produced close to the centre of the British government during a different war – on London stages at the time of the Iraq war (2003–8). Many of these plays also critically interrogated the 'skênês' of appearance supporting liberal democracy's management of the ob-scene. What critical possibilities are offered by theatre in the political centres of the colonial present? How did these plays reinforce or critique the obfuscating appearances of liberal democracies in times of crisis?

Notes

1 The Special Reconnaissance Regiment was reportedly deployed in the operation that led to the lethal shooting of Jean Charles de Menezes at Stockwell underground station in London in July 2005, shortly after the suicide attacks on the London transport system on 7 July 2005. De Menezes was a Brazilian-born electrician falsely suspected of planning a suicide attack (see Norton-Taylor 2005).

2 Thatcher's comment here has all too familiar overtones, evoking the infamous 'either you are with us or you are with the terrorists' statement made by US President George Bush as part of his announcement of a 'war on terror' shortly after the 9/11 attacks (http://archives.cnn.com/2001/US/09/20/gen.bush.transcript/ [accessed 19 August 2010]).

3 For accounts of the FRU see Davies (2004) and Ingram and Harkin (2004), and for a supportive view see Lewis (1999). For information about the struggle for truth and justice of the families who lost loved ones as a result of the activities of the FRU see the Relatives for Justice website – www.relativesforjustice.com/ [accessed 22 July 2010].

4 The worth of Scappaticci's earnings of £75,000 a year in 1986 is equivalent to £216,095 a year in 2007 (results provided by www.measuringworth.com/ukcompare/ [accessed 22 July 2010]).

5   Journalist Peter Taylor gives a slightly different account, suggesting that the
    FRU gave Notarantonio's details to a Loyalist paramilitary group because
    they had heard from their agent in that paramilitary that Scappaticci was on
    that paramilitary's list of targets. Here, Notarantonio's details were given
    to divert Loyalist rather than Republican attention away from Scappaticci
    (Taylor 2001: 295–6).

4

A crisis of voice: democratic performance on the London stage

Democracy and freedom. Freedom and democracy. I offer them to you. I'm giving them to you. Don't be frightened. Don't be alarmed. Do they seem – nurse in flames – like big difficult words? Well, they're not, they're not, they're – Women of Troy, *Shoot/Get Treasure/Repeat* [Ravenhill 2008: 13]

The word 'democracy' has featured prominently in the rhetoric of wars on terror, with military operations justified on the grounds of defending and extending democratic freedoms around the world. Contrary to such rhetoric, the war on terror of the first decade of the twenty-first century led to an actual deterioration of democratic freedoms with, for example, the abrogation of military norms in the treatment of prisoners of war, and the introduction of legislation threatening civil liberties in domestic contexts. This deterioration of democracy was symptomatic of a widely reported 'crisis of democracy' contemporaneous with the war, characterised by evermore evident constraints on democratic powers in the face of unbridled economic globalisation, the limited representativeness and accountability of key decision-making bodies, and unprecedented levels of public disengagement from electoral processes, especially in older, stable democracies (see Ginsborg 2008 for a useful account).

British playwright David Edgar has commented that 'the war on terror brought politics on to the world stage, and it's no surprise that politics returned to theatrical stages as well' (Edgar 2008). New playwriting, revivals of canonical antiwar plays, verbatim and documentary theatre, and protest events hosted by theatres were all part of an 'upsurge in political theatre' concomitant with this war (Megson 2005: 369). This chapter focuses on the examination of the crisis of democracy that took place as part of this upsurge in political theatre, particularly exploring how theatre both reproduced and interrupted the mimetic circulation of threat and frailty that made up the broader political and cultural milieu of this moment. On the other side of the Atlantic, performance scholar Jon McKenzie notes that the emergence of performance as a means by which an examination of democracy might be carried out coincided with the US administration's admonition to countries around the world to 'perform' democracy to a narrow and, one might add, duplicitous set of standards. McKenzie asks a question that reverberates across this chapter: 'what is the relation between these two sites of democracy's performance: those resistant sites we study so closely, and those dominant sites of the new world order?' (McKenzie 2003: 120).

The prominence of verbatim theatre, constructed from the words of people involved in the events dramatised on stage, and drawn from documented records, personal testimony and interview material, was a notable feature of political theatre on the London stage during this period. Verbatim theatre has been termed 'a remarkably democratic medium' (Hammond and Steward 2008: 12). A verbatim play provides an encounter with a diverse range of voices, and, as theatre scholar Chris Megson comments, exhibits an attempt 'to annex the resources of documentary theatre to expose the democratic deficit in the wider political culture' (Megson 2007: 113). Verbatim theatre is defined by a democracy of process – with actors often taking responsibility for the development of dramatic material – as well as a democracy of event – with performances offering the opportunity of 'communing silently with your fellow human beings with a multitude of different voices alive for you', and to sit in an auditorium with society's 'movers and shakers' reportedly attracted to these plays (Kent in Hammond and Steward 2008: 122–3, 161). However, any sense of democratic goodness claimed for verbatim theatre here requires urgent qualification. In dramatising the democratic *deficit* noted by Megson, these plays reflect an *absence* of democracy at least as much as they embody an activist or restorative democratic project. In this chapter I explore the ways in which the affective capacities of the voice in verbatim theatre are enlisted as part of this playing out of democracy's crisis. As part of this, I argue that the critical potential of verbatim theatre resides in its dramatisation of the diminishment and abjection of the voice during a time of crisis, rather than its revitalising contribution to democracy in practice.

In an article in which he originated the term 'verbatim theatre', Derek Paget offers a useful two-way categorisation of verbatim plays as either 'celebratory' or as exploring national 'controversy'. Celebratory plays provide a platform for the expression of marginalised or unheard voices, and are more prevalent in regional theatres, whilst national 'controversy' plays, 'cater for a metropolitan audience with its sense of presiding over issues of "national" importance' (Paget 1987: 322). Although this categorisation is not always secure, it does suggest that the proliferation of verbatim plays on the London stage that responded to the war on terror evidenced a metropolis profoundly implicated by the contemporaneous crisis, reflecting on the paradoxes of democracy that frame its everyday life and international status. The two previous chapters have shown how power in democracies is organised, in part, through overt and ob-scene performances of violence. Here, I engage with performances of democracy in the form of 'onstage' happenings of a theatre scene situated a stone's throw away from the Houses of Parliament, a site of pre-eminent significance to democracy's history. The manner in which this body of work does and does not acknowledge the exceptional realities of the war on terror is a prominent aspect of the discussion that follows.

Whereas previous chapters have focused on one event (a beheading) or motif (the obscene), in this chapter I examine a series of plays connected by their concern to engage critically with a time of terror. From this, three categories of verbatim theatre are offered, each of which denotes distinct dramatisations of the voice: the 'forensic', the 'exceptional' and the 'composed'. The 'forensic' refers to Tricycle Theatre's 'Tribunal plays', a form of verbatim theatre that stages edited transcripts of Public Inquiries and draws on precise, legalistic framings of the voice. The Tribunal plays were pioneered by Richard Norton-Taylor, the Security Affairs editor of the British newspaper the *Guardian*, and Nicolas Kent, director of the Tricycle Theatre. My discussion here focuses on *Half the Picture* (1994), *Justifying War* (2003) and *Called to Account* (2007). The second category, the 'exceptional', refers to the staging of testimony from spaces of exception, and the discussion here focuses on Victoria Brittain and Gillian Slovo's *Guantánamo: Honour Bound to Defend Freedom* (2004, originally staged at the Tricycle Theatre), Robin Soans' *Talking to Terrorists* and Alan Rickman and Katharine Viner's *My Name is Rachel Corrie* (both originally staged at the Royal Court Theatre in 2005). The third category, the 'composed', refers to plays that combine 'found' speech drawn from documented records and 'made' speech devised by playwrights, and this section focuses on David Hare's *Stuff Happens* (produced by the National Theatre in 2004). The analysis of verbatim theatre in this chapter is accompanied by an exploration of three non-verbatim plays that historically frame the war on terror and also exhibit concerns for the fate of the voice in times of crisis: Caryl Churchill's *Far Away* (Royal Court Theatre, 2000), Michael Frayn's *Democracy* (National Theatre, 2003) and Mark Ravenhill's *Shoot/Get Treasure/Repeat* (originally staged across a number of London venues in 2008, following readings at the Traverse Theatre in Edinburgh 2007).

The consideration of the plays is supported by the use of theoretical writings that draw attention to the uncertain properties of the voice in the democratic realm. A critical comparison of Habermas' 'ideal speech conditions', with Lacan's notion of the voice as *objet petit a*, underpins the discussion here. The following section lays out this territory by exploring a particularly emotive moment in verbatim theatre's drama-tisation of the voice: the faltering testimony of Janice Kelly given as part of the Public Inquiry into the death of her husband, Dr David Kelly, the British government's chief advisor on Iraq's weapons programme. Mrs Kelly's testimony was staged as part of Tricycle's Tribunal play, *Justifying War* (2003).[1]

A crisis of voice

He was a very modest, shy, retiring guy. He did not boast at all and he was very factual and that is what he felt his job was. That is always what he tried to be, to be factual. (Janice Kelly, *Justifying War* [Norton-Taylor 2003: 95])

Freud and Breuer's identification of the verbal ticks, stutters and stam-mers of their patients as symptoms of underlying psychological disor-ders introduced the voice as a primary site for staging the crisis of the subject at the turn of the nineteenth century (Freud and Breuer 1991). Given the overwhelming mass of competing voices in our contempo-rary, highly mediatised and crisis-ridden context, it is tempting to read the verbal ticks, stutters and stammers of Freud and Breuer's patients as prescient of a generalised condition of uncertainty. Social crisis has often stimulated renewed concerns for and changing practices of the voice in the theatre. In terms of contemporary theatre, for example, the working-class voices introduced by John Osborne's *Look Back in Anger* at the Royal Court in 1956 had an explosive impact on British theatre. Highlighting the uncertainty of the voice in performance, however, these voices, and the critical commentary that they stimulated, were also founded upon an exclusion and repression of others (see Rebellato 1999). In the United States, Herbert Blau provides a history of the voice in performance that directly parallels successive crises of democracy, interpreting the quiet murmurings of method actors during the 1950s as a refusal to participate in the Cold War and the political activism of the 1960s as a moment when 'stridency in the streets was matched by primal screams in the workshops' (Blau 2002: 125). Taken together, this commentary highlights how the uncertain affectivity of the voice in performance materialises dislocating reverberations that are repeated across personal, political and theatrical space during different moments of democracy's crisis.

At the end of the Tribunal play, *Justifying War* (2003), the actress Sally Giles presented the testimony of Janice Kelly, the wife of deceased scientist Dr David Kelly, the British government's chief advisor on Iraq's chemical and biological weapons programme. Dr Kelly had been quoted anonymously on BBC radio as a 'senior official' involved in drawing up the dossier of evidence of weapons of mass destruction (WMD) in Iraq in 2002. He had raised concerns over the dossier's claim that Iraq could attack within forty-five minutes of a given order, reportedly suggesting that the dossier had been 'sexed up' to present a stronger case for war. After being named as the source, Dr Kelly became the focal point of a very public controversy and within two months of his name appearing in the press, his body was found near his home in Oxfordshire. The Public Inquiry into the circumstances surrounding his death found that he had committed suicide as a result of a severe loss of self-esteem following the emotional strain of this period.[2] In a replication of the manner in which Mrs Kelly's testimony was given during the Inquiry, the audience *aurally* witnessed the testimony via a phone link, with Giles standing offstage and her voice drifting in and out of hearing according to the variable performance of the technology. In a change in the order of witnesses at the actual Inquiry, the testimony of Mrs Kelly was not presented until the final moments of the play, a move which highlighted 'the very human cost of the WMD debacle' (Megson 2007: 116).

Mrs Kelly's testimony received a great deal of attention at the time of the Inquiry as well as in the critical reception of the play. Giles' deliberately restrained performance was described as extraordinarily moving, 'the climactic scene, in which the unseen Mrs. Kelly . . . describes her husband's drift to suicide, deluges you with emotion' (De Jongh 2003). According to another reviewer, the difficult-to-bear and difficult-to-hear auditory witnessing of this highly charged moment starkly contrasted with the 'language of buck passing and exaggeration' prominent in the performed testimonies of journalists, politicians and government officials that preceded it (P. Taylor 2003). It is notable that the sense of immediacy and power credited to Giles' performance was created by multiple layers of mediation of an offstage, disembodied voice, rather than a moment of direct address. The audience heard Mrs Kelly's voice via the registers of Giles' physiological and psychosocial-linguistic interpretation of the original testimony. In addition, her voice was mediated by the stage technology of the Tricycle, the inflections of sound within the spatial architecture of the theatre and processes of collective and individual listening which are also muscular, psychological and socio-political. Less directly, Mrs Kelly's testimony was mediated by Richard Norton-Taylor's editing of the transcript of the Inquiry, which reduced almost an hour's worth of testimony to ten minutes of stage time. Then there was the mediation of Janice Kelly's voice by the framing of a Public Inquiry, the intervening questions of the legal counsel, the Inquiry's sound technology and the psychosocial-linguistic interpretation and vocal muscularity of the witness herself. Each mode of mediation facilitated the circulation of the faltering, offstage voice of Mrs Kelly, and, in the process, dramatised the uncertain affectivity of the voice in the pressured and performative environments of legal discourse, political rhetoric and the theatre stage during a time of extraordinary personal and political crisis.

One possible interpretation of this powerful moment of performance is that the inclusion of Mrs Kelly's voice as part of a public examination of war signifies a hopeful and critical incarnation of a democratic public sphere. I am going to argue against this interpretation, which might be said to constitute a Habermasian reading of the performance. For Jürgen Habermas, deliberative democracy might be extended, and democracy's crisis therefore resolved, by the generation of more opportunities for 'communicative action' in an intersubjectively constituted public sphere. Communicative action is supported by the creation of 'ideal conditions' for speech, which include a commitment to test validity claims via rational discussion, equal and symmetrical participation and a non-coercive and regulated contest for the better argument based on the best available information (see Habermas 1996: 228–30). Such idealisations of the rational basis of communication invite critical interrogation. In particular, they make a number of assumptions about the possibility of reasonably and equitably regulating the power of the live voice. This might be questioned with respect to the live voice in performance, and perhaps especially with regards to the status of the voice as part of the performance of democracy. For example, Philip Auslander provides an analysis of performance in legal settings that questions any easy association of liveness with critical communicative practices.

He insists that live performance's unpredictable power and resistance to definition makes it *amenable* rather than resistant to exclusionary, repressive forces (Auslander 1999). Slavoj Žižek extends this point directly to the voice, arguing that 'the voice is that which, in the signifier, resists meaning' and that underneath the semblances of civilisation generated by text, discourse and, one might add, notions of rationally constituted communication, there is a 'shadowy paralegal domain' that has a *vocal* status and depends upon the undecidability of the voice as an effect of power (Žižek 1995: 103).

Working inside a conceptual framework similarly influenced by Lacan's notion of the voice as *objet petit a*, and drawing a connection to Agamben's state of exception, Mladen Dolar echoes these references to the ambivalent powers of the voice. The voice in performance is always already constituted by estranging forces, and in giving voice to experience, a human subject is both exposed to and circulates the effects of power: 'the voice cuts both ways: as an authority over the Other and as an exposure to the Other . . . *One is too exposed to the voice and the voice exposes too much*' (Dolar 2006: 80–1. Italics in original). Taking up this suggestion, it becomes possible to consider the ways in which the voice plays a particularly ambivalent role in times of crisis and exception. Here, the voice participates in the circulation of fears in an uncertain world, and in terms of political performance the voice mobilises a process by which the anomalous power of the extra-discursive realm comes to be ascribed to sovereign power. Inviting a direct connection between the uncertainty of the voice and democracy's crisis, Dolar argues that a democratic system is dependent on the voice to institute the political fiction of an ideal democracy in which 'everybody could hear everybody else's voices' (*ibid.*: 109). However, the power of the voice in such performances of democracy is also strictly regulated by means of legal, educational and electoral processes. The undecidable affectivity of the voice noted by Žižek and Dolar suggests that Habermas' ideal speech conditions are impossible to attain, and, also that their idealisation and attainment impose their own exclusions. The voice is leaky – its affects and effects are neither made nor controlled by discrete human subjects operating together as part of rational communicative exchanges. The voice in performance carries certain kinds of critical potential, but these are not limited to and also are disruptive of the principles and practices of rational discourse.

The impact of Mrs Kelly's testimony at the end of *Justifying War*, therefore, arguably demonstrates little other than an appropriation of the power of her voice in order to maintain the political fiction of a democratic, rule-bound universe during a time of democracy's crisis. This moment of performance highlights how political theatre plays a role in the regulative maintenance of the political fictions of liberal democracy which supposedly provides the right to speak and to be heard to all. However, there is more to be said here about the power of this moment in the play, and, in turn, about the critical potential of a diminished voice. Dolar defines the voice as carrying 'the excrement of the signifier', arguing that whilst the voice *bears* meaning, its materiality also unsettles sense-making processes (Dolar 2006: 20). As a floating substance that cannot be securely shaped into a fixed meaning, the voice evokes the abject and exceptional, which gains tangible presence as the bits of the human that get stuck in the teeth (or, in this case, the ear) in an inter-subjective and performative encounter (to reference Kelleher's 'cycle of shit', discussed in chapter 1). The voice thus introduces a rupture or dislocation which produces an effect of uncertainty and crisis. Here, the critical potential of the voice resides in maintaining fidelity to the waste, *objet petit a* – or *lack* of meaning that cannot be appropriated and that also brings about a diminishment and decay of sense. As such, in the same moment as generating a political fiction of inclusivity and concern for the human cost of war, Mrs Kelly's voice destroys the democratic grounds on which it rests – and the faltering, failing, distorting media-tions of her voice in performance dramatise a terrifying exposure to the disorder of sense in an alienating, terrifying world. According to this reading then, the diminishment of Mrs Kelly's faltering voice unset-tles rather than reproduces the ideal conditions for speech and ration-ally constituted democratic public sphere, and it is precisely this that generates the critical impact of the performance.

During the play, the audience witnesses the betrayal of sense by a series of voices belonging to politicians and the media – voices that dominated the public sphere during this moment of democracy's crisis. The play powerfully evokes the frailty of the voice when speaking in this realm, and the fading in and out, diminished quality of Mrs Kelly's voice also inflects this circulating public rhetoric with uncertainty. However, the play also expresses a desire for the return of sense. Here, the change in the order of the original Inquiry created by moving Mrs Kelly's testimony to the end of *Justifying War* arguably undermines the critical potential of the play. Whilst it prizes the uncertainty of the voice over the textual liberties and rhetoric of media and government spin, this move also restores a *sensation* of justice being done, rather than a sense of justice being critically interrogated. It is important to emphasise here that the disruptive potential of Mrs Kelly's voice was not permitted to inflect all of the voices in the play with uncertainty. In this case, the Tribunal frame of the performance mimetically reproduced the narrow terms of reference of the original Inquiry, which did not permit an extensive examination of the evidence base for war. Whilst the speech economies of politicians and the mass media become inflected with uncertainty, the legal discourses framing the voices in the play remain reassuringly authoritative (I return to this point in the following section). In addition, in valorising the final testimony of Mrs Kelly, the play frames the war as an individual tragedy and further narrows the terms of reference of the original Inquiry as well as constructs a debilitating and gendered personification of victimhood. As such, the play's dramatisation of political crisis provides the comfort of witnessing the ethical probity of an apparently equitable public sphere, participating in a mimetic circulation of threat and frailty that ultimately works to maintain the political fictions of an orderly, rule-bound universe.

Alison Forsyth and Chris Megson argue that the diversification of documentary forms represented by verbatim theatre reflects a 'self-conscious acknowledgement of the complexity of "reality"' which situates 'historical truth as an embattled site of contestation' (Forsyth and Megson 2009: 3). Their comment usefully emphasises the uncertainties of verbatim theatre's representations of apparently 'real' experience, and draws attention to questions relating to how the complex and difficult experiences of a democracy in crisis might be dramatised and interrogated in the theatre. These questions reflect a generalised uncertainty about the critical functions of performance in a postmodern context. Such uncertainties are examined and exacerbated rather than resolved by a turn to 'real life' in the theatre. In verbatim theatre, the interrogation of experience is pursued by means of a foregrounding of the 'real' in the aesthetics of the form. Drawing on 'real' voices, verbatim *certainly* represents the *uncertain* status of the voice in a highly mediatised, performative and crisis-ridden context. As such, the hyper-reality of verbatim theatre uncannily replicates postmodern performance's 'hyper-representation' (Reinelt and Roach 1992: 1). Both kinds of aesthetic betray fundamentalist attitudes to the 'real' – one utterly rejecting, the other utterly replicating – one playfully intervening in the commodified representation of experience and the other commodifying 'reality' in an attempt to negotiate a loss of meaning and diminishment of being in an uncertain world. The performance of Mrs Kelly's 'real' voice, mediated by the legalistic framing of the Tribunal, the technology of the theatre, and psycho-linguistic, socio-political and muscular structures of performer and spectator, highlight the points of connection between postmodern theatre and verbatim theatre. Both express cultural anxieties about the lack of stability and veracity of the 'real' world. Again, the critical potential of Mrs Kelly's voice in *Justifying War* resides in the shadow it casts over 'reality', including the authenticity of the formal political record and mediatised representations of the war, and also the supposed ethical probity of the critical subject in a democratic public sphere. In other words, what is critical here is the play's dramatisation of an uncertainty about how to act in a complex and changing world, rather than its institution of certainty and affirmation of democracy.

It is useful to turn again to Lacan here, for whom the psychoanalytic process consists of 'playing all the many staves of the score that speech constitutes in the registers of language' (Lacan 2001: 86). This denotation of the voice does not promise any resolution to an endless replaying of its uncertain affectivity, but it does urge us to explore the voice's musicality as a site of critical and creative potential. Similarly, Roland Barthes' concept, the 'grain of the voice', describes how the voice works to radically uproot the subject, as in aesthetic experiences that 'bear traces of *signifiance* . . . [that] escape the tyranny of meaning' (Barthes 1990: 185). An encounter with the *signifiance* of the voice moves the subject 'which means that it shifts something in the chain of the signifier' (*ibid.*: 187). When we hear the restrained grief in the voice of Janice Kelly, we are alert to the power of her voice to threaten the stability of our sense of self. As auditory witnesses, we are moved, the ground shifts under our feet and the suffering of the other presides momentarily and painfully over the self. It is by paying attention to such moments of decay and diminishment evoked by the voice in performance that its critical potential might be located. The attention given over to ethical discussions about performing verbatim material in discussions of verbatim theatre highlights the challenges and potential of engaging with such moments of *signifiance*. Unsurprisingly, there is a strong focus on aural registers in these discussions; for example, Nicolas Kent comments that actors use microphones in Tribunal plays so as to not falsely exert their own vocal muscularity when representing the testimony of another (Hammond and Steward 2008: 156). Similarly, actors have described the challenges of replicating the uncertain affectivity of the voice, that is, the difficulty of replicating the ways in which a speaker simultaneously succeeds and fails to control the communication of their thoughts and feelings through the voice, especially when expressing pain and suffering (Paget 1987: 330–1).

The doubling and diminishment of political fictions mobilised by the affectivity of the voice in verbatim theatre dramatise the uncertainty and *signifiance* of life in times of crisis. The stuttering rhythms and repetitions, shifts in breath, pauses, contradictions and faltering pauses of real voices culminate in a public staging of a crisis of democracy. *Justifying War* encountered uncertainty by directing the decaying and diminishing affects of the voice towards certain voices and excising them from others. Do other verbatim plays support different uses of the wasting affects of the voice's materiality? The power of verbatim theatre does not reside in its revelation of truth but in its attentive engagements with wasted life – creating an imperative to explore the decay and diminishment of the voice's materiality in specific performances for its musicality and critical potential. A turn to the plays themselves will facilitate such an exploration.

Forensic voices: *Half the Picture* (1994), *Justifying War* (2003), *Called to Account* (2007)

There is a distinction between a half truth and an untruth. Your seventy-five per cent is not a half, it is a three-quarter truth. Then there is an untruth, which is just not true. It is not just a question of being true to a point. (Lord Justice Scott, *Half the Picture* [Norton-Taylor 1995: 224–5])

Tricycle Theatre's Tribunal plays stage legalistic explorations of moments of political crisis. They are edited re-enactments of Public Inquiries, a 'peculiarly British' form of legal practice consisting of an independent review of the performance of democratic institutions during events of national import (Twining in Runciman 2004: 34). Tricycle's first venture here was Richard Norton-Taylor and John McGrath's *Half the Picture* (1994). This play staged an edited version of the Scott Inquiry into the UK government's sanctioning of arms deals between British businesses and Iraq in the late 1980s. It provides an interesting counterpoint to two later plays, *Justifying War* (2003), introduced above, and *Called to Account* (2007). *Called to Account* is an edited version of a *mock* inquiry set up by Tricycle Theatre itself into the case for indicting British Prime Minister Tony Blair for the crime of aggression against Iraq. The play explores the extent to which Blair's actions in the lead up to the invasion of Iraq in 2003 can be proved to be criminal, and as such it tests the strengths and limitations of legal discourses when bringing power to account for its decisions in a time of crisis.

A preoccupation with exploring the uncertainties of the voice in the public sphere is an important focus of each of these plays, and is pursued by means of an increasing verisimilitude or what Megson calls 'hardcore illusionism' over the period of development of the Tribunal play (Megson 2007: 116). *Half the Picture* included fictional monologues written by the playwright John McGrath; however, later plays strictly adhered to the spoken testimony of the original Inquiries. Norton-Taylor comments that the Scott Inquiry was characterised by 'dissembling, buck-passing, hiding behind euphemisms, word play, facetious use of aphorisms', and that the play, 'dramatised the methodical process of cutting through these layers of duplicity' (Hammond and Steward 2008: 106). The testimony of government officials in *Half the Picture* evidenced a series of distortions of sense inside the supposed transparencies of democratic speech. Former government minister William Waldegrave responded to a question about whether selling arms to Iraq should have been subject to a public discussion with the comment that 'a mature democracy means . . . it is going to be necessary not for everything to be said in detail' (Norton-Taylor 1995: 235). Alan Clarke, also a former government minister, states that in encouraging arms manufacturers to deal with Iraq under the broad category of providing parts for 'engineering' rather than military purposes 'there was an implied invitation to them to participate in a fiction' (*ibid.*: 249). The critical reception of the play is notable for its repetition of the comment that witnessing the testimony was like entering a 'looking glass world' performed by these reversals, exaggerations and manipulations of speech. Theatre critic Irving Wardle commented that the actors deserve admiration for committing this 'verbiage' to memory: 'speeches that seem to be heading in a clear direction perform a stupefying *volte face* at the last moment, grind to a halt on a point of unargued dogma, or expire into the semantic stratosphere' (Wardle 1994).

During *Justifying War* the audience witnesses a more subtle set of prevarications as a result of the different mediations of the voice presented in the play and the original Inquiry. *Half the Picture* drew on reams of government memos, briefings and reports as textual evidence. At one point, British Prime Minister Margaret Thatcher asks 'is there more paper? I have never seen so much paper' to which the legal counsel replies 'that is only part of it. There is much more' (Norton-Taylor 1995: 241). *Justifying War* included transcripts of media broadcasts, electronic diaries projected onto screens and voice link-ups as well as ministerial briefings and dossiers. These contrasts are significant. *Half the Picture* dramatises a skilled legalistic deconstruction of the textual record to critique the dissembling vocal performances of politicians. *Justifying War* dramatises the falters and breaks in mediations of the evidence, and as a result inflects the evidence relating to the death of Dr Kelly, and, in association, the case for and against war, with uncertainty. One of the concerns identified by the Public Inquiry staged by *Justifying War* was the lack of formal records of decision-making processes at the highest levels of government. The lack of precision in the vocal and textual practices of an informal style of government is reflected in the dossier of evidence on weapons of mass destruction in Iraq, and the media furore that this provoked, which included the 'radically ambiguous' use of sound bites such as 'weapons of mass destruction', 'sexed up dossier' and '45 minute claim' (Twining in Runciman 2004: 31). It is this uncertainty in the textual and vocal record of war that constitutes the central drama of *Justifying War*.

This is dramatised by the gradual decay and diminishment of Dr Kelly's forensic voice over the course of the play. The audience first encounters Dr Kelly through the testimony of his close colleague, who describes him as a trusted expert 'who could verify the accuracy' of the dossier of evidence of WMD in Iraq whilst it was being prepared (Norton-Taylor 2003: 10). Following this, we encounter Dr Kelly via the testimony of journalist Andrew Gilligan, whose initial report on BBC radio stimulated the controversy. Gilligan reads out, from notes made at the time, a conversation with Dr Kelly recorded in the form of a dialogue: 'He said, "It [the dossier] was transformed in the week before publication". I said: "To make it sexier?" And he said: "Yes, to make it sexier"' (*ibid.*: 14). Gilligan's mediations of Dr Kelly's statements reveal how the scientist's forensic voice was reinvented in the moment of encounter by the response of the journalist ('To make it sexier?'). In the next segment of Gilligan's testimony, he reads from transcripts of two radio reports that drew on the detail of his conversation with Dr Kelly, both of which distort the original encounter to some extent. For example, the second broadcast presents the encounter in the form of 'reported speech' – reflecting the way it was originally recorded in Gilligan's notes. However, in the radio broadcast the actor playing Dr Kelly reads out a line that slightly, but crucially, misrepresents the original dialogue as recorded. The actor playing Dr Kelly says 'it was transformed in the week before it was published, to make it sexier' (*ibid.*: 18) The line as broadcast therefore seems to attribute the phrase 'to make it sexier?', originally offered by Gilligan, to Dr Kelly. In the play, this encounter is followed by an excerpt of a transcript of a recorded conversation between Dr Kelly and another reporter, Susan Watts. She testifies to his concerns with the dossier, and reads from the transcript his assertion of the importance of a precise use of language: 'the word-smithing is actually quite important' (*ibid.*: 28).

Justifying War presents multiple and conflicting versions of Dr Kelly's statements as they were variously reinvented and parodied across different speech economies. Here, the forensic voice of the scientist is ultimately inflected with the soundbite speech of a journalist in pursuit of a story. Later in the play this voice comes up against the aggressive and defensive speech patterns of politicians and government officials and these circulations gradually strip Dr Kelly's forensic voice of its precision. Contrary to the director Nicolas Kent's claims that Tribunal plays engage the audience in the project of 'trying to sort out the truth' (Kent in Hammond and Steward 2008: 139), what is staged in this play is the failure of a forensic voice in a time of crisis. The final moments, depicting the fading in and out of Mrs Kelly's voice, is therefore an appropriate culmination of the play's critical preoccupation. However, the play also stages a contest between legalistic and political voices, with the forensic qualities of the former contesting the dissimulating capacities of the latter. Legalistic forensic voices, engaged in 'trying to sort out the truth', are reassuringly secure throughout the course of the play, which means that the terms of reference of the original Inquiry are also left secure. Notably, these terms of reference excluded attention as to whether or not the evidence on which the government's case for war rested was accurate (Twining in Runciman 2004: 39–40). This results in the urgent *political* questions relating to responsibility for war being left unaddressed by the play, as they were by the original Inquiry.

Called to Account: The Indictment of Anthony Charles Lynton Blair for the Crime of Aggression against Iraq – A Hearing (2007), to give the play its full title, explicitly explores questions of responsibility for war via a mock inquiry initiated by the Tricycle Theatre (Figure 2). The play's adoption of a legal frame to carry out this examination is outlined at the start of the play in the opening statement for the defence 'this case is not about politics. It is about law' (Norton-Taylor 2007: 10). Testimony is provided by a series of witnesses closely involved in diplomatic events leading up to the invasion of Iraq, and, as with other Tribunal plays, this testimony offers startling insights into the workings of government. However, because this was a mock trial it was not possible to subpoena witnesses who could provide the most compelling evidence. In addition, the final case rested on an argument about whether it was the Prime Minister's *intention* to deceive, a proposition very difficult to evidence. As such, the play makes an unintentionally stark statement about the limitations of forensic voices across legal, political and theatrical spaces. The play's director, Nicolas Kent, comments that audiences arrived at the theatre with an expectation that there was a strong case for the indictment of the British Prime Minister, but went away with a more complex appreciation of the legal questions. Also, he describes how the prosecutor and defence employed to carry out the mock inquiry were so intensely engaged by the problems of evidence in this case that 'people

Figure 2 *Called to Account*, Tricycle Theatre, London, 2007. Photograph by John Haynes.

were not on speaking terms for some days at the end. It resolved itself but it became unbelievably dramatic offstage' (Kent in Hammond and Steward 2008: 147).

The limits of the legalistic forensic voices uncritically reproduced in *Called to Account* are clear: a play examining issues of responsibility for war becomes preoccupied with a nuanced argument about evidence of *intention*, to the neglect of issues of social and political justice. For Habermas, during times of crisis 'the structures that actually support the authority of a critically engaged public begin to vibrate. The balance of power between civil society and the political system then shifts' (Habermas 1996: 379). This becomes possible because in the structure of the public sphere 'the players in the arena owe their influence to the approval of those in the gallery' (*ibid.*: 382). Habermas suggests that during times of crisis powerful elites enact deliberative democracy as part of a competition for legitimacy and credibility. However, the Tribunal plays, and the Inquiries themselves, limit opportunities for critical intervention to the formal, adversarial vocal styles of a legal realm. Habermas' use of a theatrical metaphor is enlightening, but in these plays the competition of forensic voices – legal, political, scientific – illustrates the constrained forms deliberation permitted during times of crisis, rather than provides an opportunity for participatory democracy, where the inclusion of more diverse voices might challenge the terms of the debate. What is witnessed by the audience is a staged contest between legal and political elites, produced at a time when national decision-making processes that formerly relied upon legal and political cooperation were becoming progressively fractured by the pressures of a war on terror. Each of the three Tribunal plays discussed here thus dramatises a desire for the reining in of political power by legal, forensic voices, rather than institutes a critical interrogation of issues of social and political justice.

Half the Picture is perhaps the most evidently critical of the three plays, in its staging of the extraordinarily blatant distortions of speech of politicians, and imagined monologues written by playwright John McGrath from members of the public that extend the terms of the debate. Conversely, *Justifying War* and *Called to Account* stage power's conversation with power during a period of uncertainty. In their mourning of forensic voices and the liberal, conscientious individual, they express cultural anxieties about a crisis of democracy and make a plea to the public on behalf of the law. However, legal speech is far from benign. The problem with the Tribunal plays is not simply that they are a rhetorical performance of democracy that does not meaningfully engage the critical voices of those in the gallery. It is that they perform an all too comfortable splitting of the discourses and practices of the law from the exceptional and obscene realities that they sustain and are sustained by, and thus beautify an inequitable system that is culpable in acts of violence against innocent civilians on the front lines of war. In their mortified mimesis of a legal realm, these plays powerfully dramatise the limitations of forensic voices, ensuring that their complicity with systemic political violence remains veiled, whilst apparently reasonable speech and faltering voices are valorised and mourned. Whilst the plays provide an opportunity to hear power speak, they do not speak back to power. Perhaps other kinds of voices in verbatim theatre demonstrate more critical potential.

Exceptional voices: *Guantánamo* (2004), *My Name is Rachel Corrie* (2005), *Talking to Terrorists* (2005)

This is not at all what I asked for when I came into this world. This is not at all what the people here asked for when they came into this world. This is not what they are asking for now. This is not the world you and dad wanted me to come into when you decided to have me. This is not what I meant when I was two and looked at Capitol Lake and said, 'This is the wide world and I'm coming to it'. (Rachel Corrie, *My Name is Rachel Corrie* [Rickman and Viner 2005: 50])

The three plays discussed here use personal testimony to bring to the stages of an anxious and implicated metropolis voices from the states of exception: a voice from Gaza, the speech of those who have engaged in acts of terrorism and the testimony of 'illegal enemy combatants' in Camp X-Ray in Guantánamo Bay. These plays present a challenge to an audience's capacities for identification by staging the exceptional realities veiled by the fictions of a democratic, rule-bound universe. Complicating any easy argument that might be made about the critical potential of such encounters, Allen Feldman argues that the display of personal testimony often replicates and reproduces the exclusionary and repressive practices of witnessing in a legal context. During truth and reconciliation processes in post-conflict zones, for example, a display of 'truth', given via a heroic articulation and incarnation of pain and suffering, is related to distant audiences who may be deeply implicated in the injustices related but remain 'secure in the supposedly post-violent space of observation and adjudication' (Feldman 2004: 191). Here, the vocalisation of suffering articulates and simultaneously masks the structural inequities of a world implicated in the testimony given. We need to pay careful attention to the repressive and exclusionary functions of witnessing narratives of crisis at one remove, therefore, as well as to the complex questions of identification that are raised by this witnessing.

A turn to Adorno's work on 'shudder' provides a conceptual framework for considering how the different kinds of identification in play here might be distinguished. Adorno describes aesthetic experience as bringing about a 'capacity to shudder': 'a memento of the liquidation of the I, which, shaken, perceives its own limits and finitude' (Adorno 1997: 319). Identification infused with shudder challenges the boundaries of the self, moves the subject and, potentially, materialises more equitable ways of relating to the world: 'that shudder in which subjectivity stirs without yet being subjectivity is the act of being touched by the other. Aesthetic comportment assimilates itself to that other rather than subordinating it' (*ibid.*: 418). This creates an imperative to look closely at how exceptional realities are represented within the mimetic circulations of threat and frailty mobilised by these plays: do they move beyond the emotive and uncritical responses that I suggest are generated by Tribunal plays' mortified mimesis of a legal realm, or do they materialise the more diminished and diminishing, critical forms of mimesis denoted by Adorno's shudder?

My Name is Rachel Corrie stages excerpts from the diaries and emails of twenty-three-year-old US activist Rachel Corrie, who was killed by a military bulldozer whilst trying to prevent the demolishment of Palestinian homes by Israeli armed forces in Gaza in 2003. The play provides a powerful and moving insight into the heart and mind of a young woman deeply concerned by issues of global justice, following Rachel's journey from her bedroom in Olympia in the US to Gaza. It was produced by the Royal Court in 2005 before making a successful transfer to the West End in London the following year. However, a planned production by the New York Theatre Workshop in the US was cancelled, reportedly because of fears that its singular, Palestinian perspective and lack of an alternative view would offend the audience, a decision that sparked a fierce public protest. Notably, the London production was indeed accused of lack of balance and partiality by some reviewers, although others accepted the play's 'achingly personal' account (Whitaker 2005).

This controversy exemplifies what Jacques Derrida calls the 'democratic paradox'. Derrida notes the semantic indecision of the paradoxically *singular* principle of *plurality* of speech and argues that, 'democracy could not gather itself around the presence of an axial and, univocal meaning that does not destroy itself' (Derrida 2005: 40). Rachel's story does not provide a balanced view, it asserts an individual voice critical of injustice, and, as such, the play certainly does not materialise a democratic principle of plurality. It is partial and partisan, and this singular perspective meant that the play was deemed undemocratic by some of its audience. However, its staging of the stark realities of a space of exception, outside the frames of recognition of many in the mainstream, can also be claimed as an extension of democracy's commitment to including a plurality of voices. For Habermas, for example, communicative action in a deliberative democracy achieves, 'the intersubjectively enlarged perspective of the first-person plural' (Habermas 1996: 228). In the case of *My Name is Rachel Corrie*, the play can be interpreted as a political performance that shows the ambiguity of this Habermasian 'we' – its singularity adds a perspective that materialises a more inclusive 'we', and as a result the democratic paradox is perhaps regulated in a more inclusive manner. However, the reaction *against* the play was also generated by a concern to protect a Habermasian 'we'. Here, fear of the play's singular perspective and its concomitant exclusions culminated in the excision of an exceptional voice – leading to the cancellation of the New York performance.

Rachel Corrie's email to her mother quoted above repeats the phrase 'this is not', a phrase that simultaneously evokes and opposes the violence of the conflict, utilising the instabilities of speech and power of refusal as a critical act of resistance. 'This is not' mobilises the power of the negative to evoke a shudder – here, a refusal to identify draws attention to an unspeakable reality and inflects the object of reference, the violence of the conflict, with *signifiance*. The impact of this speech, close to the end of the play, *moves* the audience as well as expresses a powerful desire for an end to the violence. However, the audience's identification with an uncontested voice evoking such *signifiance* also, perhaps, brings about a sublimation of critical subjectivity and an exclusion of alternative frames of reference, and enacts what performance scholar Elin Diamond calls the 'violence of the "we"' (Diamond 1995). The force of the collective 'for' and 'against' responses to the play evidences the powerful effects of and critical reaction against this sublimation of critical autonomy.

However, Diamond also draws on a reading of Freud's work on identification to argue that a spectator's personal history constitutes a resource for multiple, continuously transforming, processes of identification that are never resolved as a secure form of 'identity': 'that places identity in an unstable and contingent relation to identification, and that works close to the nerves that divide/connect the psychic and the social' (Diamond 1992: 397; also see Diamond 1995). Echoing Adorno's 'shudder' (which she draws on in the later essay), Diamond infers that such shifting processes of identification – also evident in the controversy provoked by this play – provide the grounds for generating critical forms of mimesis in performance. It might thus be argued that an encounter with *signifiance* in performance, here created by the repeated repudiation of Rachel's 'this is not', disturbs the comfortable anchoring of subjectivity that may be secured by a Habermasian 'we' and also resists the 'violence of the "we"' noted by Diamond. As a result of such disturbances, the play opens up a space for encountering the *uncertainties* of diminished forms of identity and identification that might then become a *resource* for critically engaging with the play, and the global crisis that it dramatises. The repeated refusal of Rachel's 'this is not' is important – and is also dimly echoed in the repudiating qualities of the diminished, frail voice of Mrs Kelly in *Justifying War*. It is perhaps this refusal to securely identify the violence of war that mobilises open-ended processes of identification, and generates abundant resources for critical engagements with an exceptional world. If this hopeful possibility is to be realised, it is imperative that the spectator remain open to utilising such resources. The history of the play's production evidences both closure and openness in this regard: the protests against the closure of the New York production led to many readings and productions of the play across the world.[3]

Talking to Terrorists, a play by Robin Soans composed from the testimony of perpetrators and victims of acts of terrorism, failed to generate the critical impact of *My Name is Rachel Corrie*, in part because its aesthetics and politics demonstrate the exclusive, sublimating force of a 'violence of the "we"'. The play includes testimonies from figures familiar to a British audience, including Terry Waite, the archbishop's envoy held hostage in Lebanon for four years (1987–91), Mo Mowlam, former Secretary of State for Northern Ireland (1997–99), and Norman Tebbit, former Member of Parliament and Chairman of the Conservative Party in the mid 1980s (1985–87). Both Tebbit and his wife, Margaret, who also features in the play, were in the Brighton hotel attacked by the IRA at the time of the Conservative Party conference in 1984, which killed five people and left Margaret Tebbit permanently disabled. The play also presents testimony from men (and one woman), 'terrorists' from different parts of the world, including Pat Magee, who was convicted of the Brighton bombing and served fourteen years in prison before being released as part of the Good Friday peace agreement in 1999. Soans values the capacity of verbatim theatre to show complexity via the juxtaposition of testimony and the rich resonances of the voice outside formal speech environments. He asserts that the most effective material comes from the first and last third of an encounter between a playwright and a research subject wherein 'you learn about them as a human being in their vulnerable state, they're not vulnerable when they're talking to you politically' (Soans 2005b). This separation of the 'political' and the 'human' is problematic: in searching for the 'human' causes and effects of political violence, the play believes in the political fictions of a democratic realm that separates itself from and obscures its own violence against the 'human'. In its juxtaposition of a range of voices within this exclusive framework, the play reifies those political fictions, rather than critically interrogates them.

This can be shown by examining the unselfconscious and unrehearsed speech of Norman Tebbit, who, as a member of Thatcher's Conservative government in the 1980s, is a far from sympathetic figure for a politically left audience. The audience first encounters Tebbit in the second act of the play, and his statement is shocking and moving: 'I was drifting in and out of consciousness . . . because I was next to my wife, I was aware that she was gradually becoming paralysed . . . the debris was holding my head in a vice' (Soans 2005a: 85). Moments after this first encounter with Tebbit, the audience is disarmingly greeted by him: he appears onstage to 'a burst of birdsong from an English woodland garden', without shoes on his feet, a strategy that he later suggests was 'an elaborate way to prove I don't have cloven hooves' (*ibid.*: 88). The testimony of Norman Tebbit and 'Caroline', a 'landowner' who was also in the hotel at the time of the

bomb, is interwoven with the testimony of Pat Magee, named in the script
as 'an ex-member of the Irish Republican Army'.

The humanity of Tebbit contrasts with the presentation of Pat
Magee. The audience first encounters Magee via his contributions to the
story of the 'terrorists' from different parts of the world, edited into a
collective narrative of alienation and violence in the first act of the play.
This collective narrative is interspersed with explanatory interventions
from psychologist 'Edward'. The first act, therefore, constructs a universal biography of a 'terrorist' that collates very different conflicts and
presents a pathological and depoliticised interpretation of violence. In
the segment of testimony juxtaposed with that of Tebbit in the second
act, Magee's commentary comprises a description of the military operation and a series of depersonalised interjections: 'it wasn't any one individual that bombed Brighton; it was the organisation' (Soans 2005a: 83);
'of course I regret the suffering I caused but circumstances made our
actions inevitable' (*ibid.*: 85); 'sitting here now . . . it's like talking about
someone else' (*ibid.*: 86). In the audience's final encounter with Magee,
he leaves the stage with an ex-member of another paramilitary group in
Northern Ireland who comments, 'people who kill someone else also kill
a part of themselves. They lose a part of their humanity', to which Magee
responds, 'very difficult . . . very difficult to live with some of the things
that happened' (*ibid.*: 89).

The audience's sympathies are won by the humour and affability of
Norman Tebbit, his shocking testimony and the presence of his wife in a
wheelchair, all of which highlight the terrible impact of political violence.
However, the sharing out of humanity in the play is not even-handed.
Soans' interest in the vulnerability of the human in times of crisis manifests itself as a refusal of the political narrative that Magee articulates.
Magee suspects that he may have given a negative impression when interviewed for the play: 'I come across very cold and calculating in it, and
maybe in the interview that's what came across, I don't know . . . a couple
of interviews can't sum up a human being, it can't do it, so it's a big leap of
faith talking to anyone like that' (Magee 2006). His narrative is located in
the history and culture of West Belfast in Northern Ireland, and his political motivations undermined his ability to successfully perform within
the frames of Soans' search for a 'human' voice. In the subsequent erasure
of his humanity there is no mention of the political violence visited by the
British State in Northern Ireland other than via Magee's interrupted personal account, only permitted within the pathologising frame of the first
act. The play privileges some voices over others and performs the 'us and
them' excisions of the war on terror through its splitting of the personal
and political. On the one side there are individuals whose humanity is

presented as having been irrevocably damaged by their violent past, and on the other side, affable, ethical and reasonable representatives of the values and anxieties of liberal democracy.

Tricycle Theatre's *Guantánamo: Honour Bound to Defend Freedom* (2004), researched and written by Victoria Brittain and Gillian Slovo, is composed of the testimony of British citizens held as 'illegal combatants' in the US internment camp in Cuba as well as their families and legal representatives. According to Nicolas Kent, one of the directors, the play was 'blatantly a campaigning piece of work' which he believed helped secure the release of some of the British detainees from the camp in 2004 (Kent in Hammond and Steward 2008: 150). In its representation of the testimony of the detainees, who are shown to be ordinary and innocent young men, the play resists the effacement of humanity performed by *Talking to Terrorists*. Performance scholar Wendy Hesford argues that the play's juxtaposition of testimony created a 'polyphonic subjectivity, which seeks to cultivate within audiences a critical subjectivity and a sense of collective rhetorical witnessing' (Hesford 2006: 35). The play certainly drew attention to the abuse of detainees and the incompatibility of internment without recourse to legal process with democratic values. However, this notion of 'witnessing' demands critical exploration. For Hesford, such witnessing was characterised by 'the audience realising how the detainees worked through the trauma and empathising with them' (*ibid.*: 37). My concerns about this reading, and the play itself, are that it garnered the audience's identification with an exceptional reality by representing familiar and recognisable figures engaged in an idealised process of 'working through' anger. The audience's empathy with young men who were able to work through their feelings raises the question of how to negotiate encounters with more alienated responses to issues of global justice, a question that became all the more pressing following the suicide bombings in London carried out by young British men a little more than a year after the premiere of this play.

Guantánamo is most effective when it stages the *difficulty* of both giving and witnessing testimony of the atrocities committed by a democracy in crisis. This is powerfully described by a statement of the human rights lawyer Gareth Peirce:

> The [boys] are three young British lads who are like all our children – they're people who are very familiar, very easy to feel immediately comfortable with. And yet the story they tell is one of stark medieval horror . . . We read, we watch, we hear about atrocities – we know what man's inhumanity to man consists of, we know all that, but we don't sufficiently register it. We don't have the capacity to take it in and register it as human beings. But when you have [in front of you] men you're getting to know

and they're talking about it, not because you're interrogating them, but it's tumbling out and they're reminding each other . . . How do you tell it? How do ordinary words tell it? (Brittain and Slovo 2004: 51–2)

Peirce effectively describes the shudder and *signifiance* of these voices, generated by their evocation of an exceptional reality. Here, the uncertain affectivity of the voice stimulates a sense of powerlessness and a pressing imperative to reconsider the frames through which we view the war and its victims. Peirce's commentary, however, also risks promoting narcissistic forms of identification through its conflation of subjectivities (the young men are like 'all our children') that may have a repressive and exclusionary impact (what about young men who are not like 'us'?).

To some extent, all three of the verbatim plays discussed here mobilise mimetic identifications that rest on sameness rather than difference – exhibiting the 'violence of the "we"' rather than Adorno's shudder of a liquidated 'I'. The *other* of the exception emerges within the frame of the familiar and comfortable and is rarely permitted to disturb those frames. Rachel Corrie evokes empathy from the audience as the rebellious young woman driven by concerns about issues of global justice: it is difficult to imagine a performance about a young Gazan woman engaged in direct political action generating the same intensity of identification or indeed dis-identification. Likewise, the difficulty of Norman and Margaret Tebbit's personal circumstances are offered as more worthy of empathy and understanding than the political narrative of Pat Magee. Hearing such testimony within the hierarchical and exclusive frames of the familiar and identifiable constitutes a careful regulation of the shudder evoked by exceptional voices. What is dramatised by these plays is an excision of those aspects of democracy's crisis that are more uncomfortable to witness, rather than democracy's critical interrogation.

Composed voices: *Democracy* (2003) and *Stuff Happens* (2004)

So many people, with so many different views and so many different voices. And inside each of us so many more people still, all struggling to be heard. (Willy Brandt, *Democracy* [Frayn 2003a: 86])

The complex relationship between the authentic and constructed, the real and made up or mediated, and its potential relevance for understanding verbatim theatre's critical potential, can be usefully explored through an analysis of plays that consist of compositions of real and imagined voices. David Hare's *Stuff Happens* (2004) focuses on the diplomatic process leading up to the war in Iraq and combines imagined scenarios with edited excerpts from documented records of events. Michael Frayn's *Democracy* (2003) stages the Chancellorship of Willy Brandt in West Germany (1969–74), a political leader who attempted to develop diplomatic relations between East and West Germany during the Cold War, and consists of imagined speech based on extensive historical research. Both plays were staged by the National Theatre in the year following the invasion of Iraq in 2003 and explore the power machinations of political elites at different moments of democracy's crisis. As such, each play provides an uncanny mirror of the internal workings of democracy, and with *Stuff Happens*, the original that is reflected, the Houses of Parliament, stands not more than half a mile away from the National Theatre on the other side of the River Thames in London.

Frayn comments that whilst *Democracy* was based on extensive research, 'very few of the words that these characters speak, however, were ever actually spoken by their real counterparts' (Frayn 2003a: 106). Hare gives a more complex picture of the relationship of factual and fictional voices in his play: 'Nothing in the narrative is knowingly untrue. Scenes of direct address quote people verbatim. When the doors close on the world's leaders and on their entourages, then I have used my imagination' (Hare 2004: preface). The recourse to imagined voices in both plays raises the question of whether audiences are treated to a more or less complex mimesis of events than delivered by the verisimilitude of verbatim: does the abandonment of verisimilitude create a quality of speech that is easier on the ear, and reduce complexity to consumable packages of truth? Or does the deliberate use of the imagination present richer opportunities to voice complexity? Frayn asserts that writing fictional speech provides an opportunity to 'bring out the things that don't get said in life, the things that no-one quite catches hold of, because life goes very fast' (Frayn 2003b). This embracing of the not quite spoken is particularly necessary in a play exploring the limitations of democracy and its assumptions about the transparency of speech in the public sphere. Hare is similarly intrigued by the complex intersection of real and fictional – the 'artistic paradox' that 'by telling lies we reach the truth' (Hare 2005: 73).

Stuff Happens has attracted negative criticism for its particular fusion of fact and fiction. For example, theatre scholar Steve Bottoms argues that more than 80 per cent of the play is imagined by Hare and that it is difficult to distinguish the real from the imagined dialogue when watching the play. Thus, 'the story's "actual" linguistic scandals become inextricably confused with Hare's own rhetorical manipulations . . . speech in *Stuff Happens* is a slippery commodity, in every respect' (Bottoms 2006: 61). However, given my focus on mimesis as a practice that collapses and subsumes the distinction between the real and fictional, a discussion of the specific compositions of 'truth' in the play is unhelpful for the argument here – the claim to truth simply adds another layer of mimesis to be analysed for its critical potential. A turn to John Deeney's reading of Hare as a playwright who, in the later stages of his career, has been preoccupied by the theme of 'goodness' is useful (Deeney 2006). Following Deeney, the problem with *Stuff Happens* is less to do with its claim to truth, or the extent to which it acknowledges its own constructedness, and more to do with the way in which democracy's crisis is played out by a drama of good versus evil. Firstly, the bad: US President George Bush is conveyed as clever, resolved and powerfully in control of events in a way that services US interests without recourse to diplomatic processes. Secondly, the good: UK Prime Minister Tony Blair is portrayed as a reasonable and compassionate humanitarian, concerned for democratic process, but fatally flawed in that his concern for issues of global justice, specifically the conflict in Israel and Palestine, leads him to work with rather than against the US administration. The badness of the US administration is conveyed through the manipulation of speech by leading officials, for example by Rumsfeld's comment the week following the 9/11 attacks: 'A war on terror. That's good. That's vague . . . That way we can do anything' (Hare 2004: 24). These distortions of speech are contrasted with Blair's concern for evidence, for example, in his exchanges with Bush, 'we can't go to war because of what we fear. Only because of what we know,' to which Bush replies, 'I see. That's putting the bar quite high' (*ibid.*: 39).

This struggle between Blair's 'good' intentions and the US administration's power-hungry manipulation is played out in a final scathing speech from US Vice President Dick Cheney: 'Tony Blair? . . . He wants the right to go into any country anywhere and bring it relief from suffering and pain . . . I don't. What I want is to follow this country's legitimate security concerns . . . If you want to go into battle with a preacher sitting on top of a tank, that's fine by me. But bear in mind, preacher's one more to carry' (Hare 2004: 103–4). The play is a historical tragedy complete with fatally flawed tragic hero. It mourns the failure of goodness at the same time as affirming the British government's liberal values, expelling the disorder and chaos of the war on terror to the other side of the Atlantic. Hare's construction of Blair as a tragic hero does not extend to questioning Blair's good intentions critically. With the benefit of hindsight, it might be argued that Blair's decision to work

Figure 3 Conleth Hill as Guillaume and Steven Pacey as Kretschmann
in *Democracy*, National Theatre, London, 2003. Photograph by
Conrad Blakemore.

with the US administration represented a fundamentalist enactment
of his own Christianity in concert with the US administration's faith in
its own moral probity rather than any concern for reason, evidence or
democratic process.[4]

Michael Frayn's *Democracy* presents a more hopeful and critical account of democracy's crisis by exploring a fascinating moment
from democracy's troubled history – Germany's attempt to 'dare more
democracy' by opening up diplomatic relations with its antagonist
during the Cold War (Frayn 2003a: 19). The play centres on West
German Chancellor Willy Brandt's unknowing but close relationship with Günter Guillaume, an East German spy who becomes the
Chancellor's personal assistant during this period. Throughout the play,
Guillaume sustains conversations with his spymaster, Kretschmann, an
ominous presence at the side of the stage (Figure 3) The extent to which
the voice of the other might be included, listened to and trusted in a
democratic process is a repeated theme of the play, which interweaves
an exploration of the deceptions of intersubjective relationship with
those of democratic process. In the first act, Brandt's public assertion
that in order to safeguard democracy east and west 'must at last be
reconciled' is interwoven with his questioning in private of the extent
to which west can trust east and Kretschmann's questioning of whether
east might trust west: 'he chooses his words so carefully. What do they
mean? . . . Can we really trust him?' Guillaume responds to Brandt's

direct question, 'can we trust these new friends of ours?' with a comment to both his eastern and western masters: to Kretschmann: 'Yes? No? Which one of me's going to answer?', and to Brandt: 'Half of me wants to say one thing. Half of me wants to say another' (*ibid.*: 13–15). The horizontal and vertical lines of the multilevel set supported this dramatisation of uncertainty by creating a sense of interconnecting worlds, and also ensured that Guillaume's traversals of east and west, good and evil, us and them, transparency and obfuscation, are central to the play's exploration of democracy's crisis.

The play's dramatisation of the progressively paranoiac and interdependent relationship between Brandt and Guillame is a profoundly ironic exploration of the strengths and limitations of democracy in a time of crisis. Its complexity unfolds through the subjectivity of Brandt himself, whose depression leaves him preoccupied by a sense of dislocation, as well as through the multiple deceptions of the relationship between Brandt and Guillaume. Brandt's increasing reliance on Guillaume highlights the rich irony of a democracy being held in place by its exceptional other. Here, the play resists democracy's tendency to excise its own disorders by constructing dangerous and threatening others onto which those disorders might be projected. The supposed transparencies of a democratic sphere are shown to be constituted by a constant interplay of openness and deception, order and disorder, and strength and frailty. The drama culminates in a tense and claustrophobic scene set in the 'long northern twilight' of Norway towards the end of the play: Brandt, who by now is suspicious of Guillaume, begins a conversation that exposes their mutual complicity in the deception that comprises their relationship. Brandt tests Guillaume by telling him how he learnt the art of deception when hiding from the Gestapo during the war, taking on different identities and working underground: 'people kept taking me for a spy. Not something anyone's ever accused you of? . . . It's what politicians do all the time. No, I could have been a spy Günter. Might be one, for all you know. Might be spying now' (Frayn 2003a: 70).

This scene plays on anxieties about the complicity of truth and illusion in democracy's performance, and accrues its dramatic tension from the risk that these complicities might be exposed and the whole edifice collapse. Brandt and Guillaume, the real and made up, rule and exception, west and east, self and other: the first occupant of each pair depends on the power of its shadow to sustain its power. The play explores how the paradoxes and deceptions of democracy in crisis might be managed and answers with an image of anxious, dislocated selves speaking in double meanings in a half light – a powerful and jarring challenge to the audience to recognise and negotiate the difficultness of critical agency and encounters with threatening others in times of crisis. Guillaume's reflections to Kretschmann during this scene have an oddly faded and uncanny quality: 'we sit there through the long Norwegian evenings, and in that unfamiliar northern light everything begins to seem strange and uncertain. I've become transparent to him, and he's playing with me, just as I am with him . . . Is it him I'm seeing in half-light, or is it a reflection of myself?' (Frayn 2003a: 72).

Failed voices: *Far Away* (2000) and *Shoot/ Get Treasure/Repeat* (2008)

I work for the good of our society. Every day I deal with the homeless and the addicted and the mad and the lost. They come to me and I try to do what I can for them. I try to mend their broken wings. I use the arts to heal them. Drama or dance or painting. We'll . . . well, we'll . . . like we put on a little play. They all heal. Which is . . . that is a good thing to do. I'm doing good while you're . . . Do you see who I am? Do you? Do you see how good I am? As we all are good. How good we all are. How good freedom and democracy truly is. So please don't hurt . . . (Women of Troy, *Shoot/Get Treasure/ Repeat* [Ravenhill 2008: 8])

The British playwright Mark Ravenhill has described Caryl Churchill's play, *Far Away*, a forty-five minute-long staging of the descent of a cosmos into genocide and war staged in 2000 by the Royal Court, as one of the most 'theatrical and thrilling', albeit prescient, responses to the 9/11 attacks (cited in Sierz 2005: 60). For Michael Kustow, Churchill's *Far Away* and Mark Ravenhill's *Shoot/Get Treasure/Repeat* (2008) are both plays that have reinvented theatrical form in their prediction and depiction of the terror of war (Kustow 2008). Ravenhill's claim for the prescient power of performance, and Kustow's comment that the depiction of terror provokes innovations in performed language and the language of performance, have significance for my investigation of the critically mimetic capacities of the voice in performance. Taken together, these two plays provide a temporal frame for the war on terror, and their powerful dramatisations of the uncertain affectivity of the voice provide the focus of the discussion that follows.

Far Away begins with a child, Joan, in a farmhouse in a rural idyll, questioning her aunt about activities in the garden at night, where she has witnessed her uncle beating people who arrive and leave in lorries.

Figure 4 *Shoot/Get Treasure/Repeat*, Royal Court Theatre, London, 2008.
Photograph by Stephen Cummiskey.

This image is gradually revealed to the audience through the tentative questions of Joan and increasingly chilling responses of her aunt. In the final scene of the play, the adult Joan returns to the farmhouse and her closing speech is a surreal emission of images of paranoia, surveillance, collective punishment, betrayal, deception, revenge and genocide, all the more terrifying for their emergence inside the broken, tumbling qualities of a naturalistic voice:

> Of course the birds saw me, everyone saw me walking along but nobody knew why . . . It wasn't so much the birds I was frightened of, it was the weather, the weather here's on the side of the Japanese . . . there were piles of bodies and if you stopped to find out there was one killed by coffee or one killed by pins, they were killed by heroin, petrol, chainsaws, hairspray, bleach, foxgloves, the smell of smoke was where we were burning the grass that wouldn't serve. The Bolivians are working with gravity, that's a secret so as not to spread alarm. But we're getting further with noise and there's thousands dead of light in Madagascar. Who's going to mobilise light and darkness? (Churchill 2000: 43)

Like *Far Away*, *Shoot/Get Treasure/Repeat* is notable for its uncanny revelation of terror within the familiar frames of naturalistic voices (Figure 4). In the play Ravenhill draws on the rhythms and breaks of real speech as well as direct address of the audience in what, at times, seems to parody verbatim theatre's vocal conventions, here employed within entirely imagined dialogue. The piece is an epic cycle of sixteen short plays, each given the title of a canonical play. In 2008, these were staged in pairs across five London venues, taking place in conventional theatre spaces as well as a café and park. Here, the obscene realities of a war on terror stage shocking entries into a middle-class world of distorted intimacies and repressed violence. Scenes featuring garden centres, SUVs, fine wines, fair-trade coffee, handmade pasta, overprotected children, 'good and decent people', are inflected with images of monstrosity – headless soldiers, cancerous growths, rape, suicide bombings and torture. Flashes of conflated goodness and terror are repeated across each of the plays and vary in intensity and inflection, with some plays staging horrifying eruptions of terror in the everyday (*War and Peace, Yesterday an Incident Occurred*), some depicting an increasingly fractured effort to repress terror (*Intolerance, Paradise Lost*), and others explicitly evoking good and decent people engaged in monstrous humanitarian escapades in ruined warscapes (*Twilight of the Gods, The Odyssey, Birth of a Nation*). The cycle of plays are held together by the repeated trope – 'freedom and democracy' – and atrocities are rationalised as an extension of freedom and democracy enacted by the 'good people'. Audiences explore the reverberations of terror via a journey that engages them in encountering the cityscape of London, which in turn gradually becomes inflected with a series of metaphors that evoke a city utterly ruined by war. In following the cycle of plays, we engage in a process of remembering that we are citizens of a country at war. The disturbing eruptions of threatening and tortured bodies flow from peripheral vision to the centre stages of an anxious and implicated metropolis, an effect well captured by one reviewer who commented that '*Shoot/Get Treasure/Repeat* has landed like a cluster bomb' (Clapp 2008).

Far Away and *Shoot/Get Treasure/Repeat* both experiment with the excremental powers of the voice, to draw on Dolar's phrase, to materialise and critique the exceptional realities of war. In a parody of the falsely heroic and mythologising excisions of good and bad or 'us and them' political rhetoric of the war on terror, at the end of the first play of *Shoot/Get Treasure/Repeat*, 'a Soldier, half-man, half-angel', steps amongst the bodies of the women killed by a suicide bomb. He kisses each of them on the lips and proclaims, 'Freedom and democracy and truth and light – the fight is never done. There are always enemies. We must fight. I promise you that gun and tank and this flaming sword will roam the globe until everywhere is filled with the goodness of the good people. There will be good everywhere' (*Women of Troy*, Ravenhill 2008: 17). The repeated phrase 'we are the good people' of Ravenhill's epic cycle carries an echo of Harper's comment to Joan at the end of the first scene of *Far Away*, 'you're part of a big movement to make things better . . . You can look at the stars and think here we are in our little bit of space, and I'm on the side of the people who are putting things right' (Churchill 2000: 20). These rhetorical voices evoke a series of terrifying images and then attempt to regulate their impact by appropriating the trope of 'goodness'. Each play stages encounters with familiar figures, and then gradually introduces doubts about their motives and behaviour, giving voice to terrifying images within patterns of prosaic speech. What is staged here is the *failure* of the voice to regulate terror – both plays dramatise a breakdown of control over the *signifiance* of the voice. The gradual inflection of the familiar visual-discursive realm with the atrocious, excremental affects and effects of the failure of 'good' voices, constitutes a critical mimetic that reverses the maintenance of political fictions performed by verbatim theatre's regulation of frail voices, and ruins the comforting and comfortable identities of the good and decent citizens in the audience.

Far Away and *Shoot/Get Treasure/Repeat* intentionally materialise a vocal realm configured by the failure of the democratic voice to expel and excise the violence and atrocity of war. For Habermas, such distorted communication is undesirable and should be relegated from the public spheres of deliberative democracy. Distortions of speech include practices linked to 'the linguistic construction of a fictive reality, wit and irony, transposed and paradoxical uses of language, allusions . . . all these accomplishments rest on intentionally confusing modalities of being' (Habermas 1984: 331). Conversely, *Far Away* and *Shoot/Get Treasure/Repeat* intentionally materialise such distortions of speech and confusing modalities of being and enact an ethical imperative to pay attention to the violence obscured by rational voices in the public sphere. Contrary to the parodies of distorted speech in the Tribunal plays, which regulated the critical potential of the diminished voice, and mourned forensic, rational and orderly speech, *Far Away* and *Shoot/Get Treasure/Repeat* stage critical, direct engagements with the failures of the voice as a political imperative. Such failures of the voice in a time of terror highlight the irregularity of order and the violence obfuscated by political fictions of democracy. In this doubling of fictions, a fictional order's doubling and deadly effects are revealed.

As part of this, both plays also include moments of profound mistrust of their own voices by reflexively commenting on the deceptions of a decorative act of performance during times of crisis. In the second act of *Far Away*, for example, Joan and her colleague, Todd, engage in making enormous and preposterous hats, and are interrupted by a procession of beaten and raggedly dressed prisoners, each wearing a hat, making their way across the stage to their execution. Conversation between the two workers centres on the qualities of the hats and the poor working conditions of the factory: Joan comments 'I don't understand yours but I like the feather' (Churchill 2000: 25). Todd, in response to Joan's sadness that the hats are burnt with the bodies, comments, 'no I think that's the joy of it. The hats are ephemeral. It's like a metaphor for something or other . . . You make beauty and it disappears, I love that' (*ibid.*: 31). This moment is a searing indictment of a society that turns to the arts and cultural practices to beautify itself, and to cover up systemic violence. *Shoot/Get Treasure/Repeat* includes a similar moment of doubt. During *Birth of a Nation*, a team of 'artist-facilitators' arrive in a ruined city, overwhelmed by their own personal crises but full of good intentions to heal the war-affected citizens of the city through dance, art, writing and performance-installation workshops. In the final moments of the play the artists coerce a blind woman whose tongue has been cut out into participating in an art workshop: 'tell us your story – please tell us of your pain and struggle so that art can be made and the healing can begin' (Ravenhill 2008: 198). Thus, as part of their journey across London the audience is faced with a piercingly ironic reflection of their quest that powerfully unsettles any presumption of goodness that might come from completing it.

From Sally Giles' performance of Mrs Kelly's faltering voice to the desperate horror of Joan's tumbling recitation of catastrophe at the end of *Far Away*, political theatre stimulated by the war on terror has drawn on the uncertain affectivity of the voice to dramatise a crisis of democracy. The most potent moments of drama counter the stabilities of speech with the disruptive and ambiguous powers of the voice in ways that *move* audiences and disturb the political fictions of the democratic realm. The explorations here repeat the suggestion of previous chapters that the sites of critically resistant potential in performance reside in encounters with decay and diminishment in the circulations of mimesis in performance. The plays that exhibit the most critical potential locate and exploit these failures of the voice, and the three fictional plays, *Democracy, Shoot/Get Treasure/Repeat* and *Far Away* – in their half-lit, deceptive, terrifyingly familiar, fractured evocations – utilise the imagination to exploit these failures more critically than the verbatim plays. The latter tend to dramatise and mourn the loss of stable and secure frames of reference for voice, speech and critical action in the public sphere, rather than critically engage with uncertainty.

Rachel Corrie's repeated statement in her email from Gaza, 'this is not at all what I asked for', provides a further possibility for understanding the critical potential of performance. That is, the power of the repeatedly performed negative to *materialise* decay and diminishment in performance that may also, in turn, generate abundant possibilities for critical identification and action. The exploration of this potential is taken up in the analysis of protest performances in the following chapter.

Notes

1   Parts of this chapter were published in an earlier version in *Contemporary Theatre Review*, 17(2) (see Hughes 2007).
2   The Hutton Inquiry was ordered by the British government to investigate the circumstances leading to Dr Kelly's death. Lord Hutton, former Lord Chief of Justice in Northern Ireland, was appointed to lead the Inquiry. The original transcript of the Hutton Inquiry can be viewed at www.the-hutton-inquiry.org.uk/ [accessed 28 July 2010].
3   For an account of the controversy see Martin (2009; 2006), and also go to www.rachelswords.org [accessed 31 July 2010].
4   Since leaving office in 2007, Blair has been preoccupied with promoting the use of religious faith to combat the negative effects of globalisation via the Tony Blair Faith Foundation (www.tonyblairfaithfoundation.org/ [accessed 31 July 2010]).

5

Camping up and camping out as antiwar protest performance

We are the mirror that is a lens that is a mirror that is a lens. We are rebelliousness. We are the stubborn history that repeats itself in order to no longer repeat itself, the looking back to walk forward . . . We are human beings doing what must be done in reality: we are dreaming. Subcomandante Insurgente Marcos [Notes from Nowhere 2003: 523–9]

A few days after the 9/11 attacks, more than one hundred artists gathered in silence for an hour in Union Square in New York. Wearing black, with dust masks covering their faces, they held placards spelling out the message 'our grief is not a cry for war'. Images of this protest performance circulated across email networks and independent media websites, and the slogan became the headline for an antiwar campaign led by the families of victims of the attacks. The ensuing years witnessed a proliferation of antiwar protests inaugurated by this moment, especially but not exclusively across the urban spaces of those countries that joined the military coalition to fight the war on terror. From the carefully devised, costumed performances of protestors during street demonstrations, to the direct action campaigns against arms manufacturers and military bases by masked agitators, performance has been repeatedly drawn upon as a tactic and strategy of the antiwar movement.

The history of protest evidences the fecund territory that exists at the intersection of performance and activism, with powerful and provocative protest performances reappearing across environmental, anti-racist, gay liberation, postcolonial, feminist, global justice as well as antiwar campaigns. The ebbs and flows of these disparate yet inter-connected movements and their diverse repertoires of protest highlight repeated patterns of bodies and text intervening in public space in ways that are profoundly theatrical and transgress the boundaries between art and life. In this chapter, three examples of antiwar protest performance are explored. Firstly, the global day of action against imminent war in Iraq on 15 February 2003, a day which mobilised millions of people in approximately 600 cities across the world, and was the largest antiwar rally in the history of the cities of London and Rome. Secondly, Brian Haw's protest camp on Parliament Square in the heart of ceremonial London (2001–): a determined occupation of a site of democracy's crisis by one body that expresses outrage at the atrocities of war, and forms an inverted mirror image of the Houses of Parliament directly opposite.[1] These two examples are compared to Ultimate Holding Company's *This is Camp X-Ray* (2003), a performance art installation situated on a piece of wasteland in the city of Manchester (UK), which created a temporary replica of the internment camp in Guantánamo Bay, Cuba. This replica camp materialised a ghostly presence of the exceptional realities of a war on terror in an urban space geographically distant from, but politically implicated, in, that war.

The term 'protest performance' alludes to three specific relation-ships between protest and performance represented by these examples. Firstly, antiwar protests that might be interpreted and analysed *as* performance. Secondly, theatrical interventions in antiwar protest by activist groups who may not define themselves as artists, continuing the 'cultural turn' in protest movements that came to prominence with the global justice movement in the late 1990s (Amoore 2005: 357). Finally, explicitly performative contributions to antiwar protests by artist-activists. The overriding imperative of each of the examples explored here is to *act*, and, through acting, to transform the public and private sphere, and as part of this activists have identified 'the limits between where reality ends and theatre begins' as a site from which protest per-formance generates its critical force (Shepard and Hayduk 2002: 199). To haze the 'performed' and 'real' is to expand the terrain of critical activity by deliberately entering the domains of mimesis, mobilising its capacities to make and unmake worlds of experience inside an uncertain present. Here, activists occupy space with their bodies and materialise a contest with a violent and inequitable world and, within the confines of such contests, revive and renew possible, alternative ways of think-ing about and being in the world in times of crisis. As the examples explored in this chapter show, this includes intentionally acting within and against the cites/sites of sovereign power and disrupting the political fictions of an orderly, rule-bound universe.

As noted in chapter 1, Jacques Rancière draws attention to the potential of critical art to create 'dissensus' – moments of aesthetic rupture whereby different senses of the world, and ways of making sense of the world, are uncannily juxtaposed, leading to 'a dissensual reconfiguration of the common experience of the sensible' (Rancière 2010: 140). The hazing of the border between art and life performed by protest events disrupts our sense of the world as orderly, natural and 'proper', and reaquaints bodies and worlds with their possibility and potential. Rancière sees critical art as lacking a clear political project outside this materialisation of multiple and shifting sensual fabrics of the world, and welcomes artistic practices that 'focus on matters of space, territories, borders, wastelands and other transient spaces, matters that are crucial to today's issues of power and community' (*ibid.*: 149). A focus on the *matter* of bodies and space in ways that draw attention to the waste and wasted life of a war on terror is a feature of the protest performances explored in this chapter. Here, I work from a repeated motif of waste and wasted life evoked by each of the performances to articulate a politics of performance that is at once more confident and more troubled than Rancière's dissensual aesthetics and politics. These examples of protest performance, in making *use* of waste, interrupt the mimetic circulation of threat and frailty in play in times of crisis, and stimulate kinds of identification and action that employ uncertainty as a site of abundant critical potential.

Whilst Rancière's dissensus is relevant to the discussion here, Giorgio Agamben's notion of the 'camp' has provided the overarching theoretical framework drawn upon to analyse the performances themselves. The 'camp', when introduced as part of a *poetics* of exception, offers a dissensual configuration of the sensible fabric of the world. As mentioned in the prologue, for Agamben the camp is the structure by which the state of exception is given form: '*the camp is the space that is opened when the state of exception begins to become the rule . . .* a permanent spatial arrangement, which as such nevertheless remains outside the normal order' (Agamben 1998: 168–9. Italics in original). The camp is a recognisable pattern of bodies and space which, like the figure of the bandit, terrorist, protestor and exile, unconceals the state of exception that underpins sovereign power. Protest performances that make use of a structure and practice of camp purposely traverse the border between the orderly, rule-bound universe and the violent and threatening realities of a state of exception. Camps process and regulate the waste and wasted life of a system in crisis, and camp protests activate the critical and affective force of waste and wasted life that is produced at the point of collapse between order and disorder, law and violence, symbolic meaning and matter.

The examples of protest performance described in this chapter repeatedly practise a poetics of camp by drawing on a practice of queer camp and protest camps. These protest performances blend the tactics of queer camp and protest camps to materialise, mirror, occupy, confront and refuse sovereign power. As a linguistic term and critical cultural practice, 'camp' is associated with the theatrical and camouflaged, determinedly sited on bodily or spatial domains but endlessly queering, difficult to locate, ironic as well serious in its intent and operation. Queer camp reproduces the stigmatising ways the queer body has been framed and destabilises those frames at the same time as materialising a protective, communicative space for queer bodies. Protest camps occupy spaces of political and military significance and profoundly unsettle the orderly fictions of those sites by forcing a display of the exceptional violence that is concealed there. Both queer camp and protest camps exhibit 'camp critical mimesis', queering a politics of exception by locating and parodying its 'camp'. To practise camp is – potentially – to make use of the force of cites/sites of diminished, anomalous life, to materialise possibility without securing power, to assimilate to the other and world without asserting mastery or control, and to participate in a mimetic circulation of threat and frailty that refuses to regulate whilst also prizing life. Queer camp and protest camps creatively negotiate the negating indistinctions of the camp, evoke the vulnerability of life and demonstrate the body's creative capacities to make habitable spaces in the environments of exception.

Not all protest performances fully exploit the possibilities of camp critical mimesis, and the distinctions between different examples constitute the focus of the discussion here. The following review of the history of contemporary protest performance highlights camp critical mimesis repeatedly emerging across different contexts, and further explicates the theoretical framework described here.

Some deviations of camp critical mimesis

My answer, for the moment, is that we must mimic mainstream culture, and when the mirror is standing between them and us, reflecting their fantasies and desires, we break it in the audience's face. If parts of the mirror get in their eyes, that's their problem. (Gómez-Peña 2005: 251)

Here, artist-activist Guillermo Gómez-Peña gives voice to the challenges of practising critical mimesis in protest performance. In particular, he responds to the challenge of generating critical art when the means of reply are constituted by a hegemonic power that has already claimed the force of an oppositional stance. It is no longer possible to assume that taking up a position that is outside or somehow in the interstices of the circulations of organised mimesis is disruptive of an alienating power. Gómez-Peña's response is to construct a series of fantastic reworkings of an eroticised, commodified, anomalous other in ways that reproduce sexualised, racist and colonial fixations and test an audience's critical and affective capacities. His work highlights the critical powers of mimesis, and he has moved from a stance of outright opposition to making a tactical use of the body to double and negate the political fictions that constitute our perceptions of each other in a globalised world. Here, a doubling of the images of diminished, negated life offered by a cultural mainstream offers abundant possibilities for critical performance practice.

Wider scholarship on protest performance echoes Rancière's discussion of the dissensual capacities of critical art noted above, by exploring performance's occupation and disruption of the cites/sites of power and generation of new, possible practices of space, body and identity in those cites/sites. For example, Baz Kershaw, in a discussion of the US and UK demonstrations against the Vietnam war, notes how the protest camps associated with the US demonstrations carried a generative power: 'the greater permanence of the camp provides the kinds of time/space needed to fashion new relations between the symbolic and the real' (Kershaw 1999: 109). Similarly, Sophie Nield argues that anticapitalist protests which reclaim public space materialise a contest to determine the use of space, creatively producing space in ways that indicate 'other spaces, other worlds . . . which, by being materialised there, become possible' (Nield 2006: 61). In her analysis of the postindustrial *flânerie* of Reverend Billy and his satirical 'Stop Shopping' tours, Jill Lane identifies how Reverend Billy's 'prayers to shopping' subvert 'programmed scripts and narratives that constitute the scenes of today's consumption' (Lane 2002: 69). Reverend Billy 'commits himself to an endless negativity in order to make possible new configurations, new revelations, new ways of imagining being in public, being a public, beyond the retail church of shopping' (*ibid.*: 80). In different ways, then, Gómez-Peña, Kershaw, Nield and Lane all draw attention to the critical and *generative* capacity of protest performance that arises from its negative, negating qualities.

The specific relationship between protest performance's generative and negating capacities, that is, between its potential to make new
worlds of possibility, and critically resist and deconstruct worlds of
violence and inequity, appears as a point of contention in activist scholarship on protest. This is particularly evident in works that pursue an
understanding of what might constitute *critical* identity and action in a
contemporary context. For example, Michael Hardt and Antonio Negri
develop a conceptual frame for understanding protest movements since
1968, a year that they see as marking the emergence of activism embedded in and reflecting a biopolitical terrain (Hardt and Negri 2004: 81–3).
This becomes evident in the ways in which the materiality of life – body,
space and identity, and the forms of subjectivity that attend to different formulations of these – become part of the strategies and tactics of
protests. Hardt and Negri's two concepts of 'Empire' and 'Multitude'
provide the overarching frame for understanding the critical potential
of these forms of resistance. 'Empire' describes the all-encompassing,
abstract, appropriating, unaccountable power associated with global
corporate capitalism. 'Multitude' describes the 'fleshy', creative, unpredictable and productive subjectivity of singularities brought together to
act in common against the operations of 'Empire' (see Hardt and Negri
2004; 2000). Hardt and Negri insist on the *productive* capacities of singular subjectivities brought together to act in common. They identify
the carnivalesque protests of the global justice movement as providing
innovatory forms of relationship and action from which new forms
of society might be identified and produced (Hardt and Negri 2004:
210–11).

Offering a counter-perspective, John Holloway, whose work, like
Hardt and Negri's, has inspired the global justice movement, argues that
the significance of the 1968 protests resides in their display of the advent
of 'abstract labour'. For Holloway, this moment of crisis represented the
historical juncture wherein an alienating, biopolitical power completed
its appropriation of all areas of life – work, leisure, sexuality, subjectivity, desire, nature, time, space – all of which therefore become sites of
contest and struggle. Here, political action becomes a struggle of 'doing
against' abstract labour – that is, 'useful-creative doing' against the
'forces of abstraction' (Holloway 2008: 14). However, Holloway resists
any easy association of his 'doing against' with a *generative* capacity
that might institute reliable models for alternative worlds. In his view,
productive activity can only mimetically reproduce the negation of life
performed by abstract labour. Instead, Holloway argues that critical
activity consists of a double refusal – a negation of the negation of life.
Rather than assuming that we are critical subjects capable of producing

coherent and stable forms of opposition, Holloway describes a blurred, hazy critical activism that exists in mimetic relationship to its alienated form – not a defined identity but a 'not' or 'not-yet', 'undefinable' or, rather, 'anti-definable':

> Human existence is . . . an existence of not-yet-ness, in which negation, by being negation of the negation of our humanity, is at the same time a projection towards that humanity . . . This not-yet-ness can be seen not just in overt political militancy, but in the struggles of everyday living, in the dreams we have, in our projections against the denial of our projections, in our fantasies, from the simplest dreams of pleasure to the most path-breaking artistic creations. (Holloway 2002: 152–3)

It is not possible to identify the seeds of a future society in the ephemeral, fleeting projections that emerge from a practice of 'doing against'. What is hopeful is not what 'path-breaking' artistic creations signify or evidence as products, but the practice of 'doing against', the double refusal, negation of the negation, in every engagement. Two dimensions of Holloway's 'doing against' are particularly important to conceptualising the 'critical' of critical mimesis in performance. Firstly, his identification of a repeated and repudiating negative as a source of critical and affective power – the lack, if you like, in lack, is what constitutes performance's critical effects, not its productivity. Again, critical mimesis here might be conceived as generating a sense of possibility and potential, rather than a plan for transforming the world according to predetermined design. Secondly, his notions of 'useful-creative doing against' and 'not-yet' being draw attention to the critical potential of adaptive and mortifying forms of mimesis, that is, mimesis of the fractured and diminished forms in which body and world appear in an alienating world.

The argument here has associations with traditional models of political performance. Perhaps most obviously in terms of contemporary performance theory there is an association with Richard Schechner's argument that the field of performance might be conceptualised as a time/space of 'not me . . . not not me . . . the embodiment of potential, of the virtual, the imaginative, the fictive, the negative, the not not' (Schechner 1985: 114). In addition, there are versions of the double refusal in each of the three historical models explored by Larry Bogad in his discussion of 'electoral guerrilla theatre' as protest performance: Brechtian distantiation, Bakhtinian carnivalesque and Boalian spect-actorship (Bogad 2005: 8). A Brechtian aesthetic utilises an *alienation* effect in order to mobilise the spectator's recognition of the *inequities* of a capitalist system. Mikhail Bakhtin's carnivalesque refers to the *reversal* of order in part materialised by a focus on the *lower bodily stratum* in popular forms of medieval performance. Augusto Boal's spect-actorship invites spectators to *undo* their exclusion from the creative function of making performance and *act against* oppression as a rehearsal for the transformation of society. Here, performance is the creative practice of a critical not-yet subject rather than a discrete product made by comfortably inhabited discrete identities. Bogad states that protest performances demonstrate 'nascent, ludic visions' of a direct participatory democracy (*ibid.*: 206), a conclusion that is notionally similar to Holloway's 'projections against'. Following Holloway, these visions are unreliable as blueprints for an alternative society, they are temporary and fleeting performances of refusal only.

To develop a discussion of the historical deviations of camp critical mimesis, which I am viewing as a form of 'useful-creative doing against' materialised by protest performance, brief mention of two prominent protest movements of the 1990s is useful. ACT UP in the US and direct action protests of the anti-roads campaigns in the UK both exemplified camp critical mimesis, the first by 'camping up' and 'queering' heteronormative space, and the latter by establishing protest camps at sites due to be demolished by road developments. The AIDS Coalition to Unleash Power (ACT UP) campaign originating in New York in the late 1980s aimed to provoke public debate about the prevention and treatment of HIV/AIDS. It utilised a deliberately queering camp to détourn the spaces of corporate capitalism, including corporate branding, marketing and ownership of public space by means of a viscerally impacting logo ('silence=death'), business cards, advertising campaigns, and obstructions of prominent sites by queer bodies as part of 'die ins' and 'kiss ins'. ACT UP practised a form of 'MTV activism' that projected a 'queer nation' as a fiction to compete with the constructed veneer of heteronormativity in everyday spaces (Solomon in Cohen-Cruz 1998: 49). The practice of queer camp, associated with a long history of queer resilience and survival, plays up stigmatised constructions of queer identified behaviour – feminine, fake, unnatural – to produce a 'troubling inauthenticity' that 'spoils' heteronormative regimes by negating the negations of stigmatisation (Cleto 1999: 13). This double negation of queer camp functions to perpetually evacuate meaning and unsettle hierarchical, exclusive representational practices. Echoing the explorations between negation and generation in the mimesis of protest performance noted above, Fabio Cleto notes that 'queer *can't* exclude, in fact, precisely because it doesn't envision an horizon of property or propriety of itself, and of its "own" discourse, which *in itself* exists as secondary, as copy of an *absent* original, and as challenging normative definitions' (*ibid.*: 22. Italics in original).

Etymologically, the word 'camp' carries associations of inclusion and exclusion, absence and presence, and protection and exposure of life: it has theatrical, vagrant, nomadic and military roots, linked to troupes of travelling actors living rough in tents, as well as camps where men connected to the sovereign would gather for ostentatious military displays in eighteenth-century France (Cleto 1999: 33; Booth in Cleto 1999: 78). As such, queer camp links to a broader set of cultural practices that are in turn connected to spaces in which the anomalous body has historically resided. My use of queer camp in this chapter assumes, with Agamben, that the state of exception has become the rule, with life held in a state of suspension and underpinned by uncertainty. Hence the universalisation of queer camp and protest camps – camp critical mimesis – in contemporary forms of protest performance. These creative engagements with the zones of non-identification mirror the uncertainty of life in a state of exception in ways that both expose and protect the body. I am claiming, then, by this extension of Agamben's camp, that there is a critically resistant potential in camp as intentionally *practised* and *poeticised*, and that this emerges from an endless negativity which perpetually undermines power's claims on meaning and being. In addition, that camp's critically resilient potential resides in its concern for the protection, resilience and survival of life in this domain.

The protests against road developments in the 1990s in the UK similarly highlight the potential of camp as a site of refusal and a paradoxical domain in which life is both exposed and protected. Here, confrontational direct action tactics, for example the obstruction of bulldozers assigned to destroy rural spaces by protestors 'locking on' – using heavy-duty chains to attach themselves to the machines – employed the bodies of protestors in deeply theatrical demonstrations of 'manufactured vulnerability' (Doherty 2000). The direct action of the roads protest camps, and associated tactics of blockade, sabotage and occupation, involved 'performing our politics with our whole body' (Notes from Nowhere 2003: 202) and produced spectacles 'predicated on such authenticity, such commitment, such rooted realness of action' (McKay 1998: 32). Protest camps provide provisional housings for bodies that, like queer camp, display the threat to life and make use of the diminished and exposed zones in which life resides in times of crisis to protect bodies and worlds. Discourses of embodied authenticity are married to spectacles of vulnerability and threatened life in a state of exception, and the critical impact of these protests is in part evidenced by their tendency to provoke violent and repressive responses from the police, producing contests of power that further unsettle the fictions of an orderly, rule-bound universe.

As such, both queer camp and protest camps run the risk of uncritically reproducing the contours and forms of alienating power as part of their mimesis of an alienating world. These camps mobilise a paradoxical alignment of discourses of authenticity and inauthenticity (the 'manufactured' vulnerability of the suspended protestor, the theatricality and vulnerability of the queer body). Such alignments disrupt the deceptive appearances of the normative realm; however, in claiming this territory, acts of protest risk becoming imprisoned by their own mimesis. An example of this mimetic capture is offered by Bogad, in his description of the queer camp of drag queen Miss Joan JettBlakk and her guerrilla 'camp-pain' for the Presidency of the United States on a Queer Nation ticket in 1992. The 'camp-pain' here culminated in uncritically mirroring the divisive and hierarchical style of electoral politics it sought to détourn (Bogad 2005: 163). In terms of roads protests, George McKay similarly notes how these forms of 'DIY culture', in their privileging of individual autonomy and creativity, reproduced the entrepreneurial spirit and competitive individualism associated with free market capitalism (McKay 1998: 20–1).

The global justice movement has utilised diverse forms of camp in its protest performances. Here, the nomadic, clandestine, ironic, theatrical and carnivalesque have become tactics and strategies of protest disseminated at global counter-summits, in activist literature and via the internet. This movement originated in the global South, most notably with the Zapatista declaration of autonomous zones for indigenous peoples in Mexico in 1994, and burst onto the scene in the global North with the day of action which closed down the World Trade Organization meeting in Seattle in 1999. Hardt and Negri provide a point of connection between the protest tactics of the global justice movement and the notion of camp critical mimesis I am tracing here, identifying the 'common performativity of queer social flesh' with the resistant possibilities of the 'multitude' (Hardt and Negri 2004: 199). In an earlier work, they comment that, 'we consciously subvert the traditional boundaries, dressing in drag, for example, but we also move in a creative, indeterminate zone *au milieu*, in between and without regard for these boundaries' (Hardt and Negri 2000: 215). The global justice movement repertoire of protest tactics includes marches and demonstrations, commonly camped up, and protest camps as part of specific campaigns, for example the global network of No Borders, No Nations camps that help refugees safely cross border posts (Notes from Nowhere 2003: 428).

How are these complexities of camp critical mimesis, together with its ambivalent effects, exemplified by protest performances against the war on terror? Drawing on Agamben's camp, activist Stefan

Skrimshire notes the emergence of a 'politics of the camp' during the war on terror, evidenced by the retreat of world leaders to remote sites surrounded by miles of fencing at global summits and police tactics of penning protestors on demonstrations. He argues that direct action protests have become a contest of space, *against* the containment of the camp (Skrimshire in Harvie *et al.* 2005). US activist Ben Shepard, drawing on queer camp, comments that antiwar protests confronted 'the limits of camp' – arguing that the camped-up carnivalesque of the global justice movement 'recedes in relevance when political situations become too dire or when there is an urgent need to engage in dialogue with the political mainstream', for example to counter threats to civil liberties during times of war (Shepard 2004). It might be argued that Shepard fails to recognise the combination of irony and deadly seriousness that I have identified in the broad terrain of 'camp' here, and that Skrimshire does not pay enough attention to the creatively negating potential of a *practice* of camp. However, their concerns about the limitations of camp critical mimesis echo across the examples of antiwar protest that follow. These warnings about forms of protest that become imprisoned by their mimesis of exception are especially important when faced with the intensification of sovereign power at a time of war. The discussion that follows highlights the ways in which camp uncritically mirrors as well as potentially refuses the operations of sovereign power.

Stop the war, fix the world? The 'astonishing street scenes' of 15 February 2003[2]

Those tens of millions worldwide constituted something unprecedented, one of the ruptures that ushered in a new era. (Solnit 2005: 22)

The global day of action against impending war in Iraq on 15 February 2003 was historically unprecedented in its reach and scale. Between eight and thirty million people took part in demonstrations in approximately 600 cities, with protests taking place across all seven continents over the course of the day. The Guinness World Records entry for this day of action records it as the largest antiwar rally in human history, with the demonstrations in London and Rome the largest in the history of protest in those cities (Guinness World Records 2003: 83).[3] The protests drew on growing anger at diplomatic machinations relating to

United Nations weapons inspections in Iraq, which became the focus for a public discussion of the legitimacy, or otherwise, of the case for invasion. This provoked a worldwide refusal of war repeated across the placards of the millions occupying prominent public spaces in multiple cities, painted in red on the sails of the Sydney Opera House, spelt out in jet stream on the skies above Cape Town in South Africa and New Zealand, and by bare bodies in nude protests across the world. Whilst there have been accounts of artist-activist groups involved in demonstrations at this time, there has been less attention paid to the day itself *as* performance. One useful example is Susan Leigh Foster's reading of choreographies of protest, which focuses primarily on non-violent civil disobedience during the civil rights movement in the US in the 1960s, and ends with a description of the demonstration in London on 15 February 2003. Foster, a dance scholar, argues that the demonstration called forth 'a perceptive and responsive physicality that, everywhere along the way, deciphers the social and then choreographs an imagined alternative' (Foster 2003: 412). This reading usefully highlights the significance of the body's presence in protest performance. However, my own reading of the day highlights the ways in which the presence of these millions of bodies arguably materialised a more uncertain and ambivalent response to a moment of crisis.

Reportedly, a group of schoolchildren in New York carried a large inflatable globe as they marched towards the main rally. During a delay caused by a puncture in the globe, a ten-year-old child commented to a nearby journalist, 'we're trying to fix the world' (McFadden 2003). The understanding of the protests as an attempt to fix the world evoked by this comment is repeated across accounts of the day in the mainstream media. For example, media reports repeatedly narrated how demonstrations 'brought together' a diverse cross-section of people. On the London demonstration, anarchists and Eton schoolboys, the middle classes and the hard left, Conservatives and Liberals, religious and secular, and old and young, traversed social and political hierarchies to march together. There were also multiple reports of demonstrations in conflict hotspots where divided communities marched together: Catholics and Protestants in Northern Ireland, Israelis and Palestinians in Tel Aviv, Greeks and Turks in Cyprus. The revolutionary zeal of Hardt and Negri's reading of the event as an example of the critical and 'monstrous' potential of the multitude faces competition from mainstream discourses of the protests as 'healing' and 'fixing' (see Hardt and Negri 2004: 215). The rhetorical power of the scale of the protest – the millions involved across seven continents – reproduced a tendency towards abstraction evident in such 'world-fixing' narratives of the day. These reports constructed a coherent narrative for the protests, following the course of the sun across the globe: 'it started in New Zealand . . . then swept over Asia, Africa and Europe. By last night the protestors were also on the move in North and South America' (Harris *et al.* 2003). Here, a coherent spectacle of global citizenry engaged in a peaceful, ordered display of refusal materialised 'a global daisy chain of largely peaceful protests' (McFadden 2003). Whilst a straightforward correspondence between these accounts and actual experiences of the protest cannot be assumed, their rhetorical quality invites critique. The experience of joining other bodies in space and walking together enacts a liberating but also abstract sense of value and significance with, perhaps, diluted critical intent. Foster's 'responsive physicality' may be associated as much with an experience of liberation from the obligation of considering the complexity and wider contingencies of the crisis as a critical act.

The London demonstration was so well attended that it was impossible to contain. Two routes were traced across the centre of the city from two separate meeting points on the Embankment of the River Thames and Gower Street, north of the river. When joining together in Piccadilly to approach Hyde Park, where a final rally was to be held, the demonstration burst the boundaries of its designated route and 'the streets became one vast, vibrant civic space' (Bunting 2003). However, this temporary disruption of public space did not evoke the critical power of the 'vortexed, whirling' pattern of unofficial mass gatherings noted by Schechner in his analysis of protest as performance (Schechner 1993: 46), nor did it represent the visceral, participatory reversal of hierarchy performed by an expansion of the lower bodily stratum associated with Bakhtin's carnivalesque. Rather, it represented an expansion of orderliness and a calmly asserted 'no' to war. This performed affirmation and expansion of order refused one aspect of the politics of exception in play at this historical juncture, that is, the threatened suspension of the rule of law represented by imminent war without UN sanction. However, the extent to which this refusal comprised a critique – or double refusal – of the more expansive circulations of violence threatened at this time is questionable: this was arguably a refusal of war without UN sanction rather than a refusal of war *per se*. This protest performance might be most accurately interpreted therefore as a refusal of a disruption to the *appearance* of order by the US administration's embracing of an unveiled form of sovereign performance. According to this reading, the 'world' here is performed as unified, coherent and aligned in opposition to the threat of disorder, and the demonstrations thus projected a nostalgic desire to conserve the political fictions of law and order in a time of crisis.

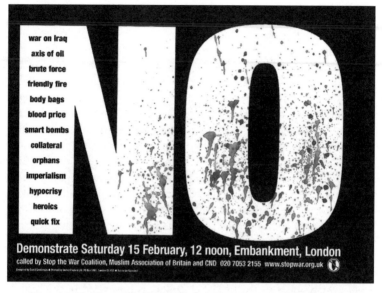

war on Iraq
axis of oil
brute force
friendly fire
body bags
blood price
smart bombs
collateral
orphans
imperialism
hypocrisy
heroics
quick fix

Demonstrate Saturday 15 February, 12 noon, Embankment, London
called by Stop the War Coalition, Muslim Association of Britain and CND 020 7053 2155 www.stopwar.org.uk

Figure 5 The 'big NO' placard, designed by David Gentleman for the
Stop the War coalition.

This can be explored further via an analysis of the refusals evidenced
by the banners and placards of the demonstration in London. An 'official' placard was commissioned by the coalition of left-wing, Muslim
and peace groups organising the march. The artist involved, David
Gentleman, gives an account of the design of the placard that expressed
his preference for 'a big NO, the two letters filling the whole space . . .
a sea of NOs that you could see half a mile off', avoiding the 'muddle'
of individually made banners (Murray and German 2005: 146) (Figure
5). Here, there is a sense that the demonstration was itself designed as a
spectacle of repeated, abstract and general refusal. Of course, this might
be interpreted as a powerful mass performance of refusal that directly
answered the attempts of governments to construct and communicate
a legitimate base for war. However, perhaps a more direct engagement
with the queering potential of camp would have generated more critical power. Such camp refusals were offered by other interventions into
the march. For example, whilst photographic records of the day testify
to the prominence of official banners, a multiplicity of 'Nos' carried
their echoes across the wider scripts of the event. These ranged from the
humorous (a man disguised as a large piece of greenery held a banner
proclaiming 'English bush – harmless'), the bizarre (the banner of a
group of 'Cornish ravers' proclaimed 'Cornish cream, not ruptured

spleen'), to the serious (banners produced by the Muslim Association of Great Britain declared 'Don't Attack Iraq – Freedom for Palestine').

Whilst these placards evidenced a more differentiated refusal than the abstract and generalised 'NO' of the organised march, and also incorporated elements of queer camp, the extent to which they embodied a doubly negative critique is questionable. For example, one of the most frequently commented-upon banners in the mainstream press, making the front cover of a right-wing newspaper the day after the demonstration, read 'Make Tea Not War', and depicted British Prime Minister Tony Blair holding a gun, with a teacup as a helmet: a quintessentially English invitation to consider a polite alternative to war (Figure 6). This banner was designed and produced by Karmarama, a creative marketing agency in the UK whose clients include multinational corporations that have attracted controversy for their questionable ethical standards, including, amongst others, Coca-Cola and Unilever.[4] The latter famously attracted criticism from Greenpeace and other environmental campaigning groups for causing damage to the environment, and Coca-Cola, widely identified with global capital, is boycotted in the Middle East. The final irony of this camp but uncritical refusal of war, is that the march in London was sponsored by both Greenpeace and Mecca Cola, a company that markets soft drinks as an alternative to Coca-Cola across the Middle East. What I am suggesting is that the invitation to 'Make Tea Not War' represented a polite refusal of an aberration in the smooth appearance of sovereign power threatened by imminent war in Iraq without UN sanction, rather than any critical contestation of the politics of war. It also supported the self-promotion of a marketing company whose existence depends upon maintenance of such appearances of order. The fetishising of 'Englishness' of 'Make Tea Not War' speaks to comfortably inhabited subjects and overpowers the more difficult to think about and act upon complexities of crisis. Echoing this, the multiple refusals of war that were performed as part of the wider scripts of the London demonstration were defined by the logic of accumulation and quantification – in design (Gentleman's 'sea of NOs'), experience (mass participation) and reception (fetishisation of numbers of participants across the mainstream press). Such discourses of accumulation assume discrete subjects and commodified identities that, multiplied together, form an abstract mass – a sum that is far from equivalent to the double refusal of the not-yet critical subject of camp critical mimesis.

I close this examination with a consideration of two examples of protest performance from the 15 February 2003 demonstrations that illustrate camp critical mimesis more effectively. My first example here is one of the images widely circulated across email networks and

Figure 6 Make tea not war placard, designed by Karmarama.

independent media sites from the day of action, and comes from the McMurdo station on Ross Island in the Antarctic. Here, scientists and technical staff used their bodies to create a peace sign against a frozen horizon of snow-covered plains. This image followed an earlier protest on 9 January 2003, again disseminated via email and internet, when ten members of staff demonstrated by stripping naked, their bodies covered by a banner with no slogan other than an exclamation mark. The nudity in this case was a response to the station manager's direction that nothing connected to the National Science Foundation, the organisation that directs research activities at the station, could be shown in the protest, including the extreme cold-weather gear issued to staff (Koch 2003: 167). This may have had something to do with the fact that McMurdo station is operated by Raytheon Polar Services, part of the Raytheon Company, a global corporation and a major US defence contractor. As a collective image, the protesting naked scientists carry multiple and competing connotations that repeat and also complicate the world-fixing critical mimetic of the larger demonstrations. For example, the setting of the photo, the research centre situated in the Antarctic, with its melting ice caps, expresses competing narratives of scientific progress and environmental damage. The peace sign of the later protest proclaims a commitment to peace and also references earlier antiwar campaigns associated with the nuclear arms race and the Cold War. The nudity of the scientists in the first protest is important: the bare bodies evoke the countercultural sexual freedom of 1970s protest performance; however, the carnivalesque excesses of former times are replaced here with an ordered display of vulnerable, exposed bodies in a way that marks the agency of the protestors *and* their powerlessness in the face of the corporation. This is an ordered display of bare life in a setting that evokes the disorder of threatened bodies – human and earthly – of impending and past war and crisis.

The protest, captured photographically, was part of a global phenomena of nude protests that brought bare bodies together to spell out antiwar messages on 15 February 2003, employing the vulnerability of bare life to express what Hardt and Negri refer to as 'the one overriding grievance, the ultimate biopolitical grievance, against destruction and death' (Hardt and Negri 2004: 284).[5] The images of nude protest evoke the vulnerability of bodies during a time of terror, exposed and at risk, stripped of clothing, rights and identity. The absence of text and exclamation mark on the banner covering the bodies of the naked protesting scientists at McMurdo is important: the deceptions of text are replaced with a protective covering marked by a defiant and hopeful exclamation of space and bodies emptied of signification. What is performed here is a right to inhabit an orderly universe materialised by a hopeful expansion of protective covering, performed by and protective of bare life. The naked protest of the McMurdo scientists asserts an imperative to ensure the protection and preservation of all bodies at times of war and crisis, queering democracy's practice of protecting some lives at the same time as threatening and destroying others.

Like the McMurdo scientists, 'the vacuum cleaner', an artist activist who prefers not to be known by his given name, materialised an

Figure 7 The vacuum cleaner, cleaning up after capitalism.

unsettling critical mimetic in his protest performances at this historical juncture (Figure 7). During the three-month period in 2003 surrounding the invasion of Iraq, the vacuum cleaner cleaned urban spaces, including Wall Street in New York and the commercial heart of London. He wore a bright yellow cleaning contractor vest with the text 'cleaning up after capitalism' printed on the back, and commented to passers-by to 'watch where you're standing, there's a lot of dirt and filth round here'.[6] This protest performance was durational and repetitive: an anonymous street cleaner slips in and out of view in the realm of the ordinary and everyday. Where possible, an upright model vacuum cleaner from the 1950s is used to clean the streets – importantly, an old model is recycled, evoking an implicit critique of a consumer-driven, throwaway society and anxieties about environmental damage. The performance mobilises a process of non-signification and non-identification that undoes the comfortable subjectivity of the spectator: the anonymous figure of the street cleaner cleans away the discarded debris of a system in crisis from the forgotten non-places of the street. Heralding the 'world-fixing' rhetoric of the protest, the critical mimesis here also mobilises a connotative regime that critiques a system which supports the destruction of life. The message on the back of his vest calls on the passer-by to look again at this figure and critiques an economic and political system that supports war, whilst the visual motif of a man engaged in domestic cleaning, together with the traditional model of the vacuum cleaner used, lightly dresses the whole performance with a layer of camp. Interestingly, like the larger demonstration, there is order in this performance – there is no confrontation with power, just a quiet repetition of a performed action that evokes devastation and decay and exhibits gentle care for a threatened environment. As such, the vacuum cleaner, cleaning up after capitalism, creates an anti-spectacle of enduring – perpetual, but also survivable – crisis rather than a fixing of the world. His careful attention to dirt and debris introduces a permanent disjuncture that refuses to settle the complexities of crisis, and is also a key operative of the camp critical mimesis of the examples of protest performance that follow here.

Spoiling the spectacle: Brian Haw's protest camp (2001–) and Mark Wallinger's *State Britain* (2006)

I'm a Christian, I'm a father, I'm a human being, I'm a British citizen and I'd seen what my country was doing to other people's innocents . . . If that had happened to your daughter wouldn't you want someone somewhere in the world to stand up and say that's not fair? . . . War begat war begat war begat war begat war, blah de blah de blah de blah . . . The good news is that most people in the world want peace. I've been here 24-7 for seven years and I've had the world visiting me here on this pavement. I've had the whole wide world and the best news is that most people are just like you and I, they want to get on with their lives. (Haw 2008)

Brian Haw's protest camp on Parliament Square in the heart of ceremonial London is situated directly opposite the main entrance to the
Houses of Parliament, in clear view of government ministers and other
officials as they arrive and leave each working day. The square is surrounded by the monuments of democracy, including the ornate structures of Parliament and Big Ben, the Treasury building and Westminster
Abbey. Haw conducts his protest alongside statues that materialise
an iconic collective remembrance of a troubled democratic tradition,
including War Prime Minister Winston Churchill, inventor of the
British police force Robert Peel, and public advocate of racial segrega-
tion Jan Christiaan Smuts. Following the death of his prematurely born
son, and moved by the contradiction between the British healthcare system's attempts to save his son's life and the government's participation
in creating an environment of violence and insecurity for children born
in Iraq, Haw set up his protest in Parliament Square on 21 June 2001.
His protest aimed to draw attention to the crisis in Iraq, with its thread-
bare healthcare service resulting from years of international sanctions,
and the risk to life created by exposure to depleted uranium in weapons
used in the first Gulf war and in air strikes through the 1990s.

From its inception therefore, Haw's protest refused a politics of
exception that supports the obliteration of some lives and the protection of others: 'isn't my neighbour's kid as precious as mine? Isn't it sad
that it's exceptional to value someone else's kid as much as mine?' (Haw
cited in Allen 2005). The camp provides a monstrous mirror image of
the grand spectacle of the Houses of Parliament opposite, reflecting the
horrors of war back to the decision-makers controlling that war. The
paraphernalia surrounding the camp includes banners and information
sheets, shocking photographs of the mutilated bodies of dead children
and unborn babies in Afghanistan and Iraq grotesquely distorted by the
effects of depleted uranium, as well as baby clothes and children's toys
covered in fake blood. Over the years of the protest, the display expanded
in size as a result of donations of banners, placards and gifts, eventually
occupying the full length of the square. After the use of local council
orders failed to remove Haw in 2002, Members of Parliament voted for a
piece of legislation, the Serious Organised Crime and Police Act (2005),
reportedly deliberately aimed at ridding the square of Haw (see Farndale
2006). The new law restricted the right to protest without prior police
authorisation within a kilometre of Parliament Square. An initial loop-
hole was identified, allowing Haw to stay as his protest began before the
introduction of the legislation. However, this was later overturned and
the majority of the banners and other paraphernalia were confiscated by
police in 2006, with Haw's protest restricted to a two-metre-square area

of the pavement and no more than twenty supporters at any time. This
diminishment of the protest prompted artist Mark Wallinger to build a
replica of the original for exhibition in the Tate Britain art gallery.[7]

Protest camps are resonant, sensate displays that generate powerful
responses from the public, ranging from direct physical attack, abuse,
determined efforts to ignore as well as active and enthusiastic support.
Haw, for example, was voted the 'most inspiring political figure' of
2007 by viewers of a major British television channel, but has also been
attacked by members of the public on at least three occasions. Protest
camps are communicatively precise: the real and metaphorical engagements of bodies and space performed by protest camps unconceal the
relations of exception between sovereign power and bare life in spectacles in which *life* is both the means and the subject of contest. Rather than
constructing a fiction of a protective order in opposition to a politics of
exception, as the 15 February demonstrations in London arguably did,
protest camps lift the veil on a fiction of order as part of a display that
highlights the violence of power. However, the mimetic effects of protest
camps are also complex and ambivalent. Here, there is a performed
contest between the two opponents, sovereign power and bare life, with
each reflecting back and forth a layered play of connotations associated
with camp critical mimesis – order and disorder, norm and anomie,
authenticity and inauthenticity, situatedness and unfoundedness, resilience and vulnerability, permanence and provisionality. The conflict
between Haw's camp and the Houses of Parliament materialises such a
contest. Haw's grief for his son triggered a display that evokes unknown
numbers of parents' grief for their own lost children in Afghanistan and
Iraq and relays that suffering to the decision-makers implicated in their
deaths. The makeshift camp critically mirrors the permanence of the
Houses of Parliament, and the world of peace lovers arriving on Haw's
pavement who are 'just like you and me' offers an inverted image of the
government's lack of democratic mandate for war.

Haw coined the term 'UN Heart Gallery' to describe his display of
a body and body parts commemorating lives damaged and obliterated
by the State (Haw cited in Millward 2002). The display, as well as the
spectacle of Haw's own permanently unhomed body, haunts the claims
to legitimacy of the democratic institutions surrounding the square and
the monuments to British statehood arranged within it, including those
statues of politicians and military men that evoke their own, untold,
uncommemorated, narratives of atrocity. The camp is an abrasive and
offensive visual and bodied reminder of the interdependency of democratic institutions and the obliteration of children's bodies – up close,
in focus and exposed. For Agamben, 'the troublemaker is precisely the

one who tries to force sovereign power to translate itself into actuality'
(Agamben 1998: 47). The politically motivated attempts to repress Haw
exemplify the success of the protest at bringing about this translation.
However, Haw also actualises sovereign power by displaying its effect on
his own, gradually thinning body, and by means of a grotesque presentation of the damaged bodies of children. By permanently exposing his
own body – placing his body outside protective sites of habitation and
inside a site of such political significance – Haw insists on the right of all
bodies to be included in a rule-bound order and presents evidence of the
crimes of government. His protest thus symbolises what Agamben calls
'modern democracy's strength and, at the same time, its inner contradiction', that is, democracy's valuing of the body as a signifier of rights,
and its production of bare life – that is, life which can be excised from
the rule-bound order, and killed without recompense (*ibid*.: 124).

Interestingly, Agamben locates democracy's contradictory relationship to the body as emerging at precisely the site of Haw's protest, with
the declaration of a principle of *habeas corpus* in Westminster in 1679.
According to this principle, it is only by having a *body to show* – by the
body's presence in the domains of formal law – that it might become a
bearer of rights. Thus, the processes by which bare life becomes a body of
value and significance are performative, and rest on a perpetually uncertain relationship between that body and State power. This uncertainty
provides law with its force and also produces democracy's coalition
with violence: '*Corpus is a two-faced thing, the bearer both of subjection
to sovereign power and of individual liberties* [. . .] the absolute capacity of the subjects' bodies to be killed forms the political body of the
West' (Agamben 1998: 125. Italics in original). Whilst Haw's protest
asserts the right to life of all bodies in all spaces, it also demonstrates
democracy's contradiction – its protection of the rights of some bodies
at the same time as annihilation of others. In its situation at this point
of contradiction, the body of the protestor and sovereign power are
both spectacularised and diminished, asserted and unfounded, but the
symmetry of the contest accounts for its critical limitations as well as
its power. The tired body of the protestor does not go away, the law
returns with evermore punitive powers and the critical mimesis in play
here creates an urgent imperative to interrupt the intensification of
vulnerability and threat. Haw calls power into question by embodying
its violent effect in the place of – and displacing – the spectacle of power
emanating from the surrounding monuments to democracy. The critical
mimetic is imprisoned in a closed cycle of verification, and the power
of the performance is confined by a competition for legitimacy that
reproduces the original contradiction of the body as an entity that has

a right to protection, and that can also be killed. Haw's body is gradually diminished by its exposure to and display of democracy's violence,
and, as such, his protest exemplifies a camp critical mimetic without the
liberating subversion of queer camp.

Haw's camp has been described as an 'eyesore', 'shanty town' and
'a rubbish dump', responsible for 'visual' and 'aural' pollution, with the
latter accusation stimulated by his regular antiwar tirades through a meg-
aphone at politicians in the Houses of Parliament opposite (Taylor 2002;
Elliott and Fitzwilliams 2004). The undesirable presence of this unkempt
spectacle in a major tourist stop in the heart of ceremonial London has
been one of the key rationales given for attempts to remove the protest.
In her anthropological study of dirt and pollution, Mary Douglas argues
that the classification 'dirt' is given to 'matter out of place' (Douglas 1966:
44). According to Douglas, subjects and objects that do not readily fit into
a social and political order are often classified as dirty. She argues that the
social and political order protects itself from that which is classified as
toxic by spatial, psychological and discursive practices of erasure, expulsion, alienation and separation – all of which are evident in the responses
of the authorities and wider public to Haw's protest. Whilst the protest
camp is imprisoned in a cycle of verification that uncritically mirrors
a politics of exception, then, this spectacle of waste and wasted life has
also produced an ongoing disturbance that the British government has
found difficult to ignore. An aura of debris and ruin emanates from the
shocking images and artefacts that are subject to continued exposure to
the elements. This refuser – Agamben's 'troublemaker' – whose presence
attracts the signifier 'waste' – also *uses* waste, debris and ruin to project
his refusal. Waste has a dislocating *signifiance*: it is that which resides
outside of a system of order only as a result of the classifications of that
order – its *use*, therefore, has the effect of diminishing that order. The
camp generates a critique of a system that classifies some lives as surplus
to value, and as dangerous or contaminating. By making use of waste,
the camp reproduces but also critically mimics that system of classifica-
tion. Following Douglas, the assignation of 'dirt' to this protest suggests
that Haw effectively makes trouble in his persistent disturbances of the
appearances of order. The camp's use of waste plays back to the authoritarian order the wasted life obscured by the crisis it controls.

A few days before the confiscation of Haw's banners and placards
in 2006, the British artist Mark Wallinger took hundreds of photographs
of the display. He built a replica of the forty-metre-long protest, including more than 600 props that Haw had accumulated, as an installation
in the Tate Britain called *State Britain*, winning the prestigious Turner
Prize for British visual art in 2007. A line across the floor of the gallery

space represented the boundaries of the 'no protest zone' surrounding the Houses of Parliament, and as some of the exhibit was inside the zone and therefore technically illegal, the installation powerfully drew attention to the suppression of Haw's right to protest. Wallinger focused on creating an authentic replica of the display, reproducing the ruin and decay of objects that had been exposed to the environment for so many years. Interestingly, the critical reception of the installation was preoccupied with the degree to which it successfully simulated the decay of the original, testifying to the significance of the ruin and dirt of the protest. Some reviewers noted Wallinger's lack of success in achieving an authentic replication, calling it a 'deodorised protest' (Cohen 2007), that lacked the 'rawness and energy' of the original (Teeman 2007), and was not 'messy enough . . . the whole thing looks too clean' (Orr 2007). Despite the fact that the artefacts had been subjected to a process of ruination by the artist at the cost of £90,000, involving a team of fifteen people, and even recreated an aroma of decomposition, the installation had the effect of sanitising the threat of the original. The aestheticisation of Wallinger's replication in the too clean spaces of the art gallery lacked the camp's materialisation of ruin and debris and it was therefore also viewed as lacking the dissensual resonances of the original.

As such, Wallinger's artwork can be most accurately interpreted as a commemoration of the right to protest rather than a continuation of the protest in another form. Whilst it is important to note that it was not Wallinger's intention to continue Haw's protest, this does raise a question about the kinds of replication that might be produced by artists as part of critically mimetic protest performances. Haw's protest camp and Wallinger's artwork both became imprisoned by a closed cycle of verification relating to questions of legitimacy and authenticity, reflecting the contradictions of bodies and space of a troubled democratic tradition. This point facilitates the introduction of the final example, *This is Camp X-Ray*, an arts installation that critically mirrored the performances of sovereign power and that, through queering the replication, produced a more disruptive camp critical mimetic.

Estranging sights/sites: *This is Camp X-Ray*, UHC Collective (2003)

Tricksters or fakes, assistants or 'toons, they are the exemplars of the coming community. (Agamben 1993: 11)

This is Camp X-Ray was an operational, life-size replica of the US internment camp in Guantánamo Bay built on wasteland in central Manchester (UK). The replica camp remained in place for ten days during October 2003, with the US national anthem played once a day and the Muslim call to prayer five times a day. Nine volunteers, one for each of the nine British prisoners believed to be detained in Guantánamo at the time, were locked up for nine days and nights, and followed the routine of the camp as closely as possible, spending hours with their hands tied behind their backs and heads covered, and undergoing simulated interrogations. The project drew attention to the injustices of internment without recourse to legal protection for prisoners of war, and the case of a local resident, Jamal Udeen al-Harath, who, at the time of the performance, had spent more than two years in Guantánamo Bay and was eventually released without charge. *This is Camp X-Ray* facilitated a ghostly emergence of a state of exception in a humdrum, routine environment, directly associating the everyday spaces of democracy with violence of war in far-off places. The replica camp disturbed the sensible fabric of common experience, producing a sense of dislocation and unsettlement in passers-by. Spectators described a haunting sense of recognition that accompanied their encounters with the camp: 'you think, what's happening to those people?'; 'it's a visual thing, you can't ignore it, a concentration camp in the middle of the city' (Mahoney 2004).

The critical mimetic here was distinct in two ways from Haw's protest camp. Firstly, to draw on Marc Augé's notion, its situation on the 'non-place' of wasteland in an inner city without apparent history or identity, daily traversed without attracting particular notice, was significant (see Augé 1995). Secondly, as a replication of the original camp, the power of which relied to a certain extent on the 'authenticity' of the copy, it was nonetheless decidedly *fake*. Haw's camp stages a competition of legitimacy with its original, the Houses of Parliament opposite, whereas the simulated replica camp *queered* the original. In a city where night-time terror raids were occurring on a monthly basis, and with growing public fears of 'extremist' elements inside the local Muslim community, *This is Camp X-Ray* critically queered a spectacle of exception in a non-place of a local community intimately, but often invisibly, implicated in the war on terror. Here, an 'illegal combatant' became a neighbour with a name, identity, history and loved ones who also frequent this space. In addition, by making *use* of this non-place – a piece of wasteland in an inner city – the performance consciously and unconsciously commemorated untold histories of waste and wasted life of significance to this particular postindustrial landscape.

UHC Collective are committed to art activism that highlights the appropriation of public space by corporate bodies across the city: 'as global capital continues its unassailed appropriation of all public space, the role of the artist should be to identify and test the boundaries of space' (Redman 2008: 41).[8] An exploration of the history of the waste-land on which *This is Camp X-Ray* was situated is useful here – it pro-vides an opportunity to extend the installation's critical interrogation of space and also highlights the broader significance of waste to under-standing critical performance's engagements with space. Until shortly before the installation of the replica camp, the wasteland was fenced off by the local authority, earmarked for leasing to corporate developers. Local residents had removed the fences, frustrated by the way they pre-vented free movement across what was formerly experienced as public space. In terms of its contemporary history, the area surrounding the installation is associated with cheap housing for working-class com-munities, regenerated through the 1990s by means of public–private partnerships that brought investment to areas of the city experiencing extraordinary levels of deprivation following the industrial slump of the 1970s. Gentrification of the area stimulated the growth of a profitable property market; however, many former residents were priced out of the area, a narrative of exclusion resulting from corporate occupation of space familiar across public space globally. Going further back in time, the area surrounding the wasteland originally became heavily populated during the prosperous period of the industrial revolution, when the name 'Manchester' was 'a household word wherever upon the face of the earth, there is anything like commercial civilisation' (Tomlinson 1887, cited in Makepeace 1995). To offer further examples of the repeated association of waste and wasted life with this space, the wasteland on which the replica camp was installed was opposite what was once a workhouse providing housing and relief for more than 300 unproduc-tive citizens of nineteenth-century Manchester, and later converted into a public washhouse.

Taken together, the replica camp, the politics of space in the con-temporary city and the historical narrative of this specific site repeatedly display waste and wasted life as it appears and disappears across histori-cal time and geographical space. The poetics of exception materialised by *This is Camp X-Ray* and its evocation of bare life mimetically reproduced a politics of exception evident in the history of this particular space. The installation highlighted an injustice of global prominence by making it visible in a local site that was itself once of global significance because of its connection to industrial capitalism. Fences of an internment camp thousands of miles away, confining neighbours now designated as 'enemies of democracy', replaced the fences around a public space enclosed for privatisation and profit. The simulation of bodies stripped of rights in Guantánamo Bay echoed the separation of the unproductive mad and poor from productive workers performed by the nineteenth-century workhouse and the removal of 'workless' classes of twenty-first-century Manchester performed by a corporate-led regeneration of public housing. This artwork both consciously and unconsciously interrogated the compartmentalisation and enclosure of space that separate the lives of a productive, profitable community from unsavoury others. Its deter-mined occupation of a piece of wasteland was of critical importance to its poetics: in revaluing wasted space, the replica camp also evoked a history of waste and wasted life, and in my commemoration of this history I am laying out the grounds for a politics of performance that has a critical significance which I hope extends beyond the contingent time and space of this particular artwork. Interestingly, the use of space here generated responses from wider publics that, in their evocation of waste, suggest that the artwork was positively disruptive: local and national reporting focused on whether the project represented a justifiable *use* of resources (it was partly publicly funded), with one politician calling it 'an outrageous *waste* of money' (A. Taylor 2003. My italics).

Waste is 'matter out of place', constantly produced but without use value in a hierarchical and exclusive stratification of human activity as productive and unproductive, citizen and bare life, hence its classifica-tion as 'waste' – dangerous, polluting, infectious, making its enforced exclusion necessary. *This is Camp X-Ray* was termed a 'waste' of money and was situated on a wasteland historically associated with the segrega-tion of human life according to its use value within a capitalist economy. It provided those bodies classified as threatening and useless, and excised from the appearances of norm and order, a tangible presence in that space. Like Haw's protest camp, and the vacuum cleaner who cleans up after capitalism, waste is utilised in this performance in a way that suggests a shift in the practice of a critical politics of performance, away from a preoccupation with radically transforming society, and towards engaging with the challenge of life's value and sustainability in a violent and inequitable world. Protest camps and queer camp mobilise an emptying of – a double negation of – alienating and exclusive systems of value, just as the *signifiance* of waste in the practice of these perform-ances does. Protest camps are provisional structures existing outside the normal order, housing bodies that have rejected hierarchical and exclu-sive stratifications of human activity as 'productive' or 'unproductive' and queer camp has an insistent inauthenticity that empties signifying regimes of their appropriating, proper meanings.

That *This is Camp X-Ray* was a fake was therefore important to its camp critical mimesis, as it queered the original and inflected the frames by which the artwork was made and perceived with the critical and affective force of waste and wasted life. The strong responses provoked by the installation were a result of the success of this simulation which, in being fake, practises a non-economy of waste, in both its symbolic and its spatial practices. Again, this is distinct from how Haw's camp stirs up trouble: he *stands in for waste* – for bodies deemed valueless and obliterable, and the terrible annihilation of these bodies is slowly materialised on his own thinning body and ruined display. The camp critical mimetic of *This is Camp X-Ray* exhibits a more successful coalition of the resilient inauthenticity of queer camp and the situated unfoundedness of the protest camp: here the artwork rather than the body stands in for waste. *This is Camp X-Ray* exposes democratic order's complicity with violence without invoking that violence – the material presence of the artwork, and its evocation of wasted life – is the source of critical disruption here. Agamben states that political action 'is that which severs the nexus between violence and law', leading to critical and creative praxis as 'pure means', that is, as releasing potential without appropriating or predetermined ends in mind (Agamben 2005: 88). Following Agamben, the queer, replica camp plays with law and order in a way that liberates them from their violent ends and generates a sense of their potential uses, outside a securing of the body in a relation of exception. The *use* of waste as part of a performance proscribed by some as wasteful is suggestive of the critical potential that emanates from engaging with waste. This protest performance challenged the making and unmaking of bodies and worlds in the normative realm – those classificatory systems that label spaces, identities, bodies as useful or useless – and as such it also redefines notions of use, and the usefulness of performance.

Agamben's 'tricksters and fakes', the 'exemplars of the coming community', denote a community of singularities that exhibit 'an absolutely unrepresentable community . . . the coming to itself of each singularity, its being whatever – in other words, such that it is' (Agamben 1993: 25). The trickster and fake reject a world of identities, properties, certain directions, predetermined ends and conditions of belonging and being. Echoing the discussion of the power of refusal discussed above – here a 'useful-creative doing against' the negations of an alienating world – opens up the space for the political. As part of its camp critical mimesis – in its fakery of a state of exception – *This is Camp X-Ray* configures just such a reconciliation of potentiality and lack, and projects a politics of performance that is not productive or transformative but *possible*. And thus, there is abundance in the contingent, uncertain times and spaces that waste and wasted life inhabit.

Waste is the product of a system of classification that claims life as useful and productive according to a narrowly defined remit, and performance can be used to reproduce these classifications. However, performance can also destabilise such classifications, and it is itself vacant until put to use. This discussion is taken up further in the following chapter, which explores performances that make explicit claims about their usefulness and that, in their critical encounters with the proliferating uncertainties of a war on terror, materialise a critical mimesis that is profoundly conservative.

Notes

1   Sadly, during the final stages of preparing this book for publication, and almost ten years from beginning his protest in Parliament Square, Brian Haw passed away. The present tense in which the section pertaining to Haw was originally written has been left untouched.

2   The phrase 'astonishing street scenes' is taken from a report in the British newspaper the *Daily Mirror* which encouraged its readers to be part of 'the biggest global appeal for peace in history' (Smith 2003).

3   Wikipedia entries on the day draw on a number of official and unofficial sources and have been used in the estimates given here. For more information go to: en.wikipedia.org/wiki/February_15,_2003_anti-war_protest [accessed 1 August 2010]. The protest on 15 February 2003 was the largest of a series of antiwar demonstrations taking place during February, March and April 2003.

4   For more information, go to www.karmarama.com/karmaprojects/ [accessed 15 August 2010].

5   For other examples of nude antiwar protests see Koch (2003) and Bare Witness – 'using the power and beauty of our bodies to send out a message of peace' – www.barewitness.org [accessed 1 August 2010].

6   For more information go to www.thevacuumcleaner.co.uk [accessed 1 August 2010].

7   For more information about Brian Haw go to his website – www.parliament-square.org.uk/ [accessed 1 August 2010].

8   For more information go to the UHC Collective website – www.uhc.org.uk [accessed 1 August 2010].

6

Performance, counterterrorism and community: cops, neighbours, lovers and double agents

This cycle of suspicion and discord must end. I've come here to Cairo to seek a new beginning between the United States and Muslims around the world, one based on mutual interest and mutual respect . . . I am convinced that in order to move forward, we must say openly to each other the things we hold in our hearts, and that too often are said only behind closed doors. There must be a sustained effort to listen to each other, to learn from each other, to respect one another, and to seek common ground. As the Holy Qur'an tells us, 'be conscious of God and speak always the truth'. (US President Barack Obama [2009])

In a historic speech given at the University of Cairo in 2009, the recently inaugurated President of the United States announced a new era of dialogue and reciprocity between his country and 'Muslims around the world'. His openness to dialogue and relationship echoed the UK Prime Minister's announcements in the period following his appointment as Prime Minister two years earlier. Here, Prime Minister Gordon Brown referred to a 'cold war' against Islamic extremism fought via new security measures, but also by means of the soft power of a 'cultural effort' devoted to winning the 'hearts and minds' of Muslim people at home and abroad (Jones 2007). The threat to the UK from international terrorism at this time (and current as I am writing this in October 2010) was officially classified as 'severe', with a terrorist attack 'highly likely'. In a rare public address in 2007, the head of MI5, the UK's security service, stated that there were at least 2000 people involved in terrorist-related activity in the country, and that a greater effort was needed to protect young people vulnerable to recruitment to extremist causes (Evans 2007). An affirmation of counterterrorism agencies' embracing of a *cultural* effort to address these concerns came with the UK counterterrorism strategy, revised following the suicide attacks in London in 2005 carried out by four young British Muslim men, and relaunched in 2009. This strategy included an unprecedented public endorsement of theatre as 'best practice' in counterterrorism, with the official strategy document noting that its successful delivery in one region had involved theatre projects in schools and colleges (HM Government 2009: 136). Here, I focus on an extraordinary series of theatre projects supported by counterterrorism funding, and aiming to win the hearts and minds of Muslim communities. As part of this, particular attention is paid to the challenges of maintaining an open dialogue during a time of ongoing security concerns, and to investigating the kinds of reciprocity on offer as part of this cultural effort.

These performances can be defined as examples of 'applied performance', a term that makes claims about the uses and usefulness of performance, and denotes a diverse tradition of theatre practice that tends to take place outside mainstream theatre, explores issues directly concerning localities of practice and often involves interactive or participatory forms of engagement. Importantly, claims of usefulness do not refer to a secure set of ideas about what performance is or what it does – performance is 'applied' within a range of communities and contexts, and to address a variety of concerns. James Thompson has questioned simplistic proclamations of the social and political *effect* of applied performance and argued for the development of scholarship and practice exploring the 'difficultness of affect' (Thompson 2009: 10). He proposes a critical politics of applied performance based on an 'affective/affectionate' practice embedded in experiences of joy, beauty and celebration, drawing on Rancière's work to explore how performance disturbs and extends the sensate and sensible worlds of its participants (*ibid.*: 189). The turn to performance by counterterrorism agencies has also, in part, been inspired by performance's affective/affectionate capacities, and the theatre projects they have supported provide an opportunity to further examine the politics and aesthetics of applied performance's affective/affectionate and reciprocal engagements. Here performance is 'applied' to engage communities in explorations of a shared, pressing concern and as part of a security drive that might be perceived as directly challenging the political aspirations of critical performance practice.

Community-based counterterrorism initiatives in the UK have targeted neighbourhoods designated by security services as potential hotspots of 'terrorist' activity, specifically areas with high concentrations of Muslim populations. Leaving aside, for the moment, the damage caused by such blanket conceptualisations of the people that live in these areas as dangerous and threatening, the evidence base for this move has been powerfully questioned.[1] Of course, the evidence base for a threat that has not yet manifested itself in a violent attack will always be partial, fragmentary and open to interpretation – hence the turn to 'institutionalising imagination' by security services in the US following the 9/11 attacks, in order to imagine scenarios of attack and better prepare for their prevention (Kean *et al.* 2004: 344). Counterterrorism's embracing of a cultural effort is a particularly fitting response to such tangible, powerfully felt and unknowable threats. Cultural practices provide a means by which a preventative response might be imagined and enacted without waiting for the evidence of an attack. In addition, cultural practices such as performance provide direct access to an affective and imaginative realm in which dialogue and preventative action might take place without the need to securely identify or apprehend the threatening other. The problem here is that these performances also risk an uncritical participation in an affect economy of a war on terror that attaches threat to all those belonging to, and perceived as belonging to, the 'Muslim communities'.

This returns the book to its starting point: Brecht's *The Exception and the Rule*, in which the insecurities caused by a violent and inequitable system came to be imagined and felt as a threat posed by the coolie. One might say that the turn to performance by security agencies in the UK substitutes for the *absence* of evidence of a *really existing* threat, and negotiates the anxiety of the unknown that is conjured by this absence. This evokes Taussig's comment about the ways in which colonial powers in early twentieth-century Colombia survived an encounter with the unknown by constructing a 'fiction of the real':

> Little makes sense. Little can be pinned down. Only the Indian in the stocks, being watched . . . If terror thrives on the production of epistemic murk and metamorphosis, it nevertheless requires the hermeneutic violence that creates feeble fictions in the guise of realism, objectivity, and the like, flattening contradiction and systematising chaos. (Taussig 1987: 132)

Taussig's 'epistemic murk' invites a provocative reading of the performances presented in this chapter as identifying and capturing Muslim communities as a threatening signifier that *stands in* for the uncertainties which configure our contemporary global context. The neighbours 'pinned down' by these attempts to script uncertainty are the living embodiments of the UK's postcolonial present: second- and third-generation children of immigrants from formerly colonised countries, making up the largest minority population and second largest religious denomination in the UK. How is this epistemic murk negotiated by the affective/affectionate performances commissioned to engage with these unknown, not-yet, perhaps-soon-to-be threatening subjects? Following the global and national focus of performances documented in previous chapters, here I explore performances that have sought direct engagements with local communities. These performances encounter the damaging and distorting impact of the war on terror on everyday relationships between neighbours in culturally diverse communities of the UK. Whilst some of these plays have performed nationally, I particularly explore performances in the postindustrial north of England, an area formerly of international significance as the centre of the industrial revolution, now struggling to negotiate the impact of a global conflict that has placed communities, and the people who work closely with them, under extraordinary pressure.

As part of these projects, artists have drawn on an ethic of care configured by a shared concern for crisis, and have sought reciprocal relationships with targeted communities in order to bring a discussion of local concerns into dialogue with a global counterterrorism agenda. The question remains though: how possible is it for artists to sustain a critical perspective when participating so directly in the organised control of mimesis of a war on terror, and its construction of certain communities as potentially threatening? The discussion below explores the ways in which such direct participations also provide opportunities for critical mimesis in performance. One way each of the plays made use of these opportunities was by scripting a drama of love – where the threatening object is also a loved person and a neighbour, with a complex subjectivity, and a valued member of the community. These performances dramatised the *difficultness* of encounters with neighbours as part of affective/affectionate practices constituted by *love* and *law*, and they demonstrate a politics of performance that is hopeful, critical and profoundly conservative. The theoretical framework supporting the development of this argument draws on discussions of love offered by Jacques Lacan, Giorgio Agamben and Terry Eagleton. Taken together, these thinkers provide a combined and at times conflicting understanding of love that is particularly useful for exploring the complex relationship between love and performance, and applied performance as an affective/affectionate practice.

Three of the four plays discussed here represent politically left traditions of performance, and their partnership with what some might see as
a right-wing security agenda reflects the complexities of performance's
politics during a time of terror. *Not in my Name* (2007–) is a verbatim
play produced by Theatre Veritae, a company committed to engaging
audiences in meaningful dialogues outside traditional theatre spaces.
The play, originally conceived for performance by young people, was
researched and written by Alice Bartlett and produced in partnership
with the Lancashire Constabulary, with the first production hosted by
Burnley Youth Theatre. It explores the consequences of a suicide attack
in an unnamed town carried out by a local young Muslim man, and
has toured to schools, colleges and community venues across the north
of England. *One extreme to the Other* (2007–) was written by Mike
Harris and produced by GW Theatre, a theatre company that specialises
in performances for young people which engage with pressing social
issues. It explores both far-right and Islamic extremism, has toured to
schools, colleges and community venues nationally, and features as an
example of 'best practice' in official counterterrorism documentation
(HM Government 2008: 38–9). Similarly hailed as an example of best
practice in counterterrorism and touring nationally, *Hearts and Minds*
(2007) was produced by Khayaal Theatre, a company that draws on
Muslim world literature and an Islamic ethos to develop theatre for
professional, heritage and education contexts. *Hearts and Minds* fuses
devised performance and Islamic storytelling, and as such it represents
an unusual contribution to applied performance, which has tended to be
configured by community theatre traditions, secular in orientation. The
final performance discussed here tackles the issue of terrorism from a different perspective – *Undercover* (2007) was devised by a group of young
Muslim women as part of a practical research project in an academic
context. It drew on the participatory ethos of applied performance, and
extended an invitation to a group of young Muslim women to engage in
a process of devising and performing their own play to a local audience.

If Taussig's 'fiction of the real' offers a provocation to consider
applied performance as a counterterrorist operative, working as part
of security agendas that pin down threat, then the title of the fourth
play here suggests an alternative invitation. Here, performance works
'undercover', as a double agent, critically engaging with and subverting
the mimetic processes of a war on terror. Practitioners of applied performance are familiar with working inside institutions and discursive
regimes that they do not necessarily support, drawing on the capacities of performance to 'rub up against and reveal the performative in
the setting, complementing or undermining it, challenging or further

heightening it' (Thompson and Schechner 2004: 13). This is a murky
territory, where it is often difficult to identify the distinction between
counterterrorist and double agent. The following section explores the
tension between these figures in the reciprocal, affectionate gestures of
applied performance, and lays out the theoretical terrain for a detailed
analysis of the performances themselves.

Reciprocity and imposture in affective/ affectionate practices of applied performance

In his imitation
No third thing rises out of him and the other
Somehow consisting of both, in which supposedly
One heart beats and
One brain thinks. Himself all there
The demonstrator stands and gives us
The stranger next door. (Extract from 'On Everyday Theatre', Brecht [1987:
178])

Writing shortly after the 9/11 attacks, Susan Buck-Morss proposed a
critical dialogue with political Islam that recognises our shared residence
in and responsibility for a crisis-ridden global context: 'the slow and
painful task of a radically open communication that does not presume
that we already know where we stand' (Buck-Morss 2003: 6). The extent
to which the invitation to dialogue configured by community-based
counterterrorism in the UK provided an opportunity to engage in 'radically open communication' is questionable; indeed, the question of *who*
to engage in dialogue was a controversial aspect of the delivery of the
strategy. Arun Kundnani argues that whilst the turn to soft power of cultural influence carefully avoided the denigration of Islam as a religion,
it has performed an attack on 'political Islam', with those having chosen
the wrong kind of politics, that is, politics that diverge from a liberal
world-view, excluded from the conversation (Kundnani 2008: 43). The
UK government specifies that organisations involved in community
initiatives should 'only work with those groups who uphold our shared
values of tolerance, respect and equality and who reject or condemn
violent extremism' (HM Government 2008: 14). The recourse made here
to vague notions of 'shared values' problematically erases any acknowledgement of State-led violence and also risks the exclusion of those who
represent *any* political opinion that diverges from the government's

views. It is important to emphasise here that the signifier 'Muslim communities' itself closes down the terms of conversation, in that it privileges religion over other markers of identity and homogenises an extremely diverse set of communities, beliefs and practices. For many commentators, these generalisations fail to recognise the heterogeneity of political Islam that has successfully diverted many young people from violent extremism by offering varied and meaningful opportunities for active and critical citizenship (see for example Mandaville 2007: 348; Lewis 2007: 144–6).

For artists involved in 'reciprocal' encounters with 'Muslim communities', the dilemma might be summarised as something like this: the war on terror has mobilised a mimetic process wherein 'Muslim communities' are deemed threatening, and excluded from dialogue if they do not conform to a deceptive, crisis-ridden political order. That is, if they do not sign up to the uncertain 'shared values' promoted by a government that has been complicit in terrible acts of violence against communities in other countries, including those with a high proportion of practising Muslims, both historically and contemporaneously. Here, an imperative to engage in reciprocal dialogue is imposed on specific communities and neighbourhoods in a way that separates those who are like 'us' (at least, as we would like to be seen) from others who, in various ways, draw attention to our complicity with violence and inequity. Žižek offers a scathing critique of the limits of such liberal forms of tolerance thus: 'the Other is just fine, but only insofar as his presence is not intrusive, insofar as this Other is not really other' (Žižek 2008: 35). There is a pressing need to conceptualise and practise kinds of dialogue and relationship with neighbours that, rather than containing and excluding, *use* the uncertainties of our contemporary global context and the undecidability of the neighbour as a common ground for encounter. To some extent, applied performance provides such a terrain – for example, an affective/affectionate model of applied performance is a response to such an imperative, as 'affect' signifies an unsettling of processes of identification and increased openness to reciprocal encounter. However, the turn to performance by counterterrorism agencies, characterised by a rhetoric of reciprocity, the imposition of conditions on encounter, and acceptance of certain kinds of critical and affective responses to the neglect of others, is troubling. Here, an affectionate/affective and reciprocal practice of performance is also an *imposture*, and an examination of performance as imposture might therefore provide critical grounds for the investigation of these performances.

Helen Nicholson's notion of the 'gift of theatre' provides an important starting point here. She argues that participatory, embodied

practices of performance in community settings have the potential
to dislodge 'fixed and uneven boundaries of "self" and "other"', and
produce open-ended, reciprocal relationships that support participants'
identifications with a range of subject positions (Nicholson 2005: 24).
However, she also highlights the ambivalence of such encounters,
drawing on anthropologist Marcel Mauss' work to argue that the 'gift
of theatre' imposes an obligation on the receiver which reflects the
self-interest of the giver and, as such, is both 'a present and a poison'
(*ibid.*: 160–1). Nicholson proposes a practice of applied performance
that moves from the homogeneity of exchange to 'the heterogeneity
of generosity, in which the gift becomes associated with shifting roles,
spontaneity, desire, loss and risk', and includes an interrogation of the
values of the giver (*ibid.*: 163). The reciprocity proposed here can be
perceived as a provocation to theatre practitioners to place uncertainty
at the centre of their encounters with participants. However, in the
context of counterterrorism – and the wider security concerns that they
are symptomatic of – the challenges of maintaining such uncertain,
open-ended encounters are multiple and substantial. Counterterrorism
initiatives try to prevent and control loss, stage-manage crisis and script
uncertainty, not evoke it. The insecurities of a time of terror make it very
difficult to maintain an open, exposed stance in relation to the other.
Arguably, such stances also risk further exposing the subjects pinned
down by these attempts to script uncertainty to wounding excisions
within a damaging public sphere that has already constructed them as
threatening and undecidable. A question that might usefully be asked
here is: how can performance offer an affective/affectionate, reciprocal
encounter, regulate participants' exposure to an alienating, punitive
public sphere and also make a critical intervention?

Part of the problem and the opportunity here is that a caring, affectionate, reciprocal encounter evokes feelings of loss, alienation, betrayal,
a sense of being overwhelmed, deceived and intensely envious – as well
as provides the deeply felt comfort of love, compassion and intimacy
and, perhaps, an experience of self as of unconditional value in the here
and now. To love is to experience estrangement and insecurity, intimacy
and contact with the world, and thus 'to know others most intimately is
in a sense to encounter them as strangers' (Eagleton 2009: 323). Here, I
understand love as providing encounters with an interchangeable series
of uncertain figures – unbearable, alien, threatening, vivifying, beautiful
and loveable. If the 'political' denotes a terrain in which we negotiate
our relationships with strangers and neighbours, then affectionate/
affective and reciprocal performance practices provide a critical but also
troubling resource in a moment of crisis in which neighbours appear as

evermore threatening and undecidable. Love, then, adds a new dimension to understanding critical mimesis in performance. To investigate the complexities of the relationship between love and performance, it is useful to turn again to Jacques Lacan, who introduces notions of imposture, *non*-reciprocity and waste as provocative and significant features of affectionate and reciprocal engagements with the world.

For Lacan, in entering the intersubjective field of encounter, the subject submits to the anonymity and impersonality of the symbolic world, through which she attains an uncertain sense of self as a discrete entity. Here, affectionate and reciprocal encounters are far from comfortable, and reproduce and recycle a *lack* of meaning in any encounter. When Lacan asked, in a seminar called 'In you more than you', '*how can we be sure that we are not imposters?*', he was proposing that we *cannot* be sure, and that we need to learn how to negotiate the imposturous, estranged and estranging experiences of self and world more critically and reflexively (Lacan 1977: 263. Italics in original). In the same seminar, Lacan explores love as an imposture in which the subject presents 'a specular mirage' of an ideal self (*ibid.*: 268). The self presented as a loveable, desirable object is a detached and fluid figure perpetually edged with uncanny, leaky, destabilising sensations. In presenting ourselves as loveable we thus also appear to ourselves as an unknowable, anamorphic stain in the field of encounter, the *objet petit a*. For Lacan, a sensation of self as a blurred, indiscrete stain signals the tangible presence of those experiences of life and world that are left out and excised from the capture and presentation of an ideal, discrete self, and also mobilise desire. Hence, a gesture of love stimulates a circulation of ideal effects and discomforting affects, described by Lacan in the following, characteristically obscure terms: '*I love you, but, because inexplicably I love in you something more than you – the* objet petit a *– I mutilate you . . . I give myself to you . . . but this gift of my person . . . Oh, mystery! Is changed inexplicably into a gift of shit*' (*ibid.* Italics in original).

Despite the obscurity of this statement, there are important echoes of Nicholson's notion of theatre as a gift here. As part of an affective/affectionate, reciprocal practice of performance we experience ourselves as meaningful and sensible, at the same time as unsure about the terms of our encounter. Our offers of performance are gifts of shit that replay the alienating uncertainties of an inequitable world, and potentially expose those engaged in such encounters to their own diminishment and unfoundedness in that world. As a practitioner and a researcher who has often worked on theatre projects generated by concerns to support young people living in difficult circumstances, and that at the same time are powerless in the face of the social and economic inequities that cause those young people damage, I find this notion of performance as loving, imposturous, estranging and toxic very resonant. Despite the deliberate provocation posed here, I also want to suggest that such impostures also configure hopeful and critical responses to a time of terror, precisely because they are situated at this point of lack of meaning. It is the way in which performance makes use of the decay of sense evoked by a gesture of love that mobilises a critical and hopeful politics of performance. Importantly, the imposture of the offer contains a gift of shit, but because of this it also generates a playful, improper domain in which to encounter self and world that might be both protective and vivifying.

What might this mean for performances that seek to engage young Muslim people in supposed hotspots of terrorist activity? Arguably, the imposture – the play – stands in for uncertainty and acts as a double agent, replaying, regulating and diverting its damaging effects. Performances also generate symbolic fictions of idealised, affectionate encounters that secure the subject, and offer a more habitable realm in which to engage with uncertainty than the alienating impostures of the counterterrorism agenda. Here, the imposture of performance 'makes strange' the counterterrorism agenda and its damaging connotations, which are recycled as lacking in meaning. The impostures of performance provide somewhere for the young person to hide, generate opportunities to understand the wider counterterrorism agenda as imposturous, and they also potentially signal a transfer of the powers of imposture to those subjects at the centre of the performance. A performance puts its own imposture on display, and in refusing to identify its subjects in proper, fixed and certain terms, power over the mimetic process is dispersed across the figures that are exposed to its decaying and estranging effects. Such combinations of symbolic fictions and circulating, sensate lack are demonstrated in the coalitions of law and love dramatised in the plays discussed below. The plays combine symbolic fictions of religious faith, brotherly love and community-friendly policing, with a circulating array of disruptive, sensate part-objects – hearts, minds, flags, excerpts from the Qur'an, broken speech, missing brothers, fragments of poetry, hijabs and hurriedly consumed chocolate – that threaten to destabilise but also test the strength of and extend these fictions.

The importance of the realm of symbolic fictions in performances of love should be stressed here and this can be explored by making reference to Agamben's discussions of love. He offers a notion of love as a lack of propertied condition – as an experience of self and other that resists the traps of identification and appropriation. For Agamben, the lover loves another being 'such as it is' rather than for a particular property or condition of personhood. Here, love opens up the possibility of

affective and reciprocal encounters that are profoundly social and exist
without propriety or coercive contractual obligations. However:

> What the State cannot tolerate in any way . . . is that the singularities form a
> community without affirming an identity, that humans co-belong without
> any representable condition of belonging . . . Wherever these singularities
> peacefully demonstrate their being in common there will be a Tiananmen,
> and, sooner or later, the tanks will appear. (Agamben 1993: 86–7)

My concern with this notion of unconditional love in the context of the
gift of a counterterrorism play, and at a historical juncture configured
by crisis, is that it leaves the subject frighteningly exposed to an alienating world. What I am proposing, through a focus on performance as
imposture, is a less radical and more conservative investiture of unconditional love. During the war on terror, the discourses and practices
of counterterrorism duly appeared in communities across Britain: not
Tiananmen's tanks, but a multiplication of anxious gazes, intensifying
fears of neighbours, unknowable threats and acts of neighbourly violence. The previous chapter explored how the trickster – the fakery of
performance – stood in for and regulated the damage of an alienating
public sphere. Here, the plays perform the same trick.

Lacan refers to the 'non-reciprocity and the twist in the return' of
an intersubjective encounter (Lacan 1977: 215). So, for example, when
I hear myself speaking to you, I become both detached from a sense of
myself and experience myself as exposed and abject. In hearing your
reply, I discover our common abjection and lack of foundedness, and
the *moving* as well as intimate grounds of our relationship. This opaque
point of double lack is identified by Peggy Phelan as relevant to performance's politics: 'the point is not so much to "find" the Other, but
rather to play the drama in such a way that the stand-ins come to reveal
that *the kernel of the drama of the Other is that the Other is always a
stand-in*' (Phelan 1997: 33. Italics in original). What is thus required by
critical mimesis in an age of uncertainty is a *competing imposture*, one
that is divorced from violence and provides the protection of a loving
contract with a neighbour without regard for his condition of being –
for whether he is known, like 'us', understandable, or willing to engage
in reciprocal encounters. The plays provide competing impostures that
present a range of stand-ins in response to sovereign power's calling
forth and capture of bodies in a state of exception. To extend Phelan's
point cited above, during times of crisis it is not just the dramatisation
of the Other as a stand-in that provides a site of critical agency. There
is also an imperative to provoke a competition between stand-ins, and

it is by means of this provocation that a more equitable order might be impostured. The plays here each materialise a distinct imposture in this regard, and the differences between them provide the focus of the discussion that follows.

Freud famously expressed bewilderment at the religious command 'love thy neighbour as thyself' (Freud 2004: 57–8). The latter might immediately be thought of as a competing imposture of relevance here, in its attempt to secure neighbourly relations at a meeting point of love and law. Freud, however, thought that this demand was impossible to meet, and was best understood as a means of negotiating the inevitable hostilities between human beings inhabiting the same world by establishing exclusive distinctions between neighbours and enemies. The command 'love thy neighbour as thyself' legitimises the removal of monstrous neighbours whilst instituting a protective realm for loved ones. In an essay called 'Fear thy Neighbour as Thyself!', Žižek similarly explores the impossibility of loving a neighbour. For him, the 'neighbour' is the one whose proximity is too much to bear, who presents us with the ultimate political dilemma of what to do about an undecidable, overwhelmingly present other. We need 'protective, symbolic walls' to keep neighbours at a distance and secure the survival of self and other (Žižek 2008: 48–9). Might other kinds of coalitions between love and law provide a better imposture – more amiable symbolic walls – than the Judaeo-Christian injunction to 'love thy neighbour'? A turn to Eagleton's discussion of the representation of faith, hope and solidarity in literature provides a way forward here. Each of these practices of love posits a lawful realm in which the threat of the other, their abjection, undecidability and impersonality, coexists with an open, equitable and mutual commitment to a practice of love. These forms of love constitute symbolic fictions that creatively negotiate the uncertainties of the world, and provide habitable realms for relationship and encounter with undecidable neighbours. It is worth quoting Eagleton at length here:

> Only on this 'inhuman' foundation can a durable human community be constructed . . . allowing ourselves to be mirrored in the very alienness, unrelatedness or deathly singularity of the other. To love another in her singularity is to love her in herself; but since what is most constitutive of the other is his or her sheer humanity, that void or vanishing-point where all differences dissolve, this love has a properly impersonal dimension which is why we can speak of charity as a law. (Eagleton 2009: 272)

This site of love and law is played out differently in the specific aesthetics and politics of the plays explored below. The conservative impulses of the plays are important, because here the subjects – young Muslim men

and women in particular – need to be protected from, rather than apprehended or transformed by, the impostures of a counterterrorism agenda
that calls forth their bodies as threatening objects. As such, these plays
do not claim anything about the usefulness of performance for bringing
about or preventing a set of outcomes – instead, they express concern
for the impact of a changing world on young people at risk. They do not
aim to make communities better or transform the world, rather, they
materialise a protective domain in which life might be preserved and
become more possible in the here and now.

Not in my Name: Theatre Veritae and policing community

Most importantly, this play is about vulnerability and in the police force
we deal with vulnerability from top to bottom . . . All of our communities
are vulnerable, and we are all vulnerable. (Senior policeman, Lancashire
Constabulary, April 2009)

A senior policeman at a performance of *Not in my Name* in a community centre in Lancashire introduced the performance with the above
statement. He called for the audience's alertness to the urgency of the
issues raised by the play, emphasised the generality of the terrorist
threat and extended a protective as well as corrective umbrella of the
law to all bodies in all communities. A collection of young people and
adults, mostly of Muslim heritage, are also told that the play is 'raw' and
that whilst the scenario of the suicide bombing depicted in the play is
fictional, the words that they will hear spoken during the play are real,
collected by the playwright from conversations with people directly
affected by terrorism.

Not in my Name, researched and written by Alice Bartlett, tells
the story of Shahid, a young Muslim man and a loved son, brother
and student, who carries out a suicide bombing in a supermarket in
his home town. Testimony from characters visiting or working in the
supermarket on the day of the bombing interweave with increasing pace
to describe the build up to and immediate aftermath of the attack, and
are followed by accounts of the long-term impact of the bombing on
victims, the family of the bomber and the wider community. The play
draws on the accounts of victims, families and emergency workers following different terrorist attacks, including the 7 July 2005 attacks in

London. It also includes accounts of the disturbances in northern towns in the summer of 2001 between Asian and white youth, and original research with people in the region about the issue of terrorism. It ends with a statement by a police officer who gives the date of the attack as a year from the date of the performance, and describes the bomber, Shahid Hussain, who did not appear in the play, as 'an angry and confused young British man' with a distorted understanding of Islam. During a post-performance interactive discussion, an actor plays Shahid and the audience is given an opportunity to advise him as to non-violent ways he might raise his concerns, and thus prevent the events depicted in the play.

Lancashire Constabulary wanted the play to communicate a 'radicalisation narrative' to audiences of young people as well as other community audiences as an awareness-raising exercise. This narrative depicts an 'age of vulnerability' to extremism, when young people look to establish an autonomous identity and sense of belonging outside the family, formal education and the mosque. During her research for the play, however, Bartlett encountered perspectives that complicated this reductive narrative, and thus the play provides a competing imposture based on more troubling and critical accounts provided by those directly affected by the issue of terrorism. The play references disturbing levels of racism and Islamaphobia, limited sympathy for extremist ideas but also powerful examples of anti-racist sentiment and outrage at British military intervention in Afghanistan and Iraq. Bartlett also heard distressing narratives of vulnerability and alienation expressed by young Muslim people, who communicated a sense that terrorism 'was somehow their community's fault', that they 'didn't understand it' and felt that 'sooner or later Asians are going to get thrown out of this country because this is our fault this is happening' (Bartlett 2009a). The verbatim aesthetic provided an opportunity to present multiple and competing perspectives of the contested and emotive issues of racism and extremism, juxtaposed in ways that encouraged culturally diverse audiences to identify points of common ground without reducing complexity. This aesthetic also provided a model for how young people might relate to each other in an environment that sets them up as in conflict with each other; in the words of one young person who saw the play: 'when you're in a situation and things like this are happening around you, it's a lot easier to see when there's a play being done . . . then you know how to deal with it' (cited in Hughes 2010).

The everyday lives of the key characters represent the interconnectedness, intersecting concerns and diversity of audiences of the play. A friendship group of young Asian and white women, including Shahid's girlfriend, opens and closes the play, and the other key voices belong to a young Muslim man who loses his mother in the bombing, Shahid's brother and sister, a Muslim policeman and a young white man who was Shahid's former best friend. The performance aesthetic was held together by the bodies of the performers, who represented the ethnic and religious diversity of characters and audiences, and were also young professional and non-professional actors. By utilising young people as performers and central characters, a hopeful future for this community is impostured, and desire for its realisation mobilised. The most provocative and compelling feature of the drama is its focus on the absent presence of Shahid, who is constructed as a confused and frustrated young man by the accounts of those who cared about him – his brother, sister, girlfriend and best friend. Importantly, Shahid is grieved for by those who loved him, and the portrait of the bomber communicated to the audience becomes increasingly complex and nuanced. During a series of powerful moments towards the end of the drama, Shahid's sister asserts that 'he wasn't bad – he was kind and gentle. He used to look out for me' and his best friend states that Shahid 'wasn't racist, I can vouch for that. He was a good friend.' Perhaps most movingly, Shahid's brother, a thoughtful and sympathetic presence throughout the play, comments: 'I still pray for my brother. Because there was a part of him, and I still believe there is a part of him that . . . that is good . . . I weep for him' (Bartlett 2009b: 82).

Not in my Name disrupts the 'us and them' discourses and practices of the war on terror by extending a gesture of grief for the young would-be suicide bomber in our community, expressed by representatives of that community's diversity and complexity. Here, the counterterrorism agenda is recycled as an affectionate/affective gesture that expresses a desire to bring a vulnerable young man under the umbrella of protection of the law. As part of this, the law constructs itself as a legitimate participant of the community, and, like that community, made vulnerable by threat and concerned for the vulnerability of young people (as expressed by the 'we are all vulnerable' comment by the senior policeman above). This is an ambivalent move, as the counterterrorism agenda has here already completed a performative act of naming this community, and especially the 'young Muslim man' in the community, as potentially engaged in terrorism. The play itself negotiates this ambivalence by focusing the drama on the *absence* of this figure – we do not meet Shahid until the play is over, and these events have *not happened*. They highlight one of a multitude of possible futures, the outcome of which relies on the critical and affective interventions of the audience in the here and now. Reinforcing this point, the play does not provide any resolution to the complexities it depicts: the overall trajectory is one that posits uncertainty and threat as features of everyday life that need to be carefully negotiated by young people. By the end, the friends who opened the play explore the possibility of renewed relationship based on respect for difference, rather than a comfortable revival of familiarity: 'we asked each other about things we wouldn't have done before'; 'and it was both ways. 'Cos even though we're all from round here and British and that – we are from different cultures and have different traditions'; 'it's not just them, it's us as well. They need to realise that not all Muslims are the same, just like we should realise not all whites are the same' (Bartlett 2009b: 81).

However, given the unhoming impostures of the counterterrorism strategy, it is important to take a closer look at the subjects that do not emerge as complex or nuanced figures within the framework of the life of the play. The verbatim aesthetic, of course, limits the discursive remit of the play to the topics those people interviewed (or represented by other sources) are prepared to say in a public forum, as well as determines to some extent the manner in which they share their experiences. Here, I explore one moment from the play in particular, paying attention to its representation of political Islam – a moment based on an edited encounter between the playwright and a group of young men in a youth club in the north-west of England. As part of the play's dramatisation of the long-term aftermath of the bomb on the community, a young man named in the script as 'Innit boy' approaches Shahid's brother, and their exchange is as follows (Figure 8):

> Innit boy: What was tragic about it? The bro, man, is living a life of luxury in his pad right now – he's chilling out. The guy's kicking man. That guy is something to follow.
> Brother: You know the type I mean – he's got a gold chain, tight jeans, Timberlands . . . them guys really annoy me.
> Innit boy: It's being a Muslim, innit? People are picking on us and shit, you know, they're doing the dirty on us [. . .] We're not gonna sit back and take it – why should we? We've gotta do exactly what your brother Shahid did [. . .]
> Brother: I said: What the hell are you talking about? He went and killed himself and five innocent people [. . .] You don't know how my brother is right now. Don't give me your crap about the seventy virgins and that [. . .] it's between him and God – but logic tells me that God's probably going to be shaking his head and saying, 'sorry mate, but that was Not in my name'. (Bartlett 2009b: 65–6)

In allowing these views a platform in the play, the playwright spoils the speaker's identity by juxtaposing his speech with the interjections of the

Figure 8 Zahoor Hussain as Innit boy and Darren Kuppan as the brother in
Not in my Name, Theatre Veritae, Lancashire, 2008.

brother, who describes the young man as more preoccupied by material
desires (Timberland shoes, tight jeans, gold chains) than religious ideas.
In performance, the unregulated quality of the young man's speech also
contrasts with the considered accounts of events given by characters
(and presumably their 'originals') in the rest of the play, undermining
Innit boy's claims to legitimacy. Importantly, the playwright's edits
undermine the speaker's claims of religious authority and thus extremist views are represented in the play but not identified with Islam. The
exchange culminates in the authoritative and regulating impact of the
brother's speech, which introduces the presence of God – and a propertied and identified condition of self – 'Not in my name' – to complete
the emasculation of the speaker. Here, the sovereignty of 'name', law and
God regulate a discordant and disruptive voice, and defuse the excessive
energy of the young man. The threatening implications of the young
man's speech are scripted within a normative imposture that, importantly, rejects violence, but also perhaps represents what the law desires
for the community, rather than a world that is actually inhabited by the
young people watching from the audience.

Interestingly, the character most frequently reported by audiences of young people as the one to whom they could most relate and
wanted to know more about was Shahid himself: 'he doesn't know who
to believe and no one listens'; 'a lot of people twist words and end up
doing something they would regret' (Bartlett and Raffle 2009). Shahid,

not present in body during the course of the play, comes on stage after the performance and talks to the audience about his disappointment at not being selected to play football professionally, his anger at wars in Muslim countries, the pressures of college and his meeting with an extremist individual who 'educated' him about Islam. Audiences encounter an active and intelligent young Muslim man with a sincere commitment to his faith and a passion for social justice. Whilst this Shahid is familiar and identifiable, the uncertainty about what happens to him next mobilises critical and affective responses in the interactive discussion following the performances. As part of the discussions that I witnessed, this included a barrage of advice that stressed the importance of Shahid's participation in the normative political realm: organise a peaceful protest, go to your Member of Parliament, ask the Imam at the mosque, talk to your parents, read the Qur'an in English, listen to others but make up your own mind. One young man in a school in Lancashire suggested that Shahid organise a college occupation. In this instance, the suggestion was reconfigured by the facilitator of the discussion, with nervous looks at the teachers surrounding the school hall: 'well, how about writing to your MP?' The provocative gap created by Shahid's absence and his critical, energetic desire for a better world are reinvented here as forms of identification and action that remain within the normative realm.

Not in my Name is a powerful play that affirms the shared values of freedom of speech and the discursive plurality of a liberal polity. It is moving in its critical engagements with the impact of a war on terror on young people, in particular drawing attention to how increasing levels of racism and prejudice have distorted their relationships with each other. Whilst I have argued that the affective/affectionate relationships configured by the drama of the play and its performance to some extent limited a critical dialogue with the counterterrorism agenda, it is important to avoid any simplistic conclusions. Here, there is a need for an imposture that values young people as members of a community without imposing conditions of identity and encounter, whilst also regulating the concomitant risk of representing young people as undecidable and threatening. This is a difficult balance, and the play pursues it by modelling lawful and loving relationships between equally valued members of a diverse community, whilst also exploring how global uncertainties are manifesting themselves in local contexts in disturbing and threatening ways. The absent presence of the loved and missed young Muslim man at the centre of the drama also prefigures a deeply hopeful politics of relationship: what is needed, perhaps, is an even greater extension of the imposturous and affective, law and love, which might include a more inviting entry point for young men in Timberlands and gold chains.

One *Extreme to the Other*: GW Theatre and flagging identities

Sara (*to Tony*): Look. (*pause*). When we were little we were friends. We were friends again later. Jess was in love with Ali, he was in love with her, and I was in love with you. Yes! And I still am. But we're standing here now like we hate each other. So.

Ali: What?

Jessica: What do we do about it? (Harris 2007: 45)

These are the final lines of *One Extreme to the Other*, a performance exploring violent extremism that started life as a response born of anger at the series of coordinated suicide attacks on the London public transport system on 7 July 2005 (Figure 9). As the playwright, Mike Harris, comments, 'I was angry because I'd regarded the bombers as my people: Northern lads, with relatives who'd worked in the cotton mills just like mine . . . and on whose behalf I had spent forty odd years

Figure 9 The cast of *One Extreme to the Other*, GW Theatre, Oldham, 2008.

arguing fiercely against the bog standard racism of my old dad' (Harris 2009: 46). The narrative of the play follows two parallel and interconnected sets of sibling relationships on one racially divided estate in a town in the north of England. Ali, Mo and Sara live on the 'Asian side' of the estate, and Tony and Karl on the 'white side'. Jessica, a successful journalist, returns to the area of her youth to investigate racial conflict on the estate stoked by outside extremists: Neville Parkin, leader of a far-right political party, and Yusef Omar, an Islamic extremist. The emotional drama resides in the history of love entanglements between the two older brothers and Sara and Jessica which have left a residual hostility. The play ends with a tentative reminder of the intimate connections between the characters indicated by Sara's speech above, but avoids any easy reconciliation. It is fast paced, with short scenes played by four actors who take multiple parts, and despite the difficult issues it raises is humorous and engaging. After the play a short interactive session provides audiences with an opportunity to question and give advice to the characters.

The parallel lives of the two families depicted provide a mimetic symmetry, and this, in turn, constructs a 'protective, symbolic wall', to evoke Žižek's useful phrase, which works to highlight points of identification between the warring neighbours, whilst also dramatising their distinct struggles. What is kept alive by this imposture is the possibility of solidarity between two families who occupy a similar, difficult position in an inequitable world. Here, each family's struggle comes to be negatively projected onto their neighbours, and the play depicts the process by which the characters find a competing, better imposture for critically engaging with the world. The mimetic symmetry is created by tracing similar events in the lives of the two sets of siblings. For example, both families lack parental figures, the older brothers have histories of drug abuse and violence, and the extremists Omar and Parkin are authoritarian figures who fulfil parental roles. Tony explains to Jessica that Parkin was someone who 'talked sense, listened and gave me advice. Just like me dad', and when she points out that he has never met his father he adds, 'like me dad does in me dreams, alright?' (Harris 2007: 19). Similarly, Ali explains to Sara that Omar offered him guidance at a time of crisis: 'I was heading back to drugs and fighting when I met the sheik. He showed me where to put the anger, OK?' (*ibid.*: 34). The symmetry culminates in a key scene in which the extremists give political speeches that are cut into each other, displaying identical messages of hatred: 'they bomb and torture Muslims all over the world'; 'Asian gangs insult old people on our streets!'; 'they hold innocent Muslim families for months without trial'; 'they bomb us in the name of Allah!' (*ibid.*: 37).

Over the course of the play, the brothers come face to face with the consequences of their hatred for neighbours and, following this, the two older brothers assume responsibility for the guidance of their younger siblings. Tony ends the play by asserting a sense of personal responsibility in the face of his younger brother's racism: 'Asians do my head in as well but it weren't them that made us dad leave, or made you mess about at school or made me take drugs . . . I've changed OK? And you've got to change with me' (Harris 2007: 41–2). Ali similarly stresses the importance of personal responsibility by giving his brother a Qur'an translated into English: 'read it! And think! Independent reasoning. Itjihad, not Jihad!' (*ibid.*: 44). In the final part of the play, the brothers are reconciled to the everyday realities of bonds of affection and disaffection with their siblings and neighbours. The overall trajectory replaces authoritarian relationships between the extremists and brothers, with brotherly affection and critical reflection. Whereas *Not in my Name* extends the protective umbrella of the law to the vulnerable young man, *One extreme to the Other* posits a different coalition of love and law, one that resists authority and is made up of solidarity between brothers and, potentially, neighbours. The problem of extremism is excised from the world of immediate relationships, and is negotiated by increased critical engagement and a commitment to brotherly love. This resolution does not imply that the characters are cured of their racist views or become 'good' neighbours. At the end of the play, Tony's relationships remain configured by love for Sara and hostility for Ali.

The struggles with neighbours are humorously staged in a scene in which Tony is discovered attaching a St George's flag to a tree in preparation for a far-right demonstration. Whilst Jessica tries to persuade him to take down the flag, Ali enters, at which point Tony hides behind the flag. When Sara enters, the scene has descended into farce:

Sara: What are you doing?
Ali: He's putting a Nazi flag up our tree.
Sara: What do you mean 'our tree'?
Ali: It's on our side of the estate. So it's an Asian tree. (Harris 2007: 27)

In the struggle that follows the flag is passed from one character to the other, and finally resolved by Tony leaving at Sara's request: 'Ali's not going to pull the flag down Tony. I won't let him. So you can go now please. For me.' In this scene, the flag is an uncertain symbol, used to aggressively mark territory, assert an exclusively white identity *and* signal the diversity of 'Englishness' – as Sara comments as part of the discussion: 'I'm telling you the original St George was a Muslim.'

The flag evokes Lacan's mythical 'lamella', an object that signifies a missing part, and is used by the subject to mark 'his place in the field of the group's relations' (Lacan 1977: 206). In this scene, the characters struggle to control multiple and competing claims on the flag, and its ultimate lack of meaning traps the neighbours in an endless cycle of claiming and contesting, humorously played out in this scene which shows both Ali and Tony's claims on the flag as both heartfelt and uncertain. The resolution of the struggle – with Sara, the young Muslim woman in hijab, replacing the flag in the tree on the 'Asian side' of the estate once Tony has left the scene – can be read as extending a more differentiated, inclusive territory within which these conflicting neighbours might recreate their relationships. However, what is interesting here is that Sara engages with the flag only when its hostile owner, Tony, has left the scene. In addition, both Sara and Tony only agree to this uneasy compromise because of their former love for each other. This is a move that does not idealise worlds of encounter, but it does express a desire to peacefully negotiate love and hostility between neighbours. As part of this, the flag does not become any one person's secure property or marker of identity, but is left hanging over the stage for the remainder of the play, posing a troubling question about what it signifies. The *lack* in this symbolic gesture also mobilises a desire for an extension of encounter: the flag was one of the most frequently mentioned features of the play during the post-performance discussions that I witnessed.

The play has toured across postindustrial landscapes deeply scarred by economic deprivation and rising levels of extremism and racial conflict. Its symmetry was an important imposture, avoiding the demonisation of one side of the community in contexts already plagued by fraught neighbourly relations. However, perhaps the most powerful moment that I witnessed whilst researching the production occurred outside the play's mimetic symmetry. Following a courageous performance for an unsettled and challenging audience in a school on a majority white housing estate, where children were regularly leafleted by members of a far-right political party when leaving school at the end of the day, a young person in the audience asked the Asian actors whether they had ever personally experienced racism and, if so, how it felt. One of the actors told a story about witnessing his mother being racially abused as a child. The reception of this story was the one moment of complete silence that occurred throughout the entire performance. The assertion of a normative injunction to 'think for yourself' performed by the play, alongside this intimate, discomforting narrative offered by an actor, was powerful and deeply moving.

The local and global context of uncertainty within which these young people are growing up does not promise them a secure future. This moment embraced the uncertainties of unrehearsed relationship and replaced questions of identity with an account of the felt effects of violence – a powerful dramatisation of the predicament of neighbourly relationships. Importantly, the audience was not being informed that 'racism is bad' in this transaction; rather, they felt bad about an experience of racism experienced by a neighbour.

Hearts and Minds: Khayaal Theatre and divine love

Break-off not the connection with me;
If nothing else, enmity, let it be. (Ghālib [2002: 565])

During performances of *Hearts and Minds*, audiences witness the build up of a succession of conflicting and intensifying pressures on Asif, a young Muslim man with a passion for hard cash, hip-hop and cooking, which culminate in his acceptance and eventual rejection of violent extremism. The play depicts the lives of three young people, Asif, Vicky and Aisha, and their struggles with their preconceptions of each other and the competing pressures of their wider social milieu, which include negotiating the vulnerability, racism and narrowly defined values of their respective parents. These lives intersect with a world in which a schoolteacher struggles against the negative perceptions of young Muslim people expressed by her school board, an extremist group plans a terrorist attack on the 2012 Olympics in London, an Islamic rap group with a peaceful message is held by police on suspicion of inciting extremism, and, in the later stages of the play, Asif's father is detained in Pakistan where he was travelling with money to support his extended family and community projects. *Hearts and Minds* was devised and produced by Khayaal Theatre, a company that makes theatre with an Islamic ethos 'to creatively and imaginatively demonstrate the reconciliation and accord that is so needed in today's world'.[2]

These principles combine to produce a moving and humorous play that explores a difficult issue within an overall frame of hope and compassion, and also critically engages with the ways in which Muslim identity is constructed by the counterterrorism strategy. Early in the play the teacher, Ms Hussain, challenges her school board:

The approach that most of you are advocating will be counter productive because it starts off with the negative implication that all young Muslims are potential terrorists because of their religious affiliation. You know, identity is so important to a human being that if you foist an erroneous one onto the vulnerable, the disconnected, the aggrieved for long enough, they will adopt it. (Khayaal 2008: 5)

This statement announces the play as critical of a counterterrorism agenda that intensifies a climate of fear and insecurity, a posture that is extended by Ms Hussain's proposal of a school project where pupils design a 'flag for humanity' to inspire people to come together 'to meet the challenges we face globally'. Vicky and Asif are assigned by Ms Hussain to work together on this project, and the hostility and tension between them is stoked by Aisha's frequent interjections of her own views, characterised by a fierce and narrow interpretation of Islam. A school scene late in the play begins with Asif angry about a racist comment he has heard directed at his father by Vicky's mother, who works with Asif's father in the same taxi company. In a conciliatory effort, Vicky mentions to Ms Hussain that a 'nice Asian man driver' (Asif's father) told her a poem that might be used as the inspiration for their flag. Asif is persuaded to write down a ghazal by the nineteenth-century Urdu poet Ghālib, often quoted by his father to explain his passive response when confronted by racist hatred. Ms Hussain translates the verse from Urdu and makes a connection to the Qur'an:

It's about unconditional love. He says: don't break relations with me, let there be some connection even if it's enmity. I think he must have been inspired by this verse in the Qur'an which says: Respond to bad with that which is better so that your enemy becomes like your best friend. (Khayaal 2008: 21)

This inspires Vicky and Asif to use the heart as inspiration for their flag, and the loving imperative of this signifier recurs in the final moment of the play. Asif's surprise encounter with his two school friends at the opening of the 2012 Olympic Games, and the announcement that their flag has won the 'International Flag for Humanity' competition, triggers his decision to pass information to the police about a planned terrorist attack with which he is involved. Importantly, the heart does not resolve the struggle here; rather, it provides a motif through which the difficultness of encounters are dramatised. The ghazal evokes the agony of a lover rejected by his loved one, for whom an abject relationship of connection is more desirable than absolute alienation. The

Figure 10 *Hearts and Minds*, Khayaal Theatre Company, London, 2008.
Photograph by Masoma Al-Khoee.

quotation from the Qur'an manifests this as a religious principle of
extending generosity to the neighbour and remaining open to encounter without obligation or condition, despite the risk of wounding,
hostile responses. Evoking Eagleton's discussions of the coalition of
love and law mobilised by the principle of faith noted above, the heart
motif is part of a wider imposture of a protective and loving symbolic
realm that focuses on the difficultness of loving and being loved in an
uncertain world. Here, there is a desire to realise a loving, lawful realm
in which abjection and alienation are acknowledged and explored as
a potential and critical condition, and at the same time carefully regulated. In the final moments of the play the heart has a privileged status
alongside, rather than as a substitute for, the flags of an international
sporting event. As such, Asif's decision to follow his heart signals a
hopeful reconciliation of the struggles of the heart with a world that
privileges the uncertainties of love for the neighbour as an organising
principle (Figure 10).

The phrase 'hearts and minds' was borrowed directly from counterterrorism discourses and deliberately reinscribed by the play: 'we
wanted to say if you really want to talk about hearts and minds . . . you
need to be talking about what's common to human beings, and about
love and about social bonds not about just how you pacify people
and get them to comply with your world view' (Ali 2009).[3] The play

is careful in its approach to depicting the hearts and minds of young people: each character is complex and untypical. For example, Asif is a young man motivated by materialist desires, he loves rap, is disengaged from education, but also has a passion for cooking and passes a proportion of the profits from his pirate DVD business to his mother. Interestingly, the extremists are denied life as part of this imposture: they are hooded and play their lines with their backs to the audience, preoccupied with financial fraud, import and export businesses, war and violence rather than matters of the heart. The damagingly abstract association of the Muslim community with extremism performed by the counterterrorism strategy is thus countered by situating the *problem* of extremism outside the symbolic order of the play, and its *prevention* as internal to the processes of identification, perception, emotion, language and action of the complex, loving and lovable figures central to the drama.

The abundant, critical potential of the symbolic dimensions of the imposture is announced early in the play by Ms Hussain during a lesson on love poetry:

> What we say and how we say it is central to who we are and how we see ourselves (holds up book). The Japanese scientist, Masaru Emoto, discovered that water is affected by words. He found that a negative word makes an ugly, deformed crystal and a positive word makes a beautifully formed crystal . . . Now since we are two-thirds water, could it not be said that we are making ourselves with our words? (Khayaal 2008: 3)

In the performance of the play, the forms of speech adopted by characters are often unsettled by the contents of the words, causing the audience to pay careful attention to a process of listening and interpreting. One example of this is the rap performed by the Islamic hip-hop group: 'when a bruvver lets rip with the troof, Boom! All hell seems to break loose, my jihad ain't bout no bullets or bombs, it's about my struggle to bring peace and calm' (*ibid.*: 14). The play is littered with other provocations to the audience to listen carefully to the spoken word, from the love poetry of Ghālib spoken first in Urdu and then in English, to the messages of exclusion in the urban cool of Aisha's speech: 'salaams to the ignorant and leave 'em to their vices. Our peeps need to keep faith and stop demeanin' themselves with all the jahiliyat' (*ibid.*: 2). This insistence on the critical potential of textual and interpretive practices is consistent with the protective extension of the symbolic realm – the competing impostures – configured by all three counterterrorism plays, performed here as an appeal to the audience to engage creatively and critically with speech acts in the public realm.

The artists involved in all three plays here echo each other's concerns at the emergence of significant amounts of counterterrorism funding for arts projects about terrorism, where there is a risk that theatre practitioners without an adequate awareness of the issues carry out ill-conceived projects. Khayaal had not been able to generate secure funding for their work in their ten years of existence prior to this period. Thus, in a letter to a national newspaper Ali comments, 'our struggle to be recognised by the gatekeepers of mainstream British drama has been repeatedly impeded by prejudice and suspicion. I hope that the theatre world's new-found interest in British Muslims is not cynical' (Ali 2008). In part, the prejudice cited by Ali arises from a suspicion of faith-based theatre, as described by Janelle Reinelt in a review of the playwright Howard Brenton's explorations of faith in two plays, *Paul* (2005) and *In Extremis* (2006). She notes that these plays were controversial as many secular artists dismiss faith as not worthy of serious attention despite being 'a vexed issue of our times' (Reinelt 2007: 167). In support of Brenton's project, Reinelt suggests that an exploration of faith needs to be undertaken outside the constraints of conservative religious doctrine and that theatre might provide such a site. However, the protective imposture of all three plays here also points to a useful role for the *conservative* in configuring a hopeful and critical politics, and that supports performance's engagements with uncertainty and complexity.

It is important to resist generalising anxieties about exclusivist faiths to all religious practices: *Hearts and Minds* is an example of faith-based theatre that draws on a conservative religious ethos to generate an imaginative response to a complex issue of pressing importance. The play's compassionate aesthetics are directly mobilised by Khayaal's Islamic ethos. It is worth quoting Ali at length here:

> We could have chosen to fuel fear and hysteria for the sake of making a splash, but the principles of the Islamic ethos prevent us from going in that direction, we also felt that it was very important to maintain a spirit of hope in the piece . . . The ethos of storytelling in Islam is that stories are very powerful, and if you do tell stories there is a certain responsibility . . . [Art] can't be about just spouting angst, one has to censor out one's ego or preoccupation with the dark side if you like, not to say that you don't deal with the dark side but that all the time your focus is on the light, your focus is on hope, some sort of aspiration or dream for development . . . Art in Islam has always been about, traditionally speaking, celebrating and paying tribute to the artistry and beauty and majesty of the divine. (Ali 2009)

In this powerful statement, the artist describes a faith in the promise of divine love, in a terrain beyond discrete identity, as facilitating a hopeful practice of relationship, and as materialised by artistic practices like performance. Importantly, such faithful performances are not constituted by crude guidelines or messages delivered by a secure or properly identified self. Rather, they directly engage with the *difficultness* of encounters between self and other in an uncertain world. The 'divine' is a complex territory, evoked here for its inspiring, unhoming, boundless, disquieting qualities and as a site in which the intimacy and interdependency of love, estrangement and hostility might be negotiated. For Freud, the 'oceanic' feeling of divine love is a residue of human personality that pre-exists the ego, and the ego, in turn, constructs a façade that separates experiences of early childhood from mature engagements with the world (Freud 2004: 255). However, as noted above, Eagleton identifies a dialectic of love and law in the divine, whereby life comes to be prized and protected regardless of its identity, ego, condition of being, and 'only on this "inhuman" foundation can a durable human community be constructed' (Eagleton 2009: 272). Threat, uncertainty and insecurity are all positively negotiated by an expression of faith in the abundant possibilities of uncertain encounters contained by love and law – to again cite Ghālib's poem – 'don't break relations with me, let there be some connection even if it's enmity'. The play thus refuses a politics of exception which calls forth Muslim bodies as a threatening symbol that stands in for the uncertainties of a time of terror. Rather, it materialises a loving law, uncoupled from violence, and draws attention to the critical potential of a relation of abjection – of beyond, outside or 'not-yet' subjectivity. The overall drama enacts this loving, lawful realm by means of a creative and carefull practice of the symbolic dimensions of performance's imposture, both inside the world of the play, and in response to the counterterrorism strategy that commissioned it.

The challenges posed by the security concerns that shaped these plays echo the argument of this book that a time of terror creates an imperative to rethink the politics of performance. Here, artists were invited to participate in a local front to the war on terror. The plays provide an inclusive and differentiated, protective symbolic world and their combinations of love and law resist the exposure of neighbours during a period of night-time terror raids, demands for vigilance in public spaces, increased surveillance in shopping centres and biometric examinations at national borders. The plays do not deny the uncertainty that underpins these developments, but, importantly, insist on the law of love in any response.

Undercover: participatory performance and the double agent

Today we are looking at the Muslim. What makes her tick? (*Undercover* 2007a)

Undercover was stimulated by the desire of a group of young women to take part in theatre project in a women-only environment, sensitive and respectful to their Islamic faith (figure 11). As such, the project echoed the impulse to extend encounters with neighbours of each of the three projects discussed above, but here as part of a venture that was not commissioned or funded by counterterrorism agencies. Led by theatre director Janine Waters and myself, the project was a partnership between *In Place of War*, an academic research project exploring performance in places of conflict, and Young Muslim Sisters (Manchester), a branch of Young Muslims UK, an Islamic youth initiative. The final performance was the culmination of three months' work, and comprised short scenes which created a playful relationship with the audience, evoking and then undermining a succession of stereotypes of Muslim women. For example, early in the play a women enters in a niqab (a veil which covers

Figure 11 In rehearsal for *Undercover*, 2007.

all of the face other than the eyes) and as she furtively looks around the audience can see she is hiding something suspicious under her jilbab: when sure she is not being watched she pulls out a chocolate box and sits down to enthusiastically consume its contents ('aahhh, that's top that is!').

Visual motifs of 'going undercover' and 'uncovering', performed by a succession of reveal gags like this early in the play, drew attention to the act of looking as well as provided audiences with objects to look at. This double looking invited the audience to read the image on stage at the same time as critically engage with the visual regimes of a war on terror that constructs a prejudicial field by which Muslim women are looked *at*. The double agency in the visual dynamic of the piece was explicitly invited early in the play by a member of the cast who paused at the side of the stage and commented to the audience: 'Today we are looking at the Muslim. What makes her tick?' Deliberately evoking fears of what might be hidden under the niqabs, hijabs and jilbabs of the Muslim women on stage, this invitation also expressed the 'looked at' object's awareness of the anxieties that configure the audience's looks. It constructed for the audience a threatening and undecidable neighbour who, in turn, *looks back, amused*. Imposturing images of Muslim women as demure, oppressed and frightening, the play captured the audience's anxious and acquiescent looks at these images, and then obliterated the visual frame by materialising a series of competing impostures that more closely depicted their dreams, aspirations and pleasures. Over the course of the play, these competing impostures included Muslim women as: dangerous drivers, chocolate lovers, shopaholics, lovers of Jane Austen heroes, leaders of an international terror cell network promoting the marriageable qualities of sons and daughters, covert agents ridding the streets of dodgy kohl and 'even dodgier' henna dealers and, most importantly, proudly self-determining in their celebration of Islam, concern for issues of social justice, education and choice of future partners.

The reception of the play by its audience testified to the unsettlement of its visual effects: 'it was an unusual watching experience'; 'you're not sure what you're laughing at, are you laughing at the racial stereotypes or are you laughing at yourself?'; 'it was very penetrating about what we think we see' (Undercover 2007b). However, the comments of audience members also featured disbelief at the young women's positive portrayal of their lives: 'there's so much in the news about how Islam supposedly treats women and some of it must be true, I find it difficult to believe that they are as liberated as they appear to be'; 'surely they feel more aggrieved about the way they're treated'; 'all that stuff about their dreams . . . do these young women fully realise the limits that might be put upon them?' (Undercover 2007b). In part, these views misunderstand the emancipatory role that Islam plays in the lives of many young women. Those who took part in the play, for example, call themselves 'culture rebels', and draw on *religious* sources to legitimise their engagement with a range of social and cultural activities, including drama. Here, Islam helps young women question the legitimacy of restrictions that are *cultural* impositions rather than doctrines of faith, and, as such, religious faith acts as a guarantee of autonomy and a source of strength, definition and learning. The women's unwillingness to perform a negative critique of their faith, their passionate political engagement and enjoyment of drama, reflect experiences of faith as guaranteeing freedom and autonomy. The play was performed by happy, faithful, Islamist women, unhappy about the capturing of Muslim women as oppressed objects inside secular discourses of Islam. Young Muslim Sisters, as signified by the attitudes of the participants here, represent the diversification and heterogeneity of political Islam that has emerged in diasporic contexts. The culture rebels participating in *Undercover* symbolise an Islam responsive to concerns of young people, and that is politically engaged and globally aware.

As such, the project evidenced a level of critical and creative engagement invisible to many of the audience; indeed, its specificities were also often invisible to the project leaders. We were unable to see or interpret anything about the encounters between Shia and Sunni Muslims in the group for instance, and were surprised to hear about them. The responses of the audience and ourselves here highlight the uncertainties of encounter, from the laughter provoked by recognition of anxious looks, to disbelief at the women's positive presentation of themselves, to the lack of awareness of the project leaders in the rehearsal process. Rather than interpreting these misunderstandings as failures of the project, they can be identified as a welcome part of a process stimulated by a mutual desire to sustain an open encounter. Here, Peggy Phelan's account of misunderstanding in performance is useful. She identifies the impossibility of ever truly seeing and knowing the other as instituting the impossibility of appropriating or being appropriated in a relational encounter. A hopeful politics of performance is signalled by a struggle to maintain connection rather than the attainment of security: '*it is in the attempt to walk (and live) on the rackety bridge between self and other – and not the attempt to arrive on one side or the other – that we discover real hope*' (Phelan 1993: 174. Italics in original). We experienced many misunderstandings during this project, too numerous to detail here. Importantly, these slippages highlight the importance of a commitment to relationship rather than a point at which relationship breaks.

The performance aesthetic – with its double agents, going 'under-cover' to expose an imposturous world – deliberately played with anxieties that underpin public controversies about the veil – hijab and niqab – worn by some Muslim women. The veil unsettles because it represents a limit to what is visible and thus knowable about the other. All of the performers wore a hijab as a marker of faith that provided definition and autonomy, describing themselves as 'doing hijab'. During one rehearsal, an invitation to imagine themselves as young women who were not Muslim for the purposes of an improvisation prompted the women to close the curtains of the rehearsal room and remove their hijabs. Whilst a secure, defining limit to seeing and being seen was still in place in this move, with the closing of the curtains, the improvisa-tion did not flow smoothly. Reflecting on this moment after the project, one participant suggested that the improvisation caused discomfort because it is not possible for a Muslim to be non-Muslim in front of a non-Muslim audience, although at parties and weddings when sketches are done it is possible to play a non-Muslim because 'everyone knows we're just pretending' (Undercover 2008). The transaction here resolves itself at the point at which both performer and observer are certain that the *imposture* is *real* – when 'everyone knows' that the pretence is real. Paradoxically, this is also the point at which the imposture is configured by *lack* – when everyone also knows that what is seen is an imposture, which is *not* real. At this point of collapse of sense, the possibilities for understanding, identification and encounter become unfathomable, infinite and abundant. After removing her hijab during the rehearsal, one of the young women commented to the project leaders 'now you know two of me' – a beautiful and intimate moment that also wonder-fully preserves the possibility of never being fully known, conclusively captured or completely finished in a world of encounter.

The cites/sites of double agency in the operations of critical mimesis in this performance were at once a place of refuge, intimate encounter and public exposure. Without imposture there can be no encounter, but the imposture had to remain a secret that 'everyone knows' in order to secure the survival of self and other in the encounter. This evokes Phelan's comment that 'the "secret" of theatre's power is dependent on the "truth" of its illusion. Enfolded within fiction, theatre seeks to display the line between visible and invisible power. Theatre has, then, an intimate relationship with the secret' (Phelan 1993: 112). It is notable that the motif of uncovering in *Undercover* made use of visibility and invisibility in the dynamics of performance. This arguably troubles Phelan's conclusion that the critical potential of performance resides in the 'immateriality of the unmarked' which 'shows itself through the negative and through disappearance' (*ibid.*: 19). In part, Phelan's 'unmarked' leaves our supposedly threatening and undecidable neighbours exposed to the prejudicial and punitive visual and discursive regimes of a war on terror. The secret – and critical and protective effect – of this performance was shared by the repeated coverings *and* uncoverings, appearances and disappearances, sense and decay of meaning, including the moment of removing the hijab and closing the curtains in the rehearsal. These veilings and unveilings generated a tangible sense of the uncertainties and abundance of encounter as well as promised the possibility of surviving their supposed terrors by providing symbolic borders that contain and regulate. Here, the covering up – the hijab and the symbolic imposture of the play – are markers of encounter that protect the subject from damaging exposures and equally damaging disappearances. As part of the repeated uncoverings of the performance, the subject goes undercover to discover, mimic and reinvent the scarring symbolisations of itself in the world, gently and humorously reminding the viewer of the secret they share about the infinite and abundant possibilities of encounter, rather than promising any ultimate revelation.

As noted above, Lacan offers the notion of a stain as the form in which the self comes to know itself – a blind spot in an imposture in which 'I' am exposed but also remain opaque. These stains are surplus bits of experience leftover from the imposture of an ideal, loveable, discrete self that we present to the world. Lacan demonstrates his argument by reference to Holbein's famous painting, *The Ambassadors*, also discussed in chapter 2. In the painting there is an indecipherable grey figure in the foreground that does not fit with the scene depicted, and when looked at awry we can see that it is a skull, and for Lacan this 'reflects our own nothingness' (Lacan 1977: 92). To map this onto the encounter between performer and spectator in *Undercover*: the unsettling experience of spectatorship provoked by the play revealed the *absence* of knowledge that configures our encounters with neighbours. Here, any claim of understanding is concomitant with opacity. However, this also provided an opportunity to decompose the deceptive effects of the visual-discursive-embodied regime that configures Muslim women as frightening, demure and oppressed. The performance continually impostured meaning and at the same time welcomed the unfathomable affectivity of the other. The lack of meaning evoked a desire for ongoing encounter in which impostures could be tested out and recycled for their relative *uses* inside the contingent performances of everyday life. This recycling, however, continues to decompose any secure knowledge of the other, rather than fill the gap between representation and the represented. The repeated uncoverings of the performance of *Undercover* did not represent a colonial claiming of foundational truth, as in the unveilings of Afghan women welcomed by the military coalition leading the war on terror as somehow display- ing the 'liberation' of the Muslim world. Instead, they shared the secret of imposture and provoked a competition of fictions, and, in the process, refused and recycled the negative and damaging images of Muslim women circulating as part of the war on terror.

Undercover supported an awry look at the war on terror. What do we see when we look at this war? Decapitated heads, as described in chapter 2 – and a succession of images that make our heads jump with fear, to again borrow a soldier's description of his experience of the First World War (cited in Bourke 2005: 195). The discussion of the beheading of Kenneth Bigley in chapter 2 made recourse to the Medusa myth, the monstrous snake-covered head of the woman which turns the onlooker into stone. In her essay, 'The Laugh of Medusa', feminist theo- rist Hélène Cixous comments that, in fact, 'you only have to look at the Medusa straight on to see her. And she's not deadly. She's beautiful and she's laughing' (Cixous in Garber and Vickers 2003: 133). The succes- sive uncoverings of *Undercover* similarly reveal a hopeful and beautiful image of the neighbour: a young woman doing hijab, laughing out loud.

Notes

1   The British counterterrorism strategy is called 'CONTEST 2' and is made up of four 'workstreams': 'Pursue', 'Prevent', 'Protect', 'Prepare' (HM Government 2009). It was launched in 2003, revised following the London bombings on 7 July 2005, and relaunched in 2009. In this chapter I refer to performances commissioned as part of the 'Preventing Violent Extremism' (Prevent) strand of CONTEST 2. A 'unique and ground break- ing range of local, national and international partners', Prevent aimed to challenge and disrupt the ideology of violent extremism, support individu- als vulnerable to recruitment to terrorist causes, increase the resilience of communities to violent extremism and address grievances exploited by extremists (HM Government 2008: 6). Funds were allocated to areas with high concentrations of Muslim populations – and this was highly controversial. Critical commentary highlights concerns that the Prevent strategy ignored the socio-economic context in which extremist ideologies thrive, supported intrusive surveillance of Muslim communities, fuelled Islamaphobia, failed to address the problem of far-right extremism in many of the targeted areas, lacked a secure evidence base and threatened existing community cohesion initiatives. For critical views of Prevent, see House of Commons Communities and Local Government Committee (2010), Thomas (2009), Khan (2009), Kundnani (2009) and Finney and Simpson (2009).

2 'Khayaal' means 'imagination' in Arabic, Urdu and Persian, and is the second of five senses that make up the human self in Sufi psychology. For more information go to www.khayaal.co.uk [accessed 1 July 2010].

3 The phrase 'winning hearts and minds' was popularised by British High Commissioner Sir Gerald Templar during the Malayan war that ran from 1948 to 1960 (Stubbs in Marston and Malkasian 2008: 113). A US military commander in Vietnam subsequently reduced 'winning hearts and minds' to the acronym WHAM (Nagl in *ibid.*: 134), which somewhat dilutes its humanising evocations, but is perhaps closer to describing the practices of forced removal of village populations, food control and mass detention that occurred as part of the war in Malaya.

Epilogue: critical mimesis, refusal and waste

Asked how he obtained the beautiful harmony of his sculptures, Michelangelo reputedly answered: 'Simple. You just take a slab of marble and cut out all the superfluous bits.' In the heyday of the Renaissance, Michelangelo proclaimed the precept that was to guide modern creation. *Separation and destruction of waste was to be the trade secret of modern creation*: through cutting out and throwing away the superfluous, the needless and the useless, the beautiful, the harmonious, the pleasing and the gratifying was to be divined [...] There can be no artistic workshop without a rubbish heap. (Bauman 2004: 21–2. Italics in original)

The theatre must in fact remain something entirely superfluous, though this indeed means that it is the superfluous for which we live. (Brecht 1978: 181)

A series of makeshift camps, constructed from litter and rubbish, appeared amongst the sand dunes of the French coastal town of Calais in late 2008. Coinciding with the US government's decision to stop using the term 'war on terror' to describe the ongoing conflict with global terrorism, the camps provided habitation for approximately 1000 refugees from Afghanistan, Iraq, Eritrea, Sudan, Somalia and the Palestinian territories, pursuing dreams of security and employment in England. In response to concerns from authorities on both sides of the English Channel, the camps were cleared by bulldozers in what was termed 'as much a public relations as a police operation' in September

2009 (Chrisafis and Travis 2009). Within hours of the departure of the bulldozers, however, the refugees had started to return to the beaches at Calais.

Despite the official end of the war on terror, the lives of many people in the world continue to be characterised by insecurity and violence caused by the conflict against international terrorism. Thus, refugees arrive on national borders, political violence occurs in sites often outside the radar of the mainstream media, 'threatening' communities are subject to ongoing surveillance and terror raids, and Afghanistan and Iraq are yet to make a promised transition to stable democracy. How can theatre makers respond to this continuing context of crisis and uncertainty? The motif of waste and wasted life repeatedly evoked by the performances documented in this book suggests that an understanding and practice of critical performance as world-transforming and world-making might be usefully substituted by a consideration of performance as a world-conserving endeavour. Here, I offer a summary of some of the implications of this suggestion and draw on a range of sources, together with the performances themselves, to provide a line of thinking about the conservative critical potential of performance's broken, ruined mimesis of a world in crisis.

The 'public relations' operation that temporarily cleared the camps on the beaches in Calais exhibited something of Michelangelo's definition of the project of art as a restoration of beauty and truth to the world by excising its 'superfluous bits'. Here, waste and wasted life – the 'unintended and unplanned "collateral casualties" of economic progress' (Bauman 2004: 39) – are removed and the beautiful fiction of an ordered, equitable world restored. Brecht's reading of the project of critical art as an exercise in superfluity provides a different perspective on this performance. In the essay, 'A Short Organum for the Theatre', Brecht describes his desire for a theatre 'enjoyable to the senses' and *lacking* in social and political utility. Instead, theatre provides forms of pleasure and entertainment in which the value of life might be encountered and measured. The coolies, beggars, prostitutes, gangsters and bandits in Brecht's plays bring audiences into close encounters with the contradictory forces conducting life's possibilities and pleasures in times of terror. His theatre is defined by the deliberate creation of alienation effects that double and estrange the bodies and worlds depicted on stage. As such, theatre offers the 'higher pleasure' of an encounter with the decay of the beautiful fictions of an ordered, equitable world. Such higher, sensual pleasures are derived from dramatisations of life's imperfection, alterability and provisionality, which allow audiences: 'to enjoy as entertainment that terrible and never-ending labour which should ensure their maintenance, together with the terror of their unceasing transformation' (Brecht 1978: 205). To apply this notion of theatre's sensual pleasures to the clearing of the camps at Calais – this public relations operation might be seen as a performance of the failure of beauty. It was also critically reinscribed by compassionate reporting in some newspapers, drawing attention to the terrible impact of war and economic crisis, and extending readers' sense of and sensibilities towards the predicaments of life for our neighbours living in camps on the borders.

Brecht's concern for theatre as a sensuous domain in which a spectator might encounter the world's doubling capacities, alterability and decay, and as a result ensure life's *maintenance* in a time of terror – provides the start and end point of the explorations in this book. This embracing of theatre as a means of transformation and protection highlights a coalition between a radical and a conservative cultural impulse, latent in Brecht's theatre, but also evidenced by many of the examples of performance explored in this book. Critical performance practices exhibit a doubling and decaying, vivifying and mortifying practice of mimesis that plays with bodily and spatial forms to provide uncertain habitations for life in a violent and alienating world. This reading of the politics of performance reflects a shift in the focus of questions asked by socially and politically conscious artists. Whereas artists have asked 'how can we change the world?', performance in a time of terror has responded to a different imperative, articulated by the Israeli playwright and screenwriter Motti Lerner cited in the prologue as follows: 'Theatre needs to ask the question, "how can we live here?"' From the frail and failed voices that disrupted the rhetoric of democracy emanating from the London stage during the years of the war on terror, to the double refusals of camp critical mimesis in antiwar protest performance, the critical potential of performance in a time of terror has resided in its encounters with waste and wasted life. The most effective examples of political performance do not attempt to fix worlds by displaying beautiful fictions of truth and order – rather, they turn to the sensate affects and effects of decay, ruin and debris to regulate the powers of mimesis in ways that protect and sustain life. At best, these performances make use of waste and decay to disperse the powers of mimesis and generate a promise of value, abundance and potential that extends to all life. As part of this, performance has turned from the certainties of left-oriented and identity politics towards engagements with the uncertainties of misunderstanding, difficult encounters, lack of definition and care-full and compassionate material and symbolic practice. It has responded to pressing issues of the survivability and resilience, rather than transformation, of life.

As noted throughout this book, Jacques Rancière locates the critical power of art in moments of aesthetic rupture or dissensus, where senses of the world, and different ways of making sense of the world, are juxtaposed, altering and extending the fabric of the sensory world, and restoring to the body a sense of possibility. In one of the pieces of writing in which he explicates this argument, Rancière works from Johann Winckelmann's eighteenth-century description of the Belvedere torso – the broken, headless and limbless ancient Greek statue thought to represent the demigod Hercules. Rancière argues that eighteenth-century fascination with this mutilated form resided in the disruption of order presented by the display of a strong and beautiful body not able to work and divorced from its productive economic function: 'a body whose dwelling is geared neither to its task nor to its determination' (Rancière 2010: 140). An extension to Rancière's argument is, perhaps, suggested by the attribution of this mutilated torso to Hercules – the mythical figure who symbolises strength, and made the world safe for human life by destroying the monsters that resided within it. Thus, might eighteenth-century fascination with the mutilated body of Hercules express cultural anxieties concomitant with the burgeoning industrialisation of this historical period, and the alienation of bodies resulting from the advent of the machine? This broken bodily form is mimetic of a period of social, economic and political crisis in Europe, and evokes the terrors of a changing world, as much as the critical potential of a body divorced from its proper function. Arguably, the perpetuity and beauty of the ruined body promise survival, and this is what accounts for its powers of fascination. Like Brecht's alienation effect, the broken statue critically mirrors a world in which bodies are appropriated and exploited – and its dissensual lines and forms communicate a sense of the body's resilience, beyond the alienating inscriptions of industry and productivity. As such, and as the examples of performance documented here also evidence, the evocation of broken, ruined forms in performance signals an attempt to regulate the power of mimesis. The fascination of such works of art attaches to their capacity to evoke, capture and mobilise the sensual domains of mortification and adaptation, decay and vivification that accompany mimesis' making and unmaking of worlds.

However, this does not present a comfortable resting place for a search for critical mimesis in an age of uncertainty – as the release of a conservative impetus in performance, just like the radical in performance, represents 'a performative process in need of direction' (Kershaw 1999: 20). The use of broken, ruined forms to claim and regulate the powers of mimesis is for example illustrated by Brian Massumi's analysis of former US President Ronald Reagan's performances as a politician. Massumi argues that the source of Reagan's popularity and power resided in his politicisation of 'the power of mime' (Massumi 2002: 40). In particular, Reagan's physical frailty and frequent verbal slippages – which introduced moments of decay, breaks and interruptions into his performance – released an 'asignifying intensity doubling his every move and phrase' (*ibid.* 41). For Massumi, Reagan's broken, frail performances produced a sense of 'incipience' – that is, a sense of potentiality or the capacity to become, which 'acted as part of the nervous system of a new and frighteningly reactive body politic' (*ibid.*). Here, Reagan's control over mimesis supported the extension of US power in a time of crisis and served a reactionary conservatism that protected some lives whilst destroying others. The reactionary conservatism of Reagan's performance creates an imperative to consider a conservative imposture of performance that uses the power of broken forms to compete with and regulate the organised control of mimesis of wars on terror. If Reagan's mimesis facilitated the mimetic circulation of threat and frailty in ways that supported violence and inequity, what other possibilities for mimesis that makes use of waste and decay are indicated by the performances explored over the course of this book?

These performances have repeatedly demonstrated the complex relationship between performance's capacities to fix, make and preserve, and alter and unmake worlds of experience. Performance has provided impostures that better protect life and make a critical and creative use of life's decay in the face of the world's terrifying and threatening alterability. In fixing the world by symbolic impostures, critical performance explicitly *refuses* a violent and inequitable world, and by decomposing meaning and sense by such imposturous refusals, performance also mobilises a competition between worlds of sense and meaning. Critical performance is responsive to the challenges of uncertainty, turning to waste for its creative potential to unfix a politics that threatens some lives and protects others, and to offer up practices of decomposition and vivification that are incipient – that materialise possibility and dramatise the resilience of life. Here, performances have drawn on the disordering force of waste and decay to inflect a hierarchical and exclusive political order with uncertainty, and pose a competing imposture that values abject, wasted life as a resource that signals life's potential and survival. As such, there are two overlapping dimensions to critical mimesis in performance, and each exhibits two competing impulses: mortifying (fixing *and* decaying) and adaptive (altering *and* making resilient).

The beheading of Kenneth Bigley, the antiwar protest performances and the community-based counterterrorism performances all privileged a mortifying, fixing and decaying practice of mimesis. Each of these performances dramatised a petrifaction that sought to stall a threatening and violent world. In the case of the beheading, this was accompanied by a mimetic display of the devastation caused by a military invasion and occupation, and an assertion of fundamental, transcendental principles in its place, signified by the Qur'an placed in the space of the head. This was a performance that attempted to fix the world by means of a violent excision that degraded the body – here, the chaos of the invasion and occupation was contained in the broken body of the enemy, and the integrity of the body of the religious nation was subsequently impostured. However, other performances of mortification, fixing and decay refused violence as part of their stalling symbolisations. The antiwar protest performances explored in chapter 5, for example, mobilised the bodies of uncountable millions to stop everyday life in urban centres across the world, and insisted on the application of international law to resolve conflict. Calling on the marchers to *stop* and look again, the vacuum cleaner participated in the demonstration in London at this time by contributing a performance that *refused* its spatial and discursive rhetoric. Similarly, the community-based counterterrorism plays in chapter 6 drew on the fixed principles of law, solidarity and faith to call for the *prevention* of violence. The conservative ethos and aesthetic of community-based counterterrorism plays was reflected in a refusal to act – these productions centred on dramatic acts that did not happen or were prevented by the critical and affective responses of young people in the worlds of each play and audiences of performances. These performances of refusal also scripted uncertainty in creative and hopeful ways, remaining open to a shared sense of unfoundedness, and mobilising social encounter. They refused the mimetic circulation of threat and frailty in an age of uncertainty and imposed coalitions of love and law in their place as competing impostures.

The aesthetics and politics of these performances support practices of identification and encounter based on assimilation, equity and reciprocity rather than mastery and hierarchical regulation. Perhaps the most significant suggestion exemplified by these examples of performance for directing the conservative impetus of mimesis in performance resides in their openness to direct encounters with life's decay rather than excision or repulsion of waste. These performances play with waste, search its domains for the forces of potential, revival and restoration, and carefully attend to loss and decay. A turn to Peggy Phelan's work on performance's politics is useful here. Phelan describes tearing out the figure of a body from a pop-up children's book as a child as her first act of performance. This act created a cut-out figure, an absent shape of the human form, and for Phelan this was an act that evokes the critical force of the body's disappearance in performance. She comments: 'the enactment of invocation and disappearance undertaken by perform-ance and theatre is precisely the drama of corporeality itself. At once a consolidated fleshy form and an eroding, decomposing formlessness, the body beckons us and resists our attempts to remake it' (Phelan 1997: 4). This notion of performance as an encounter with the body's decay in the face of the world's alterability has inspired my investigations here, perhaps especially in its insistence on the importance of performance's materiality to the discovery and articulation of its politics. For Phelan, the fading or disappearance of the body in performance is the site of performance's critical potential – by remaining 'unmarked', the appro-priation and exploitation of our bodies in an alienating world might be resisted. To introduce waste into a politics of performance inspired by Phelan is to substitute 'the immateriality of the unmarked' (Phelan 1993: 19) with the tangible materiality of the abject – the surplus, leftover, waste – generated by performance's ongoing failure to fix the world and refuse its violence. Here, it is the significance and *signifiance* of the lost bit of cardboard body torn away and left out of Phelan's account that become important – and that our attempts to direct performance's power in a way that enhances our ability to live in the world must care-fully attend to. The critical potential of performance thus resides in its cyclical processes of materialisation, mortification and decay, rather than its ephemerality or disappearance.

These cycles of mortification and decay were especially evident in the camp critical mimesis of protest performance – which made use of provisional life in the camp to materialise, display and refuse the waste and wasted life of a violent world. These protest performances drew accusations of waste from wider publics and they made use of waste in critical reinscriptions of life as valuable, as in the situating of *This is Camp X-Ray* on the inner-city wasteland, and the gentle care for the non-spaces of the streets of London and New York exhibited by the vacuum cleaner, cleaning up after capitalism. It is notable that the coun-terterrorism plays prefigured a hopeful politics of relationship by recy-cling those identities spoiled by the security agenda as loved and valued members of a community. To draw again on Douglas' useful phrase – here, performances made use of the critical and affective force of waste as 'matter out of place'. That is, performance made use of subjects and objects designated as waste by an exclusive and hierarchical order, to produce estranging displays that inflected that order with decay and pose a competing imposture. Performance is energised by waste – it is superfluous, lacks defined or predetermined use or end, decomposes sense and provides unsettling encounters with the egalitarian nature of life's decay. Here, decay also generates an intense sense of life's material presence – its abundance and resilience – and performances of waste deliberately intensify this sensual domain to disrupt political fictions, resist attempts to perfect, evoke destitution, escape detention and at the same time secure life to a sense of potential and possibility.

Bodiless heads, exposed bodies, frail voices, vulnerable hearts and minds: the circulation of these broken and ruined objects as part of performance's mimesis of the world inverts and negates fictions of bodies and worlds as secure, discrete and rule-bound. Importantly, through dramatising these unfixed and unfixing, discarded, unsettling objects, the secret that is shared (to again draw on Phelan's useful suggestion of performance's affinity with secrets) is that of the unfoundedness, but also profoundly material presence, of life. The mottling and shattering of line and form brought about by the body's decay in performance provide a site/cite from which to forge uncertain but also more habitable impostures of body and world – and embody more hopeful responses to the difficulty of encounter in times of crisis. Performances of refusal and waste highlight the complicities of performance in the degradation of the other, but they also provide an opportunity to re-cite/re-site waste and wasted life as determinedly part of desirable and desired encounters. Rather than excising uncertainty in the process of producing beautiful truths, these performances look to waste and wasted life as offering resilient and adaptive forms of habitation in the face of the world's threatening alterability. Here, terms such as preservation, salvage, protection, restoration and repair provide more critical resonance than transformation, transgression or excess, and the radical and conservative are interdependent rather than opposed concepts and practices of performance. Etymologically, the term 'radical' derives from 'radix' or 'root', and, according to Raymond Williams, it only came to mean the opposite of political 'conservatism' in the twentieth century (Williams 1976: 210). If we consider the possibility that the sense of 'uprooting' pertaining to the radical also denotes processes of cutting away and replanting that ensure survival, the term also carries associations with the conservative – with the care, nurturance and preservation of life. In terms of performance in a time of terror, a radical political project is also one that gestures towards the protection of life, and such conservative gestures constitute radical acts in a context of crisis.

The search for a politics of performance carried out by this book thus ends with a troubling, but also hopeful, notion of a conservative aesthetics and politics of performance. It is important to emphasise again that this is not a comfortable resting place. The counterinsurgency performances in Northern Ireland explored in chapter 3, for example,

made use of performance's conservative aesthetics and politics to materialise forms of protection for counterinsurgents engaging in acts of
violence, most notably in the use of the life of an innocent civilian as
protective cover for an agent at the cost of that civilian's life. A counter-
balance to these particular performances of violence is provided by the
performance of *Undercover* described in chapter 6, which drew on the
motif of the double agent in a way that protected the performers from
further exposure to a world that constructs them as threatening and vulnerable subjects. Importantly, the culture rebels of *Undercover* shared
the secret of unfoundedness rather than claimed any certain or secure
identity. This conservative performance made use of the generative
potential of imposture and decay in an encounter – rather than sought
to secure performers and spectators in a knowable world.

In his discussion of rhythm in the structure of the work of art,
Agamben states that 'by opening to man his authentic temporal dimension, the work of art also opens for him the space of his belonging
to the world, only within which he can take the original measure of
his dwelling on earth' (Agamben 1999: 101). Performance provides a
means by which we take a measure of life in space and time, and this
process of taking measure also generates a space and time for dreaming.
Performance is an imaginative and embodied practice that encounters
and generates worlds beyond the borders of ego, identity, secure relationship and determinable use of space and time. At the end of the first
act of *Somewhere over the Balcony*, produced during the war on terrorism in Northern Ireland in 1987, Ceely and Kate pause on the balcony
of the flats to take a measure of their life in a space and time of crisis.
Wearing a nightdress and a stolen army uniform respectively, they agree
that it is a 'beautiful day' and that 'on a day like today you could be anywhere', before leaving the balcony to the sounds of a controlled explo-
sion (Harris 2006: 204). The women determinedly dream of a beautiful
and habitable world in the space and time of here and now. The play's
female characters negotiate terror and uncertainty by means of self-
conscious, humorous dramatisations of the extraordinary realities of
their everyday life and determined habitation of a provisional space and
site of dreaming. Providing an important turning point in this book, the
play signalled a shift from exploring examples of performed violence to
investigating examples of theatrical performance. Here, performance is
an artful, intentional, embodied, imaginative practice that takes place
in a boundaried time and space devoted to dreaming. The series of
performances that followed this moment in the book repeatedly materialised a dream of habitable space and time as part of their conservative
politics and aesthetics.

At the same time as seeing in art the possibility of taking a measure of life's dwelling, Agamben warns that 'we must expect more camps' (Agamben 1998: 176) – temporary and provisional structures, in which life exists in a permanent state of suspension, underpinned with uncertainty and signalling the waste and wasted life of a violent and inequitable world. Our contemporary time of terror has indeed witnessed a proliferation of camps. Protestors build camps next to sites causing environmental damage and in sites of political and military significance. 'Tent cities' are larger forms of protest camps – mimicking the temporary refuges of populations fleeing war and emergency – and tent cities in the city centres of Kiev, Ukraine (2004–5) and Beirut, Lebanon (2006–7) have sought to pressure illegitimate governments into democratic reform. Camps continue to provide protective and provisional cover for unprecedented millions of refugees in Chad, Sudan, the Democratic Republic of Congo, the Palestinian territories and numerous other sites of crisis. This book has also explored examples of camp critical mimesis in performance – examples of critical art-making in spaces and states of exception that sought to restore to life a sense of its value and possibility, and promised a practice of mimesis that makes worlds without seeking mastery and control over the bodies that inhabit the space and time of those worlds. The proliferation of camps means that we need more, rather than less, performance in a time of crisis, and that we need evermore careful assessments of the politics of performance, focusing on the ways performance is enlisted by as well as stages critical interruptions of wars and crisis. I hope this book has participated in such an endeavour.

The camp appeared as part of the dramatisations of violence and inequity introduced at the start and end point of the book – the camp in the desert in Brecht's *The Exception and the Rule* and the camps constructed from litter on the beaches in Calais. These camps materialise a politics of exception, evidencing crisis and uncertainty, but they also echo Ceely and Kate's dream of a beautiful day in *Somewhere over the Balcony*. In their critical mimesis, many of the performances documented here sought to defend and extend worlds of experience in ways that evoke dreams of habitable environments and affirm life as *possible* in a time of crisis. A *poetics* of camp imagines the defence and extension of habitable space and the resilience and survivability of life, and such imaginings resist the ghettoisation of people and space. For Bachelard, the poetic force of the 'primeval hut' in literature resides in its dream of a place of refuge in which to imagine life beginning again. Hut dreams: 'give us back areas of being, houses in which the human being's certainty of being is concentrated, and we have the impression that, by living in such images as these, in images that are as stabilising as these are, we could start a new life, a life that would be our own, that would belong to us in our very depths' (Bachelard 1994: 33). The camp, in its provisional offer of refuge, evokes a more uncertain, risky dream of the perpetuity of life in times of crisis. By imposturing ongoing lives and worlds in such sites, the camp demonstrates and presents life's resilience. The poetics of camp takes a measure of life in a moment of crisis, and evokes dreams of beginning again, on a more beautiful day. However, such dreams do not escape meaning or detention; rather, they are viscerally confined and confining – and they remind us of the secrets we share, of our mutual strangeness, fear and frailty. In its broken, ruined mimesis of a space of refuge, the camp says, with the global justice movement, 'we are everywhere – out of place, without name or property, ever-present and always returning', and also, with Shakespeare's Hamlet, 'the time is out of joint'.

REFERENCES

Adams, G. (2003) *Hope and history: Making peace in Northern Ireland*, Kerry, Ireland: Brandon.

Adorno, T. (1997 [1970]) *Aesthetic theory*, trans. R. Hullot-Kentor, London: Continuum.

Adorno, T. & Horkheimer, M. (1997 [1944]) *Dialectics of enlightenment*, trans. J. Cumming, London/New York: Verso.

Agamben, G. (2005 [2003]) *State of exception*, trans. K. Attell, Chicago/London: University of Chicago Press.

Agamben, G. (2000 [1996]) *Means without end: Notes on politics*, trans. V. Binetti and C. Casarino, Minneapolis/London: University of Minnesota Press.

Agamben, G. (1999 [1994]) *The man without content*, trans. G. Albert, Stanford: Stanford University Press.

Agamben, G. (1998 [1995]) *Homo Sacer: Sovereign power and bare life*, trans. D. Heller-Roazen, Stanford: Stanford University Press.

Agamben, G. (1993 [1990]) *The coming community*, trans. M. Hardt, Minneapolis/London: University of Minnesota Press.

Ali, L. (2009) Unpublished interview with Jenny Hughes.

Ali, L. (2008) 'More recognition needed for the role of black and Asian theatre', *Guardian*, 10 May.

Allen, J. (2005) 'British unable to hush Parliament protester', *International Herald Tribune*, 23 August.

Amoore, L. (ed.) (2005) *The global resistance reader*, London/New York: Routledge.

Appadurai, A. (2006) *Fear of small numbers: An essay on the geography of anger*, Durham/London: Duke University Press.

Artaud, A. (1977 [1964]) *The theatre and its double*, London: John Calder Publishers.

Ashley, J. (2004) 'We are still free not to watch this gormless explicitness', *Guardian*, 28 October.

Augé, M. (1995 [1992]) *Non-places: Introduction to an anthropology of supermodernity*, trans. J. Howe, London/New York: Verso.

Auslander, P. (1999) *Liveness: Performance in a mediatised culture*, London/New York: Routledge.

Bachelard, G. (1994 [1958]) *The poetics of space*, trans. M. Jolas, Boston: Beacon Press.

Barthes, R. (1990 [1977]) *Image, music, text*, London: Fontana.

Bartlett A. (2009a) Unpublished interview with Jenny Hughes.

Bartlett, A. (2009b) *Not in my name*, London: Oberon.

Bartlett, A. & Raffle, A. (2009) 'Evaluation summary for Not in my name, Phase 4, Lancashire tour', Theatre Veritae (unpublished report, kindly supplied by Theatre Veritae).

Baudrillard, J. (2002) *The spirit of terrorism*, trans. C. Turner, London/New York: Verso.

Bauman, Z. (2007) *Liquid times: Living in an age of uncertainty*, Cambridge: Polity Press.

Bauman, Z. (2004) *Wasted lives: Modernity and its outcasts*, Cambridge: Polity Press.

Bhabha, H. (1994) *The location of culture*, London/New York: Routledge.

Blau, H. (2002) *The dubious spectacle: Extremities of theatre, 1976–2000*, Minneapolis/London: University of Minnesota Press.

Bobbitt, P. (2008) *Terror and consent: The wars for the twenty-first century*, London: Allen Lane.

Bogad, L. (2005) *Electoral guerrilla theatre: Radical ridicule and social movements*, London/New York: Routledge.

Borradori, G. (ed.) (2003) *Philosophy in a time of terror: Dialogues with Jurgen Habermas and Jacques Derrida*, Chicago: University of Chicago Press.

Bottoms, S. (2006) 'Putting the document into documentary: An unwelcome corrective?', *TDR: The Drama Review*, 50(3): 56–68.

Bottoms, S. & Goulish, M. (eds) (2007) *Small acts of repair: Performance, ecology and Goat Island*, London/New York: Routledge.

Bourke, J. (2005) *Fear: A cultural history*, London: Virago Press.

Brecht, B. (2001 [1957]) *The measures taken and other lehrstücke*, ed. J. Willet & R. Manheim, New York: Arcade Publishing.

Brecht, B. (1987) *Bertolt Brecht poems 1913–1956*, ed. J. Willett & R. Manheim, London/New York: Methuen.

Brecht, B. (1978 [1957]) *Brecht on theatre*, ed. & trans. J. Willett, London: Methuen.

Brittain, V. & Slovo, G. (2004) *Guantánamo: Honour bound to defend freedom*, London: Oberon Books.

Buck-Morss, S. (2003) *Thinking past terror: Islamism and critical theory on the Left*, London/New York: Verso.

Bunting, M. (2003) 'We are the people', *Guardian*, 17 February.

Burke, J. (2004a) 'Theatre of terror', *Observer*, 21 November.

Burke, J. (2004b) 'Zarqawi has method in his madness', *Observer*, 26 September.

Burke, J. (2003) *Al Qaeda: The true story of radical Islam*, London: Penguin Books.

Butler, J. (2009) *Frames of war: When is life grievable?*, London/New York: Verso.

Butler, J. (2004) *Precarious life: The powers of mourning and violence*, London/New York: Verso.

Byrne, O. (ed.) (2001) *State of play: The theatre and cultural identity in 20th century Ulster*, Belfast: The Linen Hall Library.

Carroll, R. (2005) 'Rebels confess to beheadings on Iraqi TV', *Guardian*, 24 February.

Charabanc Theatre Company (1987) *Somewhere over the balcony* (theatre programme). Public archive held at Linen Hall Library, Belfast, Northern Ireland.

Chrisafis, A. & Travis, A. (2009) 'Riot police clear Calais camp as ministers accused over asylum', *Guardian*, 22 September.

Churchill, C. (2000) *Far away*, London: Nick Hern.

Clapp, S. (2008) 'Shoot/get treasure/repeat', *Observer*, 13 April.

Claude, P. (2004) 'Barbarity can be effective', *Guardian*, 15 October.

Cleary, J. (1999) 'Domestic troubles: Tragedy and the Northern Ireland conflict', *The South Atlantic Quarterly*, 98(3): 501–37.

Cleto, F. (ed.) (1999) *Camp – queer aesthetics and the performing subject: A reader*, Ann Arbor: University of Michigan Press.

Clough, P., with Halley, J. (2007) *The affective turn: Theorising the social*, Durham/London: Duke University Press.

Cohen, N. (2007) 'The Turner judges have been hoodwinked', *Observer*, 9 December.

Cohen-Cruz, J. (ed.) (1998) *Radical street performance: An international anthology*, London/New York: Routledge.

Colleran, J. & Spencer, J. (eds) (1998) *Staging resistance: Essays in political theater*, Ann Arbor: University of Michigan Press.

Conrad, J. (1973 [1902]) *Heart of darkness*, London: Penguin Books.

Corera, G. (2005) 'Iraq's danger for foreigners', BBC News, 28 November. Available at: http://news.bbc.co.uk/1/hi/uk/4479038.stm [accessed 18 July 2010].

Coulter-Smith, G. & Owen, M. (eds) (2005) *Art in the age of terrorism*, London: Paul Holberton Publishing.

Coyle, J. (1988) 'Stage tribute to women of Divis', *Irish News*, 31 May.

Curtis, L. (1984) *Ireland: The propaganda war: The British media and the 'battle for hearts and minds'*, London: Pluto Press.

Curtis, N. (1998) *Faith and duty: The true story of a soldier's war in Northern Ireland*, London: André Deutsch.

Davies, N. (2004) *Dead men talking: Collusion, cover-up and murder in Northern Ireland's dirty war*, London/Edinburgh: Mainstream Publishing.

Debord, G. (2006 [1967]) *Society of the spectacle*, trans. K. Knabb, London: Aldgate Press.

De Certeau, M. (1984) *The practice of everyday life*, trans. S. Rendall, Berkeley/London: University of California Press.

Deeney, J. (2006) 'David Hare and political playwriting: Between the third way and the *Permanent way*', in M. Luckhurst (ed.) *A companion to modern British and Irish drama*, Oxford: Blackwell.

De Jongh, N. (2003) 'Justifying war', *Evening Standard*, 5 November.

Derrida, J. (2005) *Rogues: Two essays on reason*, Stanford: Stanford University Press.

Diamond, E. (1997) *Unmaking mimesis*, London/New York: Routledge.

Diamond, E. (1995) 'The shudder of catharsis in twentieth-century performance', in A. Parker & E. Kosofsky-Sedgwick (eds) *Performativity and performance*, London/New York: Routledge.

Diamond, E. (1992) 'The violence of "we": Politicising identification', in J.G. Reinelt & J.R. Roach (eds) *Critical theory and performance*, Ann Arbor: University of Michigan Press.

DiCenzo, M.R. (1993) 'Charabanc Theatre Company: Placing women centre-stage in Northern Ireland', *Theatre Journal*, 45(2): 175–84.

Dillon, M. (1990) *The dirty war*, London: Arrow Books.

Doherty, B. (2000) 'Manufactured vulnerability: Protest camp tactics', in B. Seel, M. Paterson & B. Doherty (eds) *Direct action in British environmentalism*, London/New York: Routledge.

Dolar, M. (2006) *A voice and nothing more*, London: MIT Press.

Douglas, M. (1966) *Purity and danger*, London/New York: Routledge.

Eagleton, T. (2009) *Trouble with strangers: A study of ethics*, Chichester, West Sussex: John Wiley and Sons.

Eagleton, T. (2005) *Holy terror*, Oxford: Oxford University Press.

Edgar, D. (2008) 'Doc and dram', *Guardian*, 27 September.

Edgerton, G. (1996) 'Quelling the "oxygen of publicity": British broadcasting and "The Troubles" during the Thatcher years', *The Journal of Popular Culture*, 30(1): 115–32.

Elliott, F. & Fitzwilliams, M. (2004) 'Blunkett legislates to silence lone protester at Westminster', *Independent on Sunday*, 24 October.

Evans, J. (2007) 'Speech: Counterterrorism and public trust', *The Times*, 5 November.

Evans, M. (2005) 'Top secret intelligence unit will quit Belfast for new role in Iraq', *The Times*, 18 April.

Farndale, N. (2006) 'The nut and the hammer', *Sunday Telegraph*, 15 May.

Feldman, A. (2005) 'On the actuarial gaze: From 9/11 to Abu Ghraib', *Cultural Studies*, 19(2): 203–26.

Feldman, A. (2004) 'Memory theaters, virtual witnessing and the trauma-aesthetic', *Biography*, 27(1): 164–202.

Feldman, A. (1991) *Formations of violence: The narrative of the body and political terror in Northern Ireland*, Chicago: University of Chicago Press.

Finney, N. & Simpson, L. (2009) '*Sleepwalking to segregation*'? *Challenging myths about race and migration*, Bristol: The Polity Press.

Fischer-Lichte, E. (2008) *The transformative power of performance: A new aesthetics*, trans. S. Jain, London/New York: Routledge.

Fisk, R. (2005) 'When nature and man conspire to expose the lies of the powerful, the truth will out', *Independent*, 24 September.

Foley, I. (2003) *The girls in the big picture: Gender in contemporary Ulster*, Belfast: The Blackstaff Press.

Forsyth, A. & Megson, C. (eds) (2009) *Get real: Documentary theatre past and present*, Basingstoke/New York: Palgrave Macmillan.

Foster, S.L. (2003) 'Choreographies of protest', *Theatre Journal*, 55: 395–412.

Foucault, M. (1977) *Discipline and punish: The birth of the prison*, trans. A. Sheridan, London: Penguin Books.

Fowler, J. (1987) 'Sanity away from the political madness', *Glasgow Herald*, 25 November.

Frayn, M. (2003a) *Democracy*, London: Methuen.

Frayn, M. (2003b) Michael Frayn on *Democracy*, interviewed by Matt Wolff, National Theatre platform paper. Available from: www.nationaltheatre.org.uk/?lid=7664 [accessed 20 August 2010].

Freud, S. (2004 [1930]) *Civilisation and its discontents*, trans. D. McLintock, London: Penguin.

Freud, S. (2003 [1919]) *The uncanny*, trans. D. McLintock, London: Penguin.

Freud, S. (1955) *The standard edition of the complete psychological works of Freud. Volume 18*, trans. J. Strachey, London: Hogarth Press.

Freud, S. & Breuer, F. (1991 [1895]) *Studies on hysteria*, trans. J. Strachey & A. Strachey, London: Penguin.

Furedi, F. (2007) *Invitation to terror: The expanding empire of the unknown*, London/New York: Continuum.

Garber, M. & Vickers, N.J. (2003) *The Medusa reader*, London/New York: Routledge.

Gardham, D. (2009) 'Abu Ghraib abuse photos "show rape"', *Telegraph*, 27 May.

George, J. with Ottaway, J. (1999) *She who dared: Covert operations in Northern Ireland with the SAS*, South Yorkshire: Leo Cooper.

Ghālib, M. (2002) *Love sonnets of Ghālib*, trans. Dr S.K. Niāzī, New Delhi: Rupa & Co.

Gilbert, H. (ed.) (2001) *Postcolonial plays: An anthology*, London/New York: Routledge.

Ginsborg, P. (2008) *Democracy: Crisis and renewal*, London: Profile Books.

Giroux, H.A. (2006) *Beyond the spectacle of terrorism: Global uncertainty and the challenge of the new media*, Boulder, CO: Paradigm Publishers.

Goffman, E. (1959) *The presentation of self in everyday life*, New York: Anchor Books.

Gómez-Peña, G. (2005) *Ethno-techno: Writings on performance, activism and pedagogy*, London/New York: Routledge.

Gove, M. (2004) 'By turning one man's anger into a media event, we allow terror a victory', *The Times*, 28 September.

Gregory, D. (2004) *The colonial present*, Oxford: Blackwell.

Guinness World Records (2003) *Guinness World Records 2004*, Guinness World Records Limited: HIT Entertainment Company.

Habermas, J. (1996 [1992]) *Between facts and norms: Contributions to a discourse theory of law and democracy*, trans.W. Rehg, Cambridge: Polity Press.

Habermas, J. (1984 [1981]) *The theory of communicative action. Volume I: Reason and the rationalization of society*, trans. T. McCarthy, Cambridge: Polity Press.

Halliwell, S. (2002) *The aesthetics of mimesis: Ancient texts and modern problems*, Princeton/London: Princeton University Press.

Hammond, W. & Steward, D. (eds) (2008) *Verbatim verbatim: Contemporary documentary theatre*, London: Oberon.

Handan, N. (2005) Unpublished interview between Jenny Hughes and Naeem Handan, director of Massafat Theatre.

Harding, L. (2004a) 'The other prisoners', *Guardian*, 20 May.

Harding, L. (2004b) 'After Abu Ghraib', *Guardian*, 20 September.

Harding, L. (2004c) 'Brutal kidnappers gaining in popularity', *Guardian*, 21 September.

Hardt, M. & Negri, A. (2004) *Multitude: War and democracy in an age of empire*, London: Penguin.

Hardt, M. & Negri, A. (2000) *Empire*, Cambridge, MA/London: Harvard University Press.

Hare, D. (2005) *Obedience, struggle & revolt*, London: Faber & Faber.

Hare, D. (2004) *Stuff happens*, London: Faber & Faber.

Harris, C.W. (ed.) (2006) *Four plays by the Charabanc Theatre Company: Inventing women's work*, Buckinghamshire: Colin Smythe.

Harris, M. (2009) 'Fighting the war against terror: Creativity, collaboration, individualism and waking up in bed with the funding devil', *Writing in Education*, Autumn 49.

Harris, M. (2007) *One extreme to the other* (unpublished play, script kindly provided by playwright).

Harris, P., Aglion-Jakarta, J., Cleaver-Berlin, S. and Arie, S. (2003) 'Iraq crisis: The peace marches: People power takes to the world's streets', *Observer*, 16 February.

Harvie, D., Milburn, K., Trott, B. & Watts, D. (eds) (2005) *Shut them down! The G8, Gleneagles 2005, and the Movement of Movements*, Leeds/New York: Dissent and Autonomedia.

Haw, B. (2008) Unpublished interview with Jenny Hughes.

Hesford, W. (2006) 'Staging terror', *TDR: The Drama Review*, 50(3): 29–41.

HM Government (2009) *Pursue, prevent, protect, prepare: The United Kingdom's strategy for countering international terrorism*, Norwich: The Stationery Office.

HM Government (2008) *The Prevent strategy: A guide for local partners in England*, Norwich: The Stationery Office.

Holloway, J. (2008) '1968 and doors to new worlds', *Turbulence*, July: 9–14.

Holloway, J. (2002) *Change the world without taking power: The meaning of revolution today*, London/Ann Arbor: Pluto Press.

House of Commons Communities and Local Government Committee (2010) *Preventing violent extremism: Sixth report of session 2009–10*, London: The Stationery Office.

Hughes, J. (2010) 'When things like this are happening around you . . .': The relationship between preventing violent extremism and theatre. An evaluation of *Not in my name'*. Available on request from author.

Hughes, J. (2007) 'Theatre, performance and the "war on terror": Ethical and political questions arising from British theatrical responses to war and terrorism', *Contemporary Theatre Review*, 17(2): 149–64.

Ingram, M. & Harkin, G. (2004) *Stakeknife: Britain's secret agents in Ireland*, Dublin: The O'Brien Press.

Iron, R. (2008) 'Britain's longest war: Northern Ireland 1967–2007', in D. Marston & C. Malkasian (eds) *Counterinsurgency in modern warfare*, Oxford: Osprey Publishing.

Itzin, C. (1980) *Stages in the revolution: Political theatre in Britain since 1968*, London: Methuen.

Janes, R. (2005) *Losing our heads: Beheadings in literature and culture*, New York/London: New York University Press.

Janes, R. (1991) 'Beheadings', *Representations*, 35 (Summer): 21–51.

Jones, G. (2007) 'Terrorism fight is cold war, says Brown', *Telegraph*, 2 July.

Jung, C. (2002 [1946]) *Essays on contemporary events 1936–1946*, trans. R.F.C. Hull, London/New York: Routledge.

Kean, T.H., Hamilton, L.H., Ben-Vensite, R., Kerrey, B., Fielding, F.F., Lehman, J.F., Gorelick, J.S., Roemer, T.J., Gorton, S. and Thompson, J.R. (2004) *The 9/11 Commission report: Final report of the National Commission on terrorist attacks upon the United States*, authorised edition, New York: W.W. Norton & Company.

Kelleher, J. (2009) *Theatre and politics*, Basingstoke/New York: Palgrave Macmillan.

Kennicott, P. (2006) 'A chilling portrait, unsuitably framed', *Washington Post*, 9 June.

Kershaw, B. (2007) *Theatre ecology: Environment and performance events*, Cambridge: Cambridge University Press.

Kershaw, B. (1999) *The radical in performance: Between Brecht and Baudrillard*, London/New York: Routledge.

Kershaw, B. (1992) *The politics of performance: Radical theatre as cultural intervention*, London/New York: Routledge.

Khan, K. (2009) *Preventing violent extremism (PVE) and PREVENT: A response from the Muslim community*, An-Nisa Society. Available at: www.an-nisa.org/downloads/PVE_&_Prevent_-__A_Muslim_response.pdf [accessed 6 September 2009].

Khayaal Theatre Company (2008) *Hearts and minds*. Unpublished play. Script kindly provided by Khayaal Theatre Company.

Kitson, F. (1971) *Low intensity operations: Subversion, insurgency and peacekeeping*, St Petersburg, FL: Hailer Publishing.

Klein, N. (2007) *The shock doctrine*, London: Penguin.

Koch, C. (2003) *2/15: The day the world said NO to war*, New York: AK Press.

Kristeva, J. (1982) *The powers of horror: An essay on abjection*, New York/ Chichester, West Sussex: Columbia University Press.

Kubiak, A. (1991) *Stages of terror: Terrorism, ideology and coercion as theatre history*, Bloomington/Indianapolis: Indiana University Press.

Kundnani, A. (2009) *Spooked! How not to prevent violent extremism*, Institute of Race Relations. Available at: www.irr.org.uk/spooked [accessed 1 July 2010].

Kundnani, A. (2008) 'Islamism and the roots of liberal rage', *Race and Class*, 50(2): 40–68.

Kustow, M. (2008) 'Plays for today', *Guardian*, 8 April.

Lacan, J. (2001 [1966]) *Écrits: A selection*, London/New York: Routledge

Lacan, J. (1977 [1973]) *The four fundamental concepts of psycho-analysis*, trans. A. Sheridan, London/New York: Karnac.

Lane, J. (2002) 'Reverend Billy: Preaching, protest and postindustrial flânerie', *TDR: The Drama Review*, 46(1): 60–84.

Latimer, J. (2001) *Deception in war*, London: John Murray.

Lefebvre, H. (1991 [1974]) *The production of space*, trans. D. Nicholson-Smith, Oxford: Blackwell.

Lehmann, H. (2006 [1999]) *Postdramatic theatre*, trans. K. Jürs-Munby, London/New York: Routledge.

Lerner, M. (2005). Unpublished interview with Jenny Hughes.

Lewis, P. (2007) *Young, British and Muslim*, London: Continuum.

Lewis, R. (1999) *Fishers of men*, London: Hodder & Stoughton.

Lloyd, M. (1997) *The art of military deception*, London: Leo Cooper.

Lojek, H. (1999) 'Playing politics with Belfast's Charabanc Theatre Company', in J.P. Harrington & E.J. Mitchell (eds) *Politics and performance in contemporary Northern Ireland*, Amherst: University of Massachusetts Press.

Luce, E. & Dombey, D. (2009) 'Obama junks "global war on terror" label', *Financial Times*, 30 June.

Mackay, N. (2003) '"UDA collusion" masterspy in top Iraq role', *Sunday Herald*, 23 February.

Magee, P. (2006) Unpublished interview with Jenny Hughes.

Maguire, T. (2006) *Making theatre in Northern Ireland: Through and beyond the Troubles*, Exeter: University of Exeter Press.

Mahoney, D. (2004) *This is Camp X-Ray*, DVD, Manchester: UHC Collective.

Makepeace, C. (1995) *Old Ordnance Survey maps, Manchester (SW) 1894 The Godfrey Edition*. Reduced from the original to 1:4 340. Dunston, Gateshead: Alan Godfrey.

Mandaville, P. (2007) *Global political Islam*, London/New York: Routledge.

Marston, D. & Malkasian, C. (eds) (2008) *Counterinsurgency in modern warfare*, Oxford: Osprey Publishing.

Martin, C. (2009) 'Living simulations: the use of media in documentary in the UK, Lebanon and Israel', in A. Forsyth & C. Megson (eds) *Get real: Documentary theatre past and present*, Basingstoke/New York: Palgrave Macmillan.

Martin, C. (2006) 'Bodies of evidence', *TDR: The Drama Review*, 50(3): 8–15.

Martin, C. (1987) 'Charabanc Theatre Company: "Quare" women "sleggin" and "geggin" the standards of Northern Ireland by "tappin" the people', *TDR: The Drama Review*, 31(2): 88–99.

Massumi, B. (2002) *Movement, affect, sensation: Parables of the virtual*, Durham/London: Duke University Press.

Mbembe, A. (2003) 'Necropolitics', *Public Culture*, 15(1): 11–40.

McFadden, R. (2003) 'From New York to Melbourne, cries for peace', *New York Times*, 16 February.

McGreal, C. (2009) 'Obama moves to postpone release of images showing alleged detainee abuse', *Guardian*, 13 May.

McKay, G. (ed.) (1998) *DIY culture: Party & protest in nineties Britain*, London/New York: Verso.

McKenzie, J. (2009) 'Abu Ghraib and the society of the scaffold', in P. Anderson & J. Menon (eds) *Violence performed: Local roots and global routes of conflict*, Basingstoke/New York: Palgrave Macmillan.

McKenzie, J. (2003) 'Democracy's performance', *TDR: The Drama Review*, 47(2): 117–28.

McKenzie, J. (2001) *Perform or else: From discipline to performance*, London/New York: Routledge.

Megson, C. (2007) 'The state we're in: Tribunal theatre and British politics in the 1990s', in D. Watt & D. Meyer-Dinkgräfe (eds) *Theatres of thought: Theatre, performance and philosophy*, Newcastle: Cambridge Scholars Publishing.

Megson, C. (2005) 'This is all theatre: Iraq centre stage', *Contemporary Theatre Review*, 15(3): 369–71.

Millward, D. (2002) 'Grudging respect of pavement protestors', *Daily Telegraph*, 27 August.

Ministry of Defence (2006) 'Operation Banner: An analysis of military operations in Northern Ireland. Prepared under the direction of the Chief of General Staff, Army Code 71842', UK: Ministry of Defence. Available at: www.serve.com/pfc/misc/opbanner.pdf [accessed 5 June 2008].

Mockaitis, T.R. (1995) *British counterinsurgency in the post-imperial era*, Manchester: Manchester University Press.

Morash, C. (2002) *A history of Irish theatre 1601–2000*, Cambridge: Cambridge University Press.

Muños Viñas, S. (2005) *Contemporary theory of conservation*, Oxford/Burlington: Elsevier Butterworth-Heinemann.

Murdock, G. (1991) 'Patrolling the border: British broadcasting and the Irish question in the 1980s', *Journal of Communication*, 41(4): 104–15.

Murray, A. & German, L. (2005) *Stop the war: The story of Britain's biggest mass movement*, London: Bookmarks.

Naughton, P. (2004) 'Retirement beckoned, but Bigley stayed in Iraq', *The Times*, 8 October.

Newsinger, J. (1995) 'From counter-insurgency to internal security: Northern Ireland 1969–1992', *Small Wars & Insurgencies*, 6(1): 88–111.

Nicholson, H. (2005) *Applied drama: The gift of theatre*, Basingstoke/New York: Palgrave Macmillan.

Nield, S. (2006) 'There is another world: Space, theatre and global anti-capitalism', *Contemporary Theatre Review*, 16(1): 51–61.

Norton-Taylor, R. (2007) *Called to account: The indictment of Anthony Charles Lynton Blair for the crime of aggression against Iraq – a hearing*, London: Oberon.

Norton-Taylor, R. (2005) 'New Special Forces unit tailed Brazilian', *Guardian*, 4 August.

Norton-Taylor, R. (2003) *Justifying war: Scenes from the Hutton Inquiry*, London: Oberon.

Norton-Taylor, R. (1995) *Truth is a difficult concept: Inside the Scott Inquiry*, London: Fourth Estate.

Notes from Nowhere (eds) (2003) *We are everywhere: The irresistible rise of global anti-capitalism*, London/New York: Verso.

Nowlan, D. (1987) 'Somewhere over the balcony at the Peacock', *Irish Times*, 29 December.

Orr, D. (2007) 'A futile gesture (and far too clean)', *Independent*, 3 February.

Paget, D. (1987) '"Verbatim theatre": Oral history and documentary techniques', *New Theatre Quarterly*, 3(12): 317–35.

Perucci, T. (2009) 'Performance complexes: Abu Ghraib and the culture of neoliberalism', in P. Anderson & J. Menon (eds) *Violence performed: Local roots and global routes of conflict*, Basingstoke: Palgrave Macmillan.

Phelan, P. (1997) *Mourning sex: Performing public memories*, London/New York: Routledge.

Phelan, P. (1993) *Unmarked: The politics of performance*, London/New York: Routledge.

Rancière, J. (2010) *Dissensus: On politics and aesthetics*, trans. S. Corcoran, London/New York: Continuum.

Ravenhill, M. (2008) *Shoot/get treasure/repeat: An epic cycle of short plays*, London: Methuen.

Rayment, S. (2007) 'Top secret army cell breaks terrorists', *Sunday Telegraph*, 5 February.

Read, A. (2008) *Theatre, intimacy and engagement: The last human venue*, Basingstoke/New York: Palgrave Macmillan.

Rebellato, D. (1999) *1956 and all that: The making of modern British drama*, London/New York: Routledge.

Redman, J. (2008) 'A public of sorts', Ultimate Holding Company, Manchester & Arts Council England. Available at: www.uhc.org.uk/website/uploads/a-public-of-sorts-report.pdf [accessed 1 September 2009].

Reinelt, J. (2007) 'The "rehabilitation" of Howard Brenton', *TDR: The Drama Review*, 51(3): 167–74.

Reinelt, J. & Roach, J.R. (eds) (1992) *Critical theory and performance*, Ann Arbor: University of Michigan Press.

Rennie, J. (1997) *The operators*, Barnsley, South Yorkshire: Pen & Sword Military Classics.

Rickman, A. & Viner, K. (2005) *My name is Rachel Corrie*, London: Nick Hern.

Rolston, B. & Miller, D. (eds) (1996) *War and words: The Northern Ireland media reader*, Belfast: Beyond the Pale.

Runciman, W.G. (ed.) (2004) *Hutton and Butler: Lifting the lid on the workings of power*, Oxford: Oxford University Press.

Samuel, R. (1994) *Theatres of memory*, London/New York: Verso.

Samuel, R., McColl, E. & Cosgrove, S. (1985) *Theatres of the left 1880–1935: Workers theatre movements in Britain and America*, London: Routledge & Kegan Paul.

Schechner, R. (1993) *The future of ritual*, London/New York: Routledge.

Schechner, R. (1985) *Between theatre and anthropology*, Philadelphia: University of Pennsylvania Press.

Scraton, P. (ed.) (2002) *Beyond September 11: An anthology of dissent*, London: Pluto Press.

Shepard, B. (2004) 'A post-absurd, post-camp activist moment', *Counterpunch*, 4 February. Available at: www.counterpunch.org/shepard02052004.html [accessed 21 January 2009].

Shepard, B. & Hayduk, R. (eds) (2002) *From ACT UP to the WTO: Urban protest and community building in an era of globalisation*, London/New York: Verso.

Sierz, A. (2005) 'Beyond timidity? The state of British new writing', *Performing Arts Journal*, 81: 55–61.

Sihra, M. (ed.) (2007) *Women in Irish drama: A century of authorship and representation*, Basingstoke/New York: Palgrave Macmillan.

Smith, J. (2003) 'A million marching: London peace demo biggest since VE-Day', *Daily Mirror*, 15 February.

Smith, M. (2007) 'Secret war of the SAS', *The Times*, 16 September.

Soans, R. (2005a) *Talking to terrorists*, London: Oberon.

Soans, R. (2005b) Unpublished interview with Jenny Hughes and Alison Jeffers.

Solnit, R. (2005) *Hope in the dark: The untold history of people power*, Edinburgh/New York/Melbourne: Canongate.

Taguba, A.M. (2004) 'Article 15-6 Investigation of the 800th Military Police Brigade'. Available at: www.npr.org/iraq/2004/prison_abuse_report.pdf [accessed 11 August 2010].

Taussig, M. (1993) *Mimesis and alterity: A particular history of the senses*, London/New York: Routledge.

Taussig, M. (1992) *The nervous system*, London/New York: Routledge.

Taussig, M. (1987) *Shamanism, colonialism and the wild man: A study in terror and healing*, Chicago/London: University of Chicago Press.

Taylor, A. (2003) 'Silly arts', *Sun*, 14 October.

Taylor, C. (2002) 'As long as it takes', *Guardian*, 20 September.

Taylor, D. (2003) *The archive and the repertoire: Performing cultural memory in the Americas*, Durham/London: Duke University Press.

Taylor, D. (1997) *Disappearing acts: Spectacles of gender and nationalism in Argentina's 'dirty war'*, Durham/London: Duke University Press.

Taylor, P. (2003) 'Justifying war', *Independent*, 6 November.

Taylor, P. (2001) *Brits: The war against the IRA*, London: Bloomsbury.

Teeman, T. (2007) 'Protest loses its potency off the street', *The Times*, 16 January.

Theatre Day Productions graduates (2005). Unpublished interviewed with Jenny Hughes.

Thomas, P. (2009) 'Between two stools? The government's "preventing violent extremism" agenda', *The Political Quarterly*, 80(2): 282–91.

Thompson, J. (2009) *Performance affects: Applied theatre and the end of effect*, Basingstoke/New York: Palgrave Macmillan.

Thompson. J. & Schechner, R. (2004) 'Why "social theatre"?', *TDR: The Drama Review*, 48(3): 11–16.

Thompson, J., Hughes, J. & Balfour, M. (2009) *Performance in place of war*, Greenford: Seagull.

Thompson, R. (1966) *Defeating communist insurgency*, reprinted 2005, St Petersburg, FL: Hailer Publishing.

Townshend, C. (1986) *Britain's civil wars: Counterinsurgency in the twentieth century*, London: Faber & Faber.

tucker-green, d. (2008) *random*, London: Nick Hern.

Undercover (2008) Unpublished interviews with participants, with Jenny Hughes.

Undercover (2007a) Unpublished play devised by Young Muslim Sisters, Manchester.

Undercover (2007b) Unpublished interviews with audience members, In Place of War team.

Urban, M. (1992) *Big boys' rules: The SAS and the secret struggle against the IRA*, London: Faber & Faber.

US Army (2007) *The US Army Marine Corps counterinsurgency field manual*. Foreword by General D.H. Petraeus, Lt General J.F. Amos & Lt Colonel J.A. Nagl. Chicago/London: University of Chicago Press.

Wardle, I. (1994) 'Half the picture', *Independent on Sunday*, 19 June.

Whitaker, R. (2005) 'My name is Rachel Corrie', *Independent on Sunday*, 17 April.

Wiles, D. (2000) *Greek theatre performance: An introduction*, Cambridge: Cambridge University Press.

Willett, J. (1977) *The theatre of Bertolt Brecht*, London: Methuen.

Williams, R. (1976) *Keywords: A vocabulary of culture and society*, London: Fontana.

Wolff, J. (2008) *The aesthetics of uncertainty*, New York/Chichester, West Sussex: Columbia University Press.

Zawahiri, A. (2005) 'Letter to Abu Musab al-Zarqawi', Office of the Director of National Intelligence (US). Available at: www.dni.gov/press_releases/letter_in_english.pdf [accessed 20 July 2010].

Žižek, S. (2008) *Violence: Six sideways reflections*, London: Profile Books.
Žižek, S. (2006) *How to read Lacan*, London: Granta Books.
Žižek, S. (2002) *Welcome to the desert of the real*, London/New York: Verso.
Žižek, S. (1995) '"I hear you with my eyes"; or, the invisible master', in R. Salecl & S. Žižek (eds) *Gaze and voice as love objects*, Durham/London: Duke University Press.

INDEX

Note: 'n.' after a page number indicates the number of a note on that page.

7 July 2005 154, 165, 171, 89n.1,
    186n.1
9/11 attacks 2, 15–16, 41, 59, 115, 158
14th Intelligence Company 60, 66,
    74–7
15 February 2003 125, 134–42,
    152n.2

abject 18, 21, 24–8, 45, 48–54, 56, 98,
    163–4, 194
Abu Ghraib prison 36, 38, 42, 49–50,
    52, 54–6
ACT UP 143
Adams, G. 65
Agamben, G. 4, 6, 16–17, 126, 144–5,
    151, 162–3, 196–7
    state of exception 4–5, 43, 109, 126,
    132
Adorno, T. 23–4, 107, 109, 113
    and Horkheimer, M. 13, 18, 23–4,
    25, 28

Ali, L. 179
anti-roads protests 131, 132–3
Appadurai, A. 45
Aristotle 11, 26
Artaud, A. 11–12
Auslander, P. 96–7

Bachelard, G. 86, 197–8
Barthes, R. 100
Bartlett, A.
    Not in my Name 157, 165–71
Bauman, Z. 10, 16–17, 188, 189
Blair, T. 36, 101, 115, 123n.4,
    138
Bogad, L. 130–1, 133
Bottoms, S. 114–15
    and Goulish 29–30, 31
Brecht, B. 1, 4, 68, 73–4, 158, 188,
    189–90
    The Exception and the Rule 1, 2,
    5–6, 155

Brittain, V. and Slovo, G.
    *Guantánamo: Honour bound to
    defend freedom* 93, 112–13
broadcasting ban (1988) 65–6
Brown, G. 153
Buck-Morss, S. 2, 158
Bush, G. 15, 89n.3 115
Butler, J. 44, 52, 54, 56

camp
    and Agamben 6, 126, 132, 148
    protest camps 127, 131–2, 144,
        150–1, 197
    queer camp 127, 131–4, 148,
        150–1
Charabanc Theatre Company
    Somewhere over the Balcony 62,
        81–9, 196, 197
Chomsky, N. 16
Churchill, C.
    Far Away 94, 118–23
community-based counterterrorism
        155–6, 186n.1, 192, 193
Conrad, J.
    Heart of Darkness 40, 41, 46
conservative (in performance) 69, 83,
        156, 163–5, 179 *see also* radical-
        conservative (in performance)
Coulter-Smith, G. and Owen, M.
        12
counterinsurgency 59–61, 66–7
    agents 72–3, 78–81
    spatial practices 70–7
    training 66–7, 71, 76
    winning hearts and minds 39, 66,
        153, 177, 187n.3

Deeney, J. 115
deliberative democracy 96, 105, 108,
        121 *see also* Habermas
Derrida, J. 41, 108
Diamond, E. 22, 109
dissensus 20, 68–9, 126, 191
Dolar, M. 97–8
Douglas, M. 146, 194

Eagleton, T. 16, 160, 164, 180
Edgar, D. 91

Feldman, A. 48, 54, 61, 107
Fischer-Lichte, E. 25
Forces Research Unit 60–1, 67–8, 76,
        79–81, 89n.3, 90n.5
Foster, S. 135, 136
Foucault, M. 40, 42, 51
Frayn, M.
    Democracy 94, 113, 114, 116–18
Freud, S. 35, 50, 78, 94, 164, 180

Gaza 6–8
Ghālib 175, 176, 178, 180
Giroux, H. 39, 54
global justice movement 129, 133–4,
        198
Goffman, E. 75
Gómez-Peña, G. 127–8
Gregory, D. 42, 58n.5
GW Theatre 157, 171

Habermas, J. 94, 96, 105, 108, 109,
        121
Hardt, M. and Negri, A. 129, 133,
        135, 140
Hare, D.
    Stuff Happens 93, 114–16
Harris, M.
    One Extreme to the Other 157,
        171–5
Haw, B. 125, 142–7, 148, 150, 151
Holbein's *Ambassadors* 46, 185
Holloway, J. 129–30, 131
Hutton Inquiry 95, 96, 104, 123n.2

institutionalising imagination 2,
        155
IRA 64–5, 71–2, 73, 76, 78, 79, 110

Karmarama
    Make Tea Not War, 138, 139
Kelleher, J. 26–7, 98
Kelly, D. 94, 95, 102, 103–4

Kelly, J. 94, 95–100, 109, 122
Kent, N. 93, 100, 104–5, 112
Kershaw, B. 18–19, 20, 128, 191
Khayaal Theatre Company 187n.1
    Hearts and Minds 157, 175–80
Kitson, F. 66
Klein, N. 15, 29, 34
Kristeva, J. 48–9, 51
Kubiak, A. 12–13

Lacan, J. 24, 27, 46–7, 69, 97, 100, 161,
    163, 174, 185 *see also objet petit a*
Lefebvre, H. 68–9
Lehmann, H. 25–6, 29
Lerner, M. 7–8, 190
love 156, 160–5, 167, 170, 173, 174,
    176–7, 178, 180

Magee, P. 111, 113
Massumi, B. 191–2
Mbembe, A. 42
McKenzie, J. 19, 22, 25, 42, 50, 92
McMurdo station protest 138–40
McQueen, S. 41, 58n.4
Medusa 46–7, 50, 186
Megson, C. 92, 95, 99, 101–2
de Menezes, J. 89n.1
mimesis 14, 21–5, 26, 43 *see also*
    wars on terror as mimetic
    process
    critical mimesis 18, 22–3, 28–9,
        68–9, 127–34, 138–42, 144, 151,
        161–5, 190–2, 194, 197
    organised control of mimesis 13,
        23–4, 64, 68, 156, 192 *see also*
        Adorno and Horkheimer
Muños-Viñas, S. 31

Nicholson, H. 159–60, 161
Norton-Taylor, R. 93, 102
    Called to Account 93, 101, 104–6
    Half the Picture 93, 101–2, 106
    Justifying War 93, 95–6, 97–9, 100,
        101–4, 106
Notarantonio, F. 79–80, 81, 90n.5

Obama, B. 56, 153
objet petit a 27–8, 97–8, 161

Paget, D. 93
Phelan, P. 28, 77, 163, 183, 184–5,
    193–4
Prevent strategy 186n.1

racism 166, 170, 174–5
radical (in performance) 3, 11, 17–19
    radical-conservative (in
        performance) 9, 11, 29–31,
        190–6
Rancière, J. 20, 68–9, 126, 191
Ravenhill, M.
    Shoot/Get Treasure/Repeat 94,
        118–23
Read, A. 20
Rickman, A. and Viner, K.
    My Name is Rachel Corrie 93,
        107–9

Samuel, R. 30
SAS 60, 71–2, 77
Scappaticci, F. 79–80, 89n.4, 90n.5
Schechner, R. 130, 136
Shepard, B. 134
Skrimshire, S. 133–4
Soans, R.
    Talking to Terrorists 93, 110–12
Stop the war placard 137–8

Taussig, M. 12, 13–14, 68, 74, 155
Taylor, D. 12, 13, 32
Thatcher, M. 65, 73, 79, 88, 102
Theatre for Everybody 6–7
Theatre Veritae 157, 165
Thompson, J. 20, 154
Thompson, R. 66

UHC Collective
    This is Camp X-Ray 125, 147–51
Undercover 181–6
US Counterinsurgency Field Manual
    67, 71

vacuum cleaner 140–2, 150, 193,
    194
verbatim theatre 92–4, 99–101, 165–6
voice
    crisis of voice 94–101, 121–3
    grain of the voice 100

Wallinger, M.
    State Britain 144, 146–7
wars on terror 2, 9–10, 59–61, 91,
    153–4, 155
    as mimetic process 14–16, 38,
      63–70

waste, wasted life 16–17 *see also*
    abject; *objet petit a*
performance and waste 17–18, 21,
    25–31, 48–51, 56, 98, 122–3, 126,
    146–7, 148–52, 188–95
Williams, R. 19, 195
Wolff, J. 10

Young Muslim Sisters 181, 183

Zarqawi, A. 35–7, 39, 46, 47, 57n.1, 60
Zawahiri, A. 39, 47
Žižek, S. 2, 28, 97, 159, 164, 172